JAPAN'S AGRO-FOOD SECTOR

Also by Albrecht Rothacher
ECONOMIC DIPLOMACY BETWEEN THE EUROPEAN COMMUNITY
AND JAPAN, 1959–81

Japan's Agro-Food Sector

The Politics and Economics of Excess Protection

Albrecht Rothacher

Second Secretary, EC Delegation, Tokyo

St. Martin's Press   New York

First published in the United States of America in 1989

Printed in Great Britain

ISBN 0–312–01691–3

Library of Congress Cataloging-in-Publication Data
Rothacher, Albrecht.
Japan's agro-food sector : the politics and economics of excess
protection / by Albrecht Rothacher.
p. cm.
Bibliography: p.
Includes index.
ISBN 0–312–01691–3 : $55.00 (est.)
1. Agriculture and state—Japan. 2. Food industry and trade–
–Government policy—Japan. 3. Tariff on farm produce—Japan.
4. Free trade and protection—Free Trade. I. Title.
HD2093.R68 1990
338.1′0952—dc19   88–18640
                                                                        CIP

For Christine

Contents

List of Tables

List of Figures

List of Abbreviations

AFF   Agriculture, Forestry and Fisheries
ASEAN   Association of South-East Asian Nations
DSP   Democratic Socialist Party (Minsanto)
EPA   Economic Planning Agency
FY   Fiscal Year
GATT   General Agreement on Tariffs and Trade
GSP   Generalized System of Preferences
HFCS   High Fructose Corn Syrup
IQ   Import Quota
IWC   International Whaling Council
JCP   Japan Communist Party (Kyosanto)
JETRO   Japan External Trade Organization
JSP   Japan Socialist Party (Shakaito)
JTS   Japan Tobacco and Salt Public Corporation
JTI   Japan Tobacco Incorporated (private)
LDP   Liberal Democratic Party (Jiminto)
LIPC   Livestock Industry Promotion Corporation
LTA   Long-Term Agreement
MAF(F)   Ministry of Agriculture, Forestry (and Fisheries) (Norin-sho)
MFA   Ministry of Foreign Affairs (Gaimusho)
MITI   Ministry of International Trade and Industry (Tsusancho)
MNC   Multinational Corporation
MOF   Ministry of Finance (Okurasho)
MP   Member of Parliament
MTN   Multilateral Trade Negotiations
NLC   New Liberal Club
NTB   Non-Tariff Barrier
OECD   Organization for Economic Development and Cooperation
PARC   Political Affairs Research Council
PMO   Prime Minister's Office
POS   Point of Sales
SCAP   Supreme Commander Allied Powers
SMP   Skim Milk Powder
STR   Special Trade Representative
TDN   Total Digestive Nutrients
USDA   US Department of Agriculture

Preface

This book deals with the political economy of Japan's agro-food sector: the interplay of political, sociological, historical and economic variables affecting the structure, performance, and the domestic and international effects of a very significant sector of the Japanese economy.

The thrust of this study ('excess protection') may appear as overly critical of Japan's agriculture, her farm policies, and those who appear to benefit from them. In fact, this author has great admiration and a strong affinity for the traditional Japanese countryside – as it is, for instance, immortalized in Kurosawa's and Kinoshita's early classics. This is, however, a world for better or for worse long since gone, destroyed by benevolent policies and economic progress. Current policies should therefore not be influenced by romantic notions of an ever more distant past, but guided and judged by the criterion of welfare maximization alone. Japan's agricultural policies have currently entered a phase of reorientation and reform. The conclusions of this study strongly favour this adjustment, which should lead to a more competitive, saner agro-food sector in Japan, and could contribute to the much needed solution of the current international farm crisis.

I was able to collect material for this study in Japan as a researcher at the International Christian University in Mitaka/Tokyo in 1979–80, as a junior attaché in the EC Commission's Delegation in Tokyo in 1981–82, and during a further research trip in summer 1984. The subsequent evaluation was stimulated greatly by student contributions, made in the course of seminars on Japan's agriculture and food industry, I held at the Free University of Berlin in summer 1985 and at Vienna University in spring 1986. This study also benefited from the in-depth analyses made by the OECD Secretariat on international agricultural issues, and by the discussions in the OECD Committee for Agriculture, in which I was privileged to be able to participate as a representative of the European Community.

It goes without saying, that all views and statements of fact expressed here, are strictly my own and are not intended to reflect the views of the Commission of the European Communities.

Brussels   ALBRECHT ROTHACHER

ADMINISTRATIVE MAP OF JAPAN

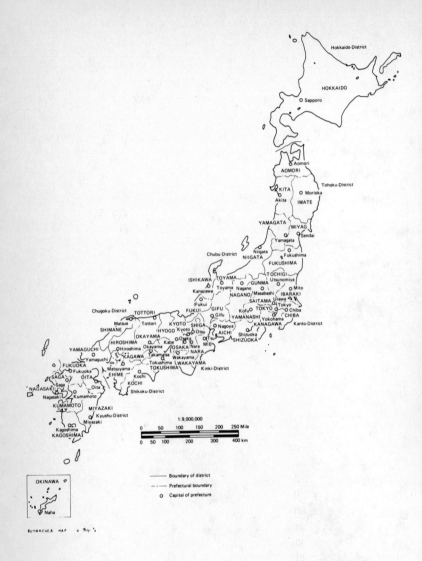

Hokkaido-District

HOKKAIDO

○ Sapporo

○ Aomori
AOMORI
Tohoku-District
KITA
Akita ○ Morioka
IWATE

YAMAGATA
MIYAG
○ Yamagata ○ Sendai
Niigata ○ Fukushima
Chubu-District NIIGATA
FUKUSHIMA
TOCHIGI
ISHIKAWA TOYAMA Utsunomiya
GUNMA ○ Mito
Kanazawa Toyama Nagano Masabashi IBARAKI
NAGANO SAITAMA Urawa
IFukui Kofu ○ TOKYO Tokyo
Chugoku-District FUKUI GIFU YAMANASHI CHIBA
TOTTORI ○ Gifu Yokohama ○ Chiba
Matsue Tottori KYOTO SHIGA ○ Nagoya KANAGAWA Kanto-District
SHIMANE IHYOGO Kyoto Otsu Shizuoka
HIROSHIMA OKAYAMA Kabe AICHI SHIZUOKA
YAMAGUCHI ○ Hiroshima Okayama ○ Osaka Nara MIE
Yamaguchi KAGAWA OSAKA NARA
FUKUOKA Takamatsu Wakayama
SAGA Fukuoka Matsuyama Tokushima WAKAYAMA
NAGASAKI OITA EHIME TOKUSHIMA Kinki-District
Saga Kochi
Nagasaki Oita KOCHI
KUMAMOTO Kumamoto Shikoku-District
MIYAZAKI
Kyushu-District
Kagoshima Miyazaki
KAGOSHIMA

1:9,000,000

0 50 100 150 200 250 Mile
0 50 100 200 300 400 km

———— Boundary of district
– – – – Prefectural boundary
○ Capital of prefecture

OKINAWA

○ Naha

ROTHACHER MAP × 54 %

1 Introduction: Analysing Japan's Agro-Food Sector

Even the most casual and short-term visitor to Japan cannot fail to make some pertinent observations about Japan's agro-food sector: landing at Narita airport he views the tidy, parcelled and densely settled paddy cultures of Northern Chiba prefecture. In food stalls and convenience stores he purchases neatly packaged high-quality foods at extravagant prices. Restaurants serve one of the world's best cuisines usually for an even more exorbitant bill. The agro-food sector accounts for 22% of all employment, 11% of all production, 30% of all consumer expenditure and easily qualifies as the most important single component of the Japanese economy. Yet with an average farm size of only 1.2 ha and the paramount food security arguments enjoyed in a traditionally relatively isolated island nation, the 'backwardness' and high cost structure of Japan's strongly protected agro-food structure at first sight might appear plausible.

This may explain why hitherto so little intellectual curiosity outside Japan was geared to her agricultural and food industry sector, while entire libraries have been written on Japan's automobile, electronics and service industries and other aspects of her modern economic and managerial system.

This study attempts to stimulate more curiosity by questioning some of the homilies and truisms on the agro-food sector generally perpetrated by the foreign media and the habitual interpreters of all things Japanese, and thus contribute to closing the perception gap. In fact, Japan's agricultural sector is undergoing a significant structural transformation. Farmers become either agro-businessmen or retire and take up gardening as a hobby. Villages turn into suburbs or are gradually being abandoned. The Japanese diet (national diets are something extremely conservative) is changing rapidly. Her farm policies and perhaps even her farm political economy equation are being altered. The food industry – so far largely isolated and heavily protected – sees itself increasingly exposed to international competition and the US and UK food multinationals' 'world food' strategies. Biotechnology and ecological concerns pose new challenges, and so

1

does an international environment which overproduces food in ever more frightful quantities. It aggressively seeks new outlets and erodes the traditional rationales for agricultural protection.

A proper analysis of the changes in the agro-food sector and its political economy can no longer view the agricultural sector in isolation. Increased vertical integration, modern farming practices, ever growing sophistication in food processing and consumer-demand diversification require a more integrated sectoral approach. It therefore appears meaningful to distinguish vertically linked sectors in an integrated agro-food chain:

1. *Input industries and distribution*: finance (rural banks), chemicals (fertilizers, pesticides, herbicides, etc.), agricultural machinery and construction, feed compounding, energy (fuels and electricity), know-how (training, extension services, R&D) and services (veterinary, insurance, accounting etc.). The suppliers of agricultural inputs evidently are a very diverse lot: they include public institutions, private professionals, multinational corporations and producer-owned cooperatives. It would be very difficult to generalize their economic and market power, except that their efficient functioning and timely supplies are essential to the proper operation of a modern mechanized and chemical-intensive agriculture for which these inputs are a major cost factor (next to labour and land) affecting farmers' net income.

2. *The agricultural sector proper*, to be differentiated in two major subsectors: crop and livestock production, with the first partly serving as input industry (feed) to the latter.

    In structural terms three major producer groups are to be discerned:
    (a) part-time farmers and retirees at varying degrees of seriousness in their agricultural pursuits;
    (b) the classical full-time ('family') farmer, who as an individual entrepreneur lives exclusively or predominantly off his farm operations; and
    (c) agro-business: industrial and trading capital venturing into agriculture, such as feed compounders or supermaket chains moving into intensive livestock production, pension funds and insurances buying up farmland, or cooperatives cultivating members' land with hired labour. Plantageons are their tropical equivalent.

3. *Processing industries of the first transformation*[1] (dairies, slaught-

erhouses, cereals and oil mills, wineries, sugar refineries, etc). These industries carry out the first processing of raw agricultural products, whose transformations only rarely are sold directly to producers (typical are products like liquid milk, cheese, sugar and flour). Usually the plants are close to agricultural producers or near importing ports. Typical for this sector are still small- to medium-sized enterprises, often family owned or in cooperatives' property. An OECD study estimates that they are still rather more linked to the agricultural sector (as firms have to rely on their local and regional suppliers).[2]

4. *The processing sector of the secondary transformation* finalizes the semi-processed products supplied by the primary transforming food industry. It comprises the drinks industry, bakeries, confectionary, producers of prepared and frozen foods, of margarine, instant coffee, etc. This industry is more diversified, more concentrated, metropolitan in location, often operated as MNC, and according to the above mentioned OECD study not different in its operations from other manufacturing industries of consumer products.[3] Their prime concern are product differentiation through technological innovation and specific marketing techniques (proper advertising, branding and direct sales promotion).

5. *Transportation and wholesales* link the agro-food production of both the agricultural and the two processing subsectors with the retail outlets for the ultimate consumers. The sector, squeezed by the growing purchasing power of the large supermarket chains, is in relative and absolute decline in most OECD countries.

6. The *Retail trade* provides the final link to consumers. Frequently also offering non-food items, competition particularly in food sales remains keen and the retail sector's structural transformation rapid: superstores and supermaket chains relentlessly increase their market shares and power, while the innumerable number of independent retailers is in persistent decline and urban department stores in stagnation.

7. *Consumers* are the ultimate outlet of the combined effort of the agro-food sector. Given the relative inelasticity of food demand, Adam Smith's observation of the limited absorptive capacity of the human stomach is indicative of the limits to growth of the entire sector. Yet consumer habits change rapidly in response to variations in lifestyles (working women, eating out, etc.) and to dietary fashions and beliefs (health foods, preferences for red meat, vegetarian food, ethnic cooking, etc.).

The interrelations within the agro-food sector are quite evident: a crisis in the agricultural sector hits input industries, such as rural banks and machinery producers, considerably. High producer prices affect the international competitiveness of the national food processing industry. The whims and fancies of ultimate consumer demand finally decide about growth and decline of entire branches of the agro-food sector. As a whole, however, while unable to 'boom', the sector by the same token is fairly stable and crisis proof in situations of cyclical demand contractions.

A comprehensive analysis of the agro-food sector anywhere will need to employ more than just applied economies and statistics: methods of historical, sociological and political analysis are equally required. This study will start out reviewing the historical bases of modern Japan's agriculture, from its pre-Meiji origins to the SCAP's land reform of 1946. It will need to cover the profound sociological and economic transformations of the post-war Japanese countryside. The roles of agricultural cooperatives, of input industries, of the food and the distribution system will be analysed, as well as subsequently the interplay of the key actors in the political economy of Japan's agriculture: government bureaucracy, LDP, the farm lobby, and its opponents in the export industry. A sectoral analysis and an investigation on good and bad effects of product policies pursued should yield estimates of costs to consumers, taxpayers and eventually any effects on the Japanese economy as a whole.

Her agricultural protection strongly affects relations with fellow OECD member countries, particularly so with the US, Australia, Canada and the EC, but also with Third World agricultural exporters, like the ASEAN nations. Next to her agricultural structural problems, international relations probably are the most significant challenge to Japan's current food policies.

The analysis should lead to better understanding and a more reasoned forecast for Japan's agro-food sector: its current sociostructural transformation, its policy constraints, and the international, ecological and biotechnological challenges and their implications for the future development of a sector which through excess-protection was induced into massive resource misallocations, but in which equally long-stifled entrepreneurial talents and innovative minds attempt to reassert economic rationality and progress over bureaucratically administered 'stability' and the network of protection rent-collecting profiteers.

Notes

1. Only relatively few (and increasingly less) agricultural products (fruit, vegetables, eggs and potatoes) still typically bypass processing and enter the distribution system directly.
2. See also OECD, *Les industries alimentaires de l'OECD dans les années '80* (Paris: OECD, 1983) p. 14.
3. Ibid., p. 14.

2 Agricultural Development until the Land Reform of 1946

This chapter will review three major elements in Japan's post-Tokugawa agricultural policies: the development in production factors (land, labour, capital), the unfolding and effects of key events and movements (Rice Riots of 1918, the interwar tenants' movement, and the post-war land reform), and the development of theories on the role of agriculture in Japan's society and economy. All these elements obviously have repercussions on contemporary structures and policies in Japan's agricultural system.

PRODUCTION FACTORS AND AGRICULTURAL OUTPUT

Agricultural output in Japan during the hundred years since the 1880s increased roughly 5 times, representing an average annual growth rate of 1.6%. According to Hayami,[1] 50% of this output growth is explained by variations of conventional production factors (land/labour and especially capital), the remainder in his estimations is largely due to improved rural education and successful public agricultural R&D. Japan's success in boosting agricultural production did also provide valuable lessons for other rice-based Asian agricultural economies facing a similar land pressure.

However, when discussing Japan's agricultural take-off its basic macroeconomic condition requires consideration: Japan's industrial development policies since the Meiji Restoration (1868) until at least the end of the Taisho period (1912–26) consciously aimed at a massive (though gradually diminishing) transfer of resources from the rural economy to the industrializing urban sector which on its own had not yet been in a position to accumulate industrial capital sufficiently. The transfer of resources took four principal avenues:

1. *The introduction of an agricultural land tax to be paid in cash.* This tax made up about 80% of the early Meiji governments' fiscal

revenue which was largely used to finance public investments for industrialization. It replaced the Tokugawa feudal rents, delivered in kind as shares of the annual rice harvest.

2. *Landlords investing in off-farm activities.* During the latter Meiji/ Taisho period rural landlords found it more worthwhile to urbanize and to invest their rural land rents as 'parasitic' absentee owners into industrial or commercial pursuits.

3. *Foreign exchange earnings made largely from silk and tea exports* which in 1870 made up about 70% of total exports.[2] They were essentially used to finance foreign machinery and industrial technology imports.

4. *Highly elastic supplies of disciplined labour to the industrial sector as well as of low-priced food to the expanding population.* The Engel's coefficient (the percentage of household expenditure spent on food) in the 1930s was still at 35%,[3] which underlines the importance food prices had for industrial wage demands and hence the competitiveness for Japan's labour intensive light industries at the time.

While this net transfer of resources took place, yet important variations in factor allocation happened within the agricultural sector leading to significant gains in productivity and output:

1. Labour employed in agriculture since the 1880s remained relatively stable at around 15 m (with a 10% fall during the World War I boom) until the early 1950s, dropping rapidly, however, thereafter to below 10 m in the late 1960s.[4] At the same time, there was a strong increase in working days per labour employed: growing from 110 days per year to 160 (1920–40), then levelling off at 150 (1972).[5] The higher labour utilization rate was due to the spread of double cropping – the growing of winter cereals harvested in late May in paddy fields – and due to the expansion of sericulture, after technological progress had allowed cocoon raising in the off-peak labour season.

   In spite of the spread of labour intensive animal husbandry since the 1950s, mechanization[6] has allowed further savings in manhours employed per agricultural worker. Total work days in agriculture rapidly declined after the early 1950s reflecting the outmigration of rural labour due to increased agricultural opportunity costs in view of more renumerative industrial employment.

2. Land use until 1920 increased by 0.5% p.a., mostly due to newly

cultivated marginal land in Tohoku and Hokkaido. Since then agricultural land gained through reclamation, irrigation and draining schemes has been off balanced by farm land converted to residential or industrial use. While total farm land stagnated until 1960 at 6 m ha, and then gradually declined to 5.4 m ha (1983) – its crop land use diminished more dramatically from 8.1 m ha (1960) to 5.6 m ha (1981) as double cropping fell into disuse due to growing opportunity costs relative to off-farm employment.

3. Capital use grew slowly prior to World War II, followed by a severe decline during the war and a rapid increase thereafter. This growth occurred with the gradual spread of chemical fertilizer application in the 1920s, and its intensification especially in the decade 1955–65.[7] Today Japan has one of the world's most intensely fertilized crop land with 138 kg nitrogen (N), 150 kg phosphonic acid (P_2O_5) and 140 kg potash (K_2O) employed per arable hectare.[8]

   After 1965, mechanization advanced fast as Japan's agricultural machinery had developed adequately light and small-sized farm appliances (small-scale tillers, tractors with less than 10 PS, rice transplanters and harvesting machines) whose relative prices compared to alternative labour use rapidly declined. Two trends are therefore evident in capital use:

   (a) until late 1960s: mainly substitution of fertilizers for land use; and

   (b) since the late 1950s: the substitution of machinery for labour.[9]

With labour and land use grosso modo stagnated after World War I and declining since the late 1950s, the growing application of capital should be the most important single production factor explaining Japan's agricultural output growth in this period. Its productivity enhancing effects are even more evident in the contemporary period, when during 1960–81 the agricultural production index rose by another 33%.

Other production factors which are less easy to quantify include:

1. *Agricultural know how*: farmers' abilities to produce and to manage efficiently and to have access to up-to-date technological information and products. Improved rural education levels, extended extension services and e.g. the spread of high yield rice varieties indicate a strengthening of this production factor.

2. *Public sector investment in agricultural R&D and rural infrastructure*:

Table 2.1 Agricultural production growth[12]

1880–1900	1.5
1900–1920	1.9
1920–1935	0.9
1935–1945	−1.8
1945–1955	3.1
1955–1965	3.3
1965–1981	1.3

although MAFF's budget, which grew steadily until 1982 (to Y3.7 bn), has declined since (to Y2.6 bn in 1988), the shares and the absolute amounts spent on these items have continued to expand. Public R&D efforts were crucial, e.g. to develop fertilizer responsive high yield crop varieties (as private agricultural R&D efforts are significant only in mechanical machinery in Japan).[11] Infrastructural investments, which are ever more publicly financed, with their irrigation, drainage and rearrangement schemes equally enhanced land productivity.

While these factors all explain why agricultural productivity grew at all over the last century, the observation of distinct growth periods (Table 2.1) requires a residual explanandum, which could by due to institutional factors or historical events. Technological knowledge and entrepreneurial initiative, pent-up during the late Tokugawa decades was released by the Meiji era's agricultural modernization policies. Its fixed-cash land tax forcefully urged producers to increase rice yields and to produce profitable cash crops. Former samurai as local landlords provided effective rural leadership for innovation and adaption. During the 1900s rural banks, cooperatives and public extension services, began operations thus enhancing output. World War I with increased overseas food demand similarly stimulated production.

The relative stagnation of the interwar period may have occurred due to the drain of resources away from agriculture effected by absentee landlords. Oppressive tenancy rents (often 50% of harvested products in kind) also discouraged production. In World War II the military draft reduced rural manpower. Shortage of labour, bombing damage and the unavailability of fertilizers and other industrial inputs reduced food production in spite of the controlled

Table 2.2   Agricultural output composition (in value)[13]

	Rice(%)	Livestock(%)	Sericulture(%)	Vegetables(%)
1874/77	67.0	0.6	2.6	–
1928/32	52.6	4.9	12.4	–
1968/72	40.0	27.9	1.9	15.9 (1970)
1979/82	31.5	28.6	1.4	18.0

production targets of Japan's war economy. After the war, once again a 'backlog' in technological innovation (chemical pesticides/ insecticides, appropriate machinery) was utilized by farmers whom the land reform had made owner-operators. High support prices since the 1960s further stimulated output, resulting first in mountains of excess rice and later also in overproduction of mikan oranges, eggs, milk, poultry and pork since the late 1970s. Administrative production controls, such as the paddy field diversion programme of 1979 and 'voluntary' production restraint arrangements for the other products have now placed an effective lid on further 'dynamic' agricultural output growth in Japan.

Table 2.2 shows considerable shifts in total output value of agricultural products over the last century and hence indicates a fairly high supply elasticity in response to price returns and public policies. The relative dominance of rice evidently is on continued decline, though it still remains by far the most important single agricultural product. Commercial livestock production as well as the vegetables sector had its take off from very modest beginnings in the late 19th century only after disposable consumer incomes started to benefit from Japan's rapid economic post-war growth in the 1960s. Sericulture which had been one of Japan's most significant foreign exchange earners until the mid-1930s (In 1922 silk products made up 48.9% of Japan's total exports), never recovered from the price collapse in the Great Depression and its suppression as non-essential agricultural production during the war, as in the post-war years highly fluctuating demand has retarded technical progress and production rationalization[14] and hence increased opportunity costs beyond alternative returns. These production shifts underline the ability of Japan's agriculture in the past to reallocate resources and to restructure effectively. Such adaptation to changing economic realities certainly would have been faster and more drastic had not agricultural policies (especially on rice) after 1961 began to distort systematically market signals to producers.

As Japan's agricultural producers throughout that period enjoyed guaranteed support prices above world price levels for most products, one should assume overallocations of capital and of labour especially in the highest assisted sectors, the inevitable adjustments of which certainly will prove painful to both producers and policy-makers.

While there were structural developments (the declining wage role of rice, growing fiscal revenues and urban incomes and the shrinking size of the agricultural sector continuing to enjoy high political leverage in the election system favouring agricultural protectionism), the more immediate origins of these support policies can be traced to very significant events in Japan's recent social history and to the development of agricultural thought in Japan.

THE RICE RIOTS OF 1918

The riots started on 22 July 1918 when housewives began to protest against out-prefectural shipment of rice in the small coastal town of Uotsu (Toyama Prefecture). They rapidly spread South and often turned violent with protesters storming rice dealers' storage depots. Though the government on 5 August started selling imported rice from Korea and Taiwan, rioting did not abate and by 11 August troops had been despatched to 60 cities which often engaged in street fighting where the protesters' violence had turned increasingly against establishments symbolic of the *nouveaux riches* (posh restaurants, usurers' offices). In Tokyo police boxes were destroyed and the ministries of agriculture and commerce and of communication stoned. In Miike on Kyushu a militant coal miners' strike erupted in which miners fought with dynamite against the military for their demands for wage hikes and reduced food prices.[15] On 18 August the government started expropriating rice cornered by dealers and landlords, and after a calming of the situation the government accepted its responsibility for the crisis and resigned on 21 September 1918.[16]

There were three underlying factors for the scale of these spontaneous disturbances (which due to the lack of leaders, organization and ideas were by no means revolutionary):

1. the war boom with its social frictions created by a rapidly expanding industrial labour force and the unequal distribution of the benefits of growth and war profiteering;
2. poor rice harvests in 1917 and 1918 stimulated massive cornering

by rice dealers and landlords, even when the prices for monthly
rice consumption exceeded average wages, the government failed
to respond; and

3. the maintenance of a protectionist system on rice, which increased
   its consumer price and guaranteed landlord's rent without giving
   incentives to tenant farmers for improved productivity. In order to
   finance the costs of the war with Russia in 1905/6, a 15% tariff on
   rice imports had been introduced, which after extensive public
   debate (which already then had pitted landed interest, represented
   by the Imperial Agricultural Association, against the Tokyo Chamber of Commerce, representing manufacturers and exporters) in
   1912 was made permanent with Y1 tariff for 60 kg of rice.[18]

The Japanese government responded with increased imports from
her colonies in Korea and Taiwan, which by 1926 covered 10% of
domestic rice consumption. The 1921 Rice Law further provided for
public adjustment in rice supplies through

(a) government storage, purchase and sales of rice (up to Y20 m
    p.a.);
(b) a more flexible import adjusting mechanism (variable quotas and
    duties).

These measures proved insufficient in 1931 where a crop failure
renewed scarcities and inspired Tokyo housewives' demonstrations.
The Rice Control Act of 1933 then tightened government intervention:[19]

(a) the government determining the annual minimum and maximum
    rice price;
(b) it intervenes through purchasing and selling with no limits to
    maintain prices within the desired range, thereby also eliminat-
    ing seasonal fluctuations; and
(c) it establishes permanent export/import control of rice and other
    grains.[20]

These regulations laid the groundwork for the 1942 Food Control
Law which introduced production and price controls, food rationing
and compulsory deliveries. The Food Agency's current rice and
cereals monopoly is still based on the 1942 Act.

THE TENANTS' MOVEMENT

While rice support prices in the inter-war period were intended to support economically depressed farmers, they (as price support policies usually do), in fact, largely benefited landowners and merchants in Japan and large producers and dealers in her colonies. Colonial rice production was sold on the – more profitable – Japanese main islands while native peoples had not sufficient rice to feed themselves. Japanese tenant farmers were obliged to pay their rent in kind in rice, and hence did not benefit from higher rice prices as rice was almost exclusively sold by their landlords for cash.

In the 1920s the government began first large-scale infrastructural improvement schemes for Japan's agriculture, thus aiding its productivity and supplying off-farm employment. The burden of the land tax diminished rapidly. In 1921–25 its share in total fiscal revenue had shrunk to 9.9% and declined continuously to a mere 1.8% share in 1936–40. To alleviate the farm debt crisis of 1930, the government ordered a debt repayment moratorium and began to subsidize farmers' interest payments.

Government policy in the 1920s already changed from one of exploiting the agricultural sector to a policy of farm assistance. P. K. Hall, in fact, contests the popular perception of a general farm crisis in Japan in the inter-war period and argues that it was largely the landlords, benefiting most from agricultural protection and development programmes, who had made up the notion of agriculture being in a state of uniform depression and crisis in order to get government assistance through their considerable political influence in the political parties and in the military.[21]

The tenant farmers' situation – with a disposable income roughly at half of that of owner-operators in 1925–29[22] – certainly was much more precarious. Average agricultural income figures, as used by Hall,[23] evidently ignore the fact that tenancy rents, which amounted to about one-third of total farming expenses, statistically are transfers *within* the agricultural sector, and hence attenuate intrasector inequalities. Nonetheless, in spite of the high indebtedness of the Japanese farm sector, the share of tenanted land remained remarkably stable at around 46% of total cultivated land between 1908 and 1942.[24] Over these years there was a small decrease in the share of owner-farmers (totalling 1.7 m in 1942) from 33.3% to 31.0% among farm families, while owner-tenant farmers' share remained stable at

39% (2.2 m in 1942), and tenant farmers' shares increased slightly from 27.6% to 28.7% (1.6 m in 1942).[25]

The expansion of landlordism clearly had taken place in the Meiji period, following the monetarization of agriculture with its excessive land taxation. During depressions farm land was then forfeited to merchants, usurers and already established local landlords. In 1872, 29% of cultivated land was tenanted; in 1887 the share was at 40%; and from 1908 on it remained stable at around 46%.[26]

With the worldwide social upheavals following the end of World War I, it was not only the Rice Riots of 1918 which alarmed the Japanese establishment, but also the newly emerging militant labour and tenants' movements, which were helped by the growing social disparities in Japan's war boom economy and her adjustment difficulties after the boom's post-war collapse. Tenancy disputes and campaigns for rent reductions found organizational backing from Socialist and trade union groups. Particularly in the crises of 1920 and 1929 conflicts spread and often took violent turns. In 1922 the Japan Peasants' Union (Nippon Nomin Kumiai) was set up as a national organization of tenant unions, demanding as a political programme, rural minimum wages and the 'socialization of all cultivated land'.[27] Japan's emerging Communist Party in 1922 similarly called for nationalized land ownership and the expropriation of the holdings of the imperial household as well as of large landlords, including shrines and temples.

In later years the Japan Peasant Union demanded an immediate reduction in rents, strengthened tenancy rights and a state rice monopoly (1925). The Unions' degree of organization was very disparate: some villages and hamlets were completely organized, in others with largely owner-farmers, for the lack of tenants, or in some for fear of powerful landlord families the Union was very weak. In 1926 sections of the more militant Peasant Union with socialist politicians formed the Farmer Labour Party (Nomin Rodoto) which advocated an alliance between the urban proletariat and the rural poor. Though plagued by internal dissension (like all left wing movements in Japan) and continuously harrassed by police, the party managed to have 8 members elected to the Diet in 1928.[28]

Tenants' more pragmatic demands were not without sympathy among agricultural bureaucrats, who saw absentee landlords (disinvesting from agriculture) and weak tenancy rights as principal obstacles to a more productive agricultural economy. In 1913 a government-sponsored tenancy law passed the National Diet's House of Representatives, but was thrown out in the House of Peers which was dominated by landlord interests.[29] The military and the right wing's peasantist convictions, aiming at food self-sufficiency and the maintenance of a traditional farm structure, with the 1938 Agricultural Land Adjustment Law and the 1939 Land Rent Control Ordinance (the latter in the context of the National Mobilization Law of 1938) froze rents and land prices, and guaranteed tenants' status, thus re-establishing rural 'peace' while preparing for war.

THE LAND REFORM OF 1946

Already before and during the war the Ministry of Agriculture had ventured some fairly moderate plans for a land reform. As public opinion in Japan after her capitulation had turned against large landowners, and as the US military administration (similar as in the case of Germany) for whatever reason[31] held Japan's landowners as co-responsible for her militaristic undertakings, it seemed appropriate for Japan's political establishment to take action.

This seemed particularly urgent as the Potsdam Declaration of 27 July 1945 had called for the democratization of Japan, which in MacArthur's public interpretation of October 1945 would also have to include a land reform.

MAFF then drafted a land reform law, which provided for:

1. rents in cash (instead of in kind);
2. rents as fixed amounts (no longer as share of the harvest);
3. expropriation of all absentee landlords;
4. expropriation of all holdings above 3 ha;
5. land committees to be established with an equal share of landowners and tenants.

A Japanese cabinet decision then enlarged the maximum allowable farm size to 5 ha. But while the Diet was debating the draft law on 9 December 1945, SCAP issued a memorandum which was notable for its rhetorics. It stressed the need to 'destroy the economic bondage which has enslaved the Japanese farmer for centuries of feudal oppression. . . .' and concluded, the Japanese government was 'ordered to submit to this HQ on or before 15 March 1946 a program of rural land reform'.[32]

The bill was now rushed through the Diet, was approved on 28

December 1945 and to be enforced on 1 February 1946. SCAP however remained dissatisfied with its provisions and in March 1946 vetoed the bill. Until June 1946 the Allied Council for Japan demanded:

1. a drastic reduction in resident landlord's land reserves;
2. a further democratization in the land committees' composition;
3. the transfer of land should be done through government purchases and resales to tenants; and
4. the reform to be concluded within 5 years.

On 14 August 1946 the Cabinet announced its revised land reform draft law:

1. all absentee landlord land would be subjected to compulsory government purchase;
2. maximum tenanted land for resident landlords would be around 1 ha in the main islands (varying between 0.6 ha in Hiroshima Prefecture and 1.5 ha in northern Aomori Prefecture) and 4 ha in Hokkaido;
3. maximum holdings for resident landlords' own cultivation would be 2 ha in the main islands and 8 ha in Hokkaido;
4. forests and wastelands would be excluded from the land reform, but Imperial Household forests transformed into national forests;
5. prices for purchases and resales were set at 758 yen per tan ($99.2m^2$) for paddies and 465 yen per tan of upland fields. Inflation later reduced these prices to purely nominal fees;
6. tenant evictions and nominal sales would be declared invalid. Expiration or cancellation of tenant leases would require approval of the prefectural governor;
7. in each village land committees (composed of 5 tenants, 3 landlords, 3 owner-farmers) were to be established determining the land to be transformed. Their decisions needed the approval of prefectural land committees; and
8. a national land committee (8 tenants, 8 landlords, 2 peasant union representatives, 5 agricultural academics) was to supervise the land distribution nationwide.

The land reform for most villages (except some largely situated in the coastal plains of central Honshu which were settled mainly by owner-farmers) had the most profound social and economic implications. As most resident landlords had rented out their land, most of their holdings exceeding 1 ha were expropriated – 400,000 of these more or rather less large landlords, the hitherto leading rural class, were affected by the land reform. By August 1950, 1.7 m ha were thus purchased and 1.9 m ha (which included public land) – one-third of Japan's arable land – transferred to tenants and landless farmers, most of which were thus elevated to the status of owner-farmers.

The share of owner-operators among Japan's farm households' drastically increased from 31% in 1945 to 62% in 1950, and to 80% in 1965. Tenant-cultivated land correspondingly declined from 46 % (1945) of the total cultivated area to 10% (1950), and further to 5% (1965). Rigid rent controls and tight tenancy rights at the time provided a strong disincentive to renting out one's land. It should be assumed however that after 1955 rent controls (and public statistics) were frequently circumvented by more sensible informal arrangements.[34]

The implementation of the land reform[35] predictably was affected by the often chaotic situation in the immediate post-war period with repatriates, bombed out urbanites and demobbed farmers returning to their old villages. The confusion was augmented by frequent changes in legal provisions and by differing discretionary interpretations of prefectural land committees. Local land committees' qualities also varied considerably from high degrees of corruption to similarly high levels of diligence and meticulousness. The stronger the local Peasants' Union was organized (its national membership had grown to 1.2 m in 1947 but was plagued by dissention thereafter, and began to decline as communists struggled for influence and moderate socialist and conservative farmer groups split off), the more radical was usually the land reforms' implementation. Overall, as evident in subsequent land distribution statistics, thorough work was done.

However various grievances persisted:

1. those who had rented large landlords' land obtained larger holdings than tenants of smaller landlords;
2. owner farmers resented that the best local land – i.e. the landlords' – was transferred to former tenant farmers;
3. small and medium landlords were reduced to holdings which were hardly enough to make a living, though still sufficiently large to tie them to the land;
4. hit hardest were 'absentee' landlords owning and cultivating land in neighbouring villages or those villagers with urban employment

and residences who had bought land for their planned retirement occupation; and

5. the exemption of private and public forest land, whose economic significance remained considerable to mountain farmers. In these villages privileged 'feudal' family rule hence continued for at least one further decade.[36]

The advantages of transforming Japan's agriculture into an owner-farmer system were more evident in the 1950s:

1. After the initial disruptions and entrepreneural lessons the new owner farmers had strong incentives to maximize output (no doubt also furthered by black market prices 13 to 14 times above the official levels in late 1945). Former tenant land was hence more fully utilized to feed Japan's starving urban population.
2. Landlord families' economic power was broken and within years most of their social and political privileged standing effectively eroded, which in many parts of rural Japan – particularly so in Tohoku – had been a prerequisite to implementing the post-war constitution's civil rights and liberties.
3. With the land reform accomplished, Japan's countryside was politically pacified. After the receipt of land titles militant tenants almost overnight turned into conservative *petit bourgeois*. To the chagrin of JSP and JCP and to the relief of the US occupation the tenants' movement soon disbanded (in the Chinese civil war lasting until 1949 landless farmers had been the backbone of the communist insurgency) after its demand for an equitable land distribution had been fulfilled. Japan's countryside for the decades to come turned into solid and reliable LDP territory.

While the land reform's political and medium-term economic effects largely followed the intentions of its originators, its structural and hence long-term implications proved fatal for the creation of an efficient crop farming sector. While in 1946 71% of farms were smaller than 1 ha, in 1950 their share was at 87%. Ownership tied farmers to their land, while a booming industrial economy would have provided more rewarding full-time employment alternatives. Industrial part-time employment – often in construction – frequently only offered second-rate working conditions and pay. Rigid rent controls and prohibitive land sales provisions – legislated to assure the durability of the land distribution – (their liberalization later was made ineffective by disproportionate land price increases) continued to prevent economies of scale for Japan's crop production, and perpetrated a structure of unviable small holdings in continous need of public subsidization.

NOHONSHUGI – JAPAN'S TRADITION IN AGRICULTURAL THOUGHT

Outdated economic theories show an astounding tenacity to life, and even worse, an obstinate staying power in policy-making. Contemporary warfare in world agricultural trade is still best explained by the curious mixtures of mercantilism and physiocratic thought pursued by the main antagonists. Japan with her historical orientation to Nohonshugi is no exception. Nohonshugi is a concept of agricultural fundamentalism considering agriculture as the basis for the entire economic system, and the farming community to be the foundation of society.

The Tokugawa social order accordingly placed farmers ahead of merchants (who challenged the feudal social system). Confucian thinkers praised agricultural frugality and farmers' diligence. Essentials, like food, should be produced, not trifles such as manufactured goods. With their essential significance for food supplies and fiscal revenue, the policy conclusion appeared plausible: the more farmers, the better for the nation.[37]

Though the subsequent Meiji period's industrialization policy strongly favoured industrial development, Nohonshugi as a peasantist ideology with its emphasis on maintaining small/medium farmers persisted. One of its representatives was Ninomiya who as one of the founding fathers of Japan's cooperative movement attempted to organize non-profit self-sustained agricultural production units which were to maintain the roots of the nation.[38] Nohonshugi became politically relevant in the rice tariff debates between 1905 and 1912. At the time, the notion of agriculture as 'root' of social and economic national life was less absurd than it may appear today. In 1900, 68% of employment was still provided by the primary sector, with an even larger share of the population living in rural communities. Agriculture supplied 32% of the net domestic product, and 44% of exports. The rural land tax equally furnished 44% of total fiscal revenue.

Right-wing ideologists have a natural propensity for the agricultural sector, as rightly or wrongly they tend to view farmers – as opposed to uprooted urban workers, intellectuals and capitalists – as standard bearers of ethnic purity, of unquestioned patriotic and religious beliefs, as keepers of tradition and suppliers of reliable and brave soldiers.[39] Also there is a timeless attraction in the romantic perception of un-alienated preindustrial work with soil and nature and of harmonious community and farm family life.

In a right-wing view, this idyllic set-up was being destroyed by capitalist (foreign) manipulation and the resulting social disparities being exploited and exacerbated to the detriment of the nation by Marxist agitators (who were again foreign-directed).

In a more conservative vein, General Taki (Minister for Agriculture and Commerce 1885–87) advocated peasantism in reasoning that Japan needed as many farmers as possible for her political stability and military strength. Japan's military expansion and her settlement programmes in Manchuria later in the 1930s offered scope for the realization of more radical designs.

Communal farms and hamlet communities of settlers – often graduates of Shinto-oriented agricultural colleges – were set up in colonial Manchuria. Right-wing associations planning and supporting these schemes had been created in Japan. Their protagonists aimed at self-governing and self-sufficient village communities, whose members would engage in physical work and brotherhood which then would extend to a system of national solidarity and military strength.[40]

While anti-capitalist notions of right-wing peasantism might have struck a positive cord also in socialist minds, orthodox Marxism does not accept the 'specificity' of agriculture. Based on Marx's contempt at the 'idiocy of country life', communist party policies aim at bridging the gap between city and country life. When in power, individual farmers are ruthlessly collectivized (notable exceptions being Poland, Yugoslavia and post-Maoist China) and agriculture – with usually disastrous results – forced into industrial modes of production.

Nonetheless, there is also a tradition of non-Marxist 'progressive peasantism', which during the inter-war flourishing of the Japan Peasants' Union grew roots in some areas of rural Japan and had repercussions in the establishment of the agricultural cooperatives and their – largely theoretical – pursuit of 'just prices', non-profit targets and supposedly non-capitalist modes of trading.[41].

Today both JCP and JSP programmes largely echo the demands of the farm lobby urging higher degrees of food self-sufficiency and increased support prices and infrastructural spending.[42] Japan's socialists also advocate improved agricultural cooperation and commercial farm machinery use, as well as a system of regionally specialized multicrop farms with collective and year-round production.

Nohonshugi in its various concepts in a highly urbanized and successful industrial and service economy like Japan may sound absurd to most Japanese. However, though no longer a coherent theory, elements of agricultural fundamentalism play a role in contemporary public debates on the direction of farm and food policies:

> We . . . are compelled to absorb a flood of agricultural products from abroad. These imports create both a yen for luxury and the illusion of plenty. Herein is born the finicky palate and the self-indulgent lifestyle. This system of satiation has led to the swelling of Japan's economic power and the creation of a vain, ostentatious subculture among its youth, who have never known adversity. Decadent though their social mores may be, the Japanese are becoming disgustingly proud of their accomplishments. . . . We seem to be changing into an arrogant race.
>
> Haven't we abandoned our roots somewhere along the line? The Japanese of old were essentially an agricultural people. . . . Through their diligency, they led this country along the road to today's prosperity.[43]

Notes

1. Hayami, Yujiro, *A Century of Agricultural Growth in Japan* (Tokyo: Tokyo University Press, 1975) pp. 195–6.
2. Nakamura, Takefusa, *Economic Development of Modern Japan* (Tokyo: Ministry of Foreign Affairs, 1985) p. 24.
3. Ogura, Takekazu, *Can Japan Agriculture Survive?: a Historical Approach* (Tokyo: Agricultural Policy Research Center, 1979) p. 708.
4. Hayami, op. cit., p. 224.
5. Ibid., p. 24.
6. In 1950 the cultivation of 10 acres for rice production took 207 hours; in 1984 this was down to 57 hours. (MAFF, *Agriculture in Japan*, Mar. 1986, p. 19).
7. Hayami, op. cit., pp. 32–4.
8. MFA, 'Agriculture in Japan', *Facts about Japan* (undated) p. 5.
9. Hayami, op. cit., p. 35.
10. Ibid., p. 125.
11. Ibid., p. 138.
12. Adapted from Hayami, p. 15.

13. Adapted from Hayami, p. 21; and *Japan Statistical Yearbook* (Tokyo, 1985) p. 172.
14. Sato, Yoshio, 'The Silk-Reeling Industry of Japan and the Catch-up Case', *Keio Business Review*, no. 11, 1972, p. 64.
15. Arthur Young. 'The Rice Riots of 1918' in J. Livingston, J. Moore and F. Oldfather (eds), *The Japan Reader 1* (Harmondsworth Middx: Penguin, 1973) p. 324.
16. Ogura, op. cit., p. 158.
17. Ibid., p. 161.
18. Hayami, op. cit., p. 61.
19. Ogura, Takekazu, *Agricultural Development in Modern Japan* (Tokyo: Fuji Publishing Co., 1963) p. 26.
20. Ogura, op. cit., p. 186.
21. P. K. Hall, 'Japan's Farm Sector, 1920–1940: a Need for Reassessment', *Journal of Agricultural History*, 1985, p. 614.
22. Calculated according to the figures provided by Ogura, op. cit., p. 687.
23. Hall, op. cit., p. 611.
24. Ogura, Takekazu, *Agricultural Development in Modern Japan* (Tokyo: Fuji Publishing Co., 1963) p. 26.
25. Ibid., p. 25.
26. Fukutake, Tadashi, *Rural Society in Japan* (Tokyo: Tokyo University Press 1980) p. 5.
27. Ogura, 1979, op. cit., p. 389.
28. Wakukawa, Seiyei, 'The Tenant Movement' in J. Livingston *et al.* (eds), op. cit., p. 254.
29. Ogura, 1979, op. cit., p. 392.
30. As refuted by R. P. Dore, 'Tenancy and Aggresion' in J. Livingston *et al.* (eds) op. cit., p. 431.
31. Usually cited are that Japan's army was inspired by the rural misery at home, by its desire for colonies to settle the landless tenants, and that the landlord system bred authoritarianism and external chauvinism to divert from domestic social cleavages and economic misery.
32. Quoted in Ogura, 1979, op. cit., pp. 407–8.
33. The US average farm size, for comparison, was at 78 ha in 1945 (US Department of Commerce, *Historical Statistics of the United States*, Washington; DC 1960, p. 278); 32% of all US farmers were tenants then.
34. Ogura, 1979, op. cit., p. 427.
35. For details see Ronald P. Dore, *Land Reform in Japan* (London: Oxford University Press, 1959) p. 192.
36. Ushiomi, Toshitaka, *Forestry and Mountain Village Communities in Japan* (Tokyo: Kokusai Bunka Shinkokai, 1968) p. 66.
37. Ogura, 1979, op. cit., p. 2.
38. Wolfgang Lemm, *Japans Landwirtschafliche Genossenschaften* (Hamburg: Institut für Asienkunde, 1977) pp. 46.
39. Ogura, 1979, op. cit., p. 34.
40. Ibid., p. 44.
41. Lemm, op. cit., p. 104.
42. Appendix 7A in Emory M. Castle and Kenzo Hemmi, *US–Japanese*

Agricultural Relations (Baltimore, Md.: Resources for the Future, 1982) pp. 270–3.

43. Nanri, Masahori, *Nihon Nogyo Shimbun*, 1 January 1985, translated in *Japan Agrinfo Newsletter*, Jan. 1985, p. 14.

3 Social and Economic Change in Japan's Post-War Agriculture

THE CONTEMPORARY FARM STRUCTURE

Japan's farm structure, similar to that of most other Western indust-rialized countries pursuing protectionist agricultural politics, is a triple one comprising:

1. the classical, viable 'family-farmers' (with a male household head of productive age engaged mainly or full-time in agriculture);
2. a majority of part-timers who derive their bulk of income from off-farm sources, or of 'full-timers' working beyond retirement age;
3. agro-industry pursuing capital intensive primary production at industrial scale.

The first two groups are well documented in Japanese farm statistics (see Table 3.1).

Table 3.1   Farm household structure (1000s)[1]

	1984	% of total
Full-time Farm Households	605	13.5
of which with males of productive age (16 to 64 years)	391	8.7
consisting of elderly people only (above 64)	214	4.8
Part-time Farm Households	3,868	86.5
of which mainly farming ('Class I')	689	15.4
of which mostly off-farm income ('Class II')	3,179	71.1
Total	4,473	100

The most striking feature of this structural farm statistic is the minority – ever more shrinking – position of viable full-time professional farms in Japanese agriculture. It reflects a profound structural weakness and an admission of failure of public policies which since 1961 have the declared principal aim of strengthening its productive structure.

The 'core farm households', which in their official definition include all households with a man under 60 who works on his own farm for 150 days at least per year, however, remain the backbone of Japan's market oriented food production. In 1980 1 042 000 farm households (23% of the total) were estimated as 'core'. They cultivated 47% of Japan's farmland and produced 61% of gross agricultural production. These professionals are strongest in the more intensive livestock and vegetable production: 92% of all dairy cattle, 80% of all crops, 71% of beef cattle and 67% of poultry production, as well as 91% of green house vegetable production, 67% of outdoor vegetables and 67% of tree fruits, but only 33% of the rice grown in Japan are produced by these farms.[2]

The focus on non-land intensive production is explained by the land distribution pattern established by the 1946 Land Reform and its concomitant transfer controls (which were relaxed only gradually in the 1962, 1970 and 1980 Land Law Amendments)[3] and land price increases,[4] far in excess of annual inflation rates during most of the post-war period have restrained part-time farmers from selling their land even more beyond their 'natural' disinclination to do so. Also price levels for paddy fields with Y17 m per ha in agricultural areas (1985)[5] have reached heights beyond any prospects for reasonable rates of return for this investment through crop production.

Given the rate and intensity of off-farm employment, renting out land is fairly widespread – especially via Nokyo – but still due to 'absentee landlordism' reminiscences not popular to admit (at least to government statisticians). By December 1984 158,000 ha of farmland had been officially leased (a significant proportion of which, however, among close relatives, e.g. by parents to their children).

A popular alternative to a straight lease among small-scale part-timers is to delegate certain labour intensive work sequences to the cooperatives or directly to full-time neighbours. More than 25% of those farmers cultivating under 0.5 ha of paddies had left raising seedlings, ploughing, rice planting and weeding to others. This percentage rose to 34% for harvesting and threshing, and to 55% for drying and crop preparation work.[6] One wonders whether with such little work left, some of these commissioning 'farmers' declare themselves as such for tax purposes mainly.

In most countries land distribution patterns are usually used to explain structures of social inequality in agriculture. In Japan, since the Land Reform, with its current 1.15 ha average land holdings, this yardstick makes little sense. In 1980 in Japan, excluding Hokkaido, 42% of all farm households owned less than 0.5 ha, 29% held 0.5 to 1.0 ha, 14% owned 1.0 to 1.5 ha (thus beginning to exceed the Land Reform's old average limitation), 7% held 1.5 to 2.0 ha, 5.3% of farmers owned 2 to 3 ha, with 2.1% being landlords of '3.0 ha or more'.

In Hokkaido with its more extensive husbandry based farming pattern, average holdings reached 9.5 ha in 1979 (for comparison, the EC 10 average farm size is: 17.1 ha, the US: 181.4 ha), up from 4.05 ha in 1960[7] (prior to the gradual land transfer liberalization of 1962). Farm land holdings are equally more sizeable in Tohoku than predictably in the major metropolitan areas of Kanto and Kansai.[8] This regional differentiation prima facie reflects differentials in population density and production modes rather than social or income disparities.

Yet, according to our earlier professional/part-time classification a clear picture of the viable full-timers and Class I part-timers owing the larger holdings emerges. Almost 50% of these households own arable land of above 1.5 ha. In contrast, the groups of Class II farmers whose head is either a regular off-farm wage-earner or day labourer, or those full-timers having no male household members of productive age, almost all (85%) own holdings of below 1 ha. Most are even smaller than 0.5 ha. More than 20% of these small holdings have no commercial sales. They just produce rice or vegetables for their personal consumption. Most other farm statistics in the developed world would count this 'subsistence farming' as extensive gardening.[9]

There is, however, a small Class II part-time household group, in which the household head is fully engaged in agriculture (the bulk of family income is derived from the off-farm employment of other family members). It forms a somewhat intermediate position in farmland ownership with 60% of farmers owning less than 1.0 ha, and only 20% of the total possessing less than 0.5 ha.[10] Among the Class II and the retired full-time farmers obviously rice is the most favourable crop, which with the current mechanized and intensive chemical input use poses few production problems in terms of know-how and labour (laborious tasks like harvesting being commissioned off on a fee basis). Equally rice production poses few marketing problems, as most of the crop is purchased by the Food Agency, the government's marketing monopoly. Nonetheless, it is evident that in rice production also economies of scale work in favour of larger holdings. In 1975 with a total cost index of 100 for paddies of less than 0.3 ha, the index stood at 59.8 for farmland of more than 3 ha. The index for work hours with only 47.9 for the largest holding was even more advantageous to large-scale operations. Modern production techniques have strengthened the economies of scale aspect: in 1960, by comparison, when traditional rice growing techniques still prevailed, the scale of operations' differential had been much less pronounced.[11] Still, the well-known natural and financial barriers to exploitation of scale economies in land extensive crop production persist.

Predictably expansion of scales of operations have hence been most pronounced in labour and capital intensive livestock production, like hog, poultry and dairy operations as well as in greenhouse vegetable and fruit production – areas in which also agribusiness found its sphere of operations in Japan. Concentration has been rapid in the past decade. In 1984 the average dairy herd consisted of 24.1 cows (in 1975: 11.2) with one of the world's highest yields per animal. The average holding of hogs reached 113.9 (1975: 24.4),[12] the flocks of laying hens were at a medium of 852 (1975: 229) and of chicken broilers at 19 500 birds (1975: 7 596). A continuation of the trend to further concentrated holdings is expected. This growth so far shows little evidence of possible environmental or political limits to this type of 'factory farming'. Greenhouses in Japan in 1983 had an average size of 0.25 ha of surface (1975: 0.15 ha).[13]

Japan's 'industrial horticulture' in 1982 already enjoyed a 92% share in all open grown melons, 89% in strawberries, 65% in paprikas, 57% in cucumbers and 48% in tomato production.[14]

As regards general income levels, it would be mistaken to associate 'rural poverty' with small land holdings. Those 'farmers' with holdings of less than 0.5 ha already in 1974 showed the largest farm family income, followed by those with between 0.5 ha and 1 ha land holdings, and then only by the 'large-scale' farmers with more than 2.5 ha of land. The first two groups were evidently dominated by those Class II farmers who were essentially wage earners with agricultural pursuits as a lucrative side activity. The medium-scale farmers owning land between 1.0 and 2.5 ha fared worst.[15] Their off-farm part-time activities appear largely as seasonal employment in industry and in public works – poorly paid as unskilled labour, forced into off-village migratory jobs by the insufficiency of the farming income alone. It comes as little surprise that this disadvantaged intermediate group shows the strongest decline in membership numbers over the years. Viewed in professional terms, it appears as if it were the full-timers who fare worst in the income statistics compared to both Class I and II part-timers.[16] It is certain, however, that the popularity of farming as a full-time retirement occupation has distorted the statistics.

In fact, compared to urban wage earners, farmers – even in official statistics (with farmers as agricultural entrepreneurs being able to conceal real income levels much more effectively to both statisticians and the fisc) – still appear significantly better off (Table 3.2).

Table 3.2 Farmer's and workers' household incomes (national average)[17]

	1965	1975	1981
Agricultural households			
No. of persons per household	5.3	4.6	4.4
No. of practising farmers per household	2.7	2.6	2.5
Income, total (Y1000)	835	3,967	5,930
disposable	775	3,577	5,069
of which agricultural	365	1,146	968
(as percentage of total income)	44	29	16
disposable income per person (Y1000)	147	784	1,152
Salaried households			
No. of persons per household	4.1	3.8	3.8
Income, total (Y1000)	797	2,897	4,468
disposable	728	2,642	3,852
disposable income per person (Y1000)	177	694	1,014

These figures clearly indicate higher total disposable farm income figures since the 1960s, and since the 1970s increasingly higher disposable income figures per rural household member. Even discounting agricultural income (which in 1981 had shrunk to a mere 16% of total farm household income), the off-farm income of farm families alone exceed that of their urban counterparts. When analysing these figures, it must be remembered that farm families usually live in their own – more spacious – housing and hence enjoy lower expenditure on rents as well as evidently on food, which should more than compensate for higher rural costs for transportation and spending on non-food items.

These data indicate that on average the 1961 Agricultural Basic Law's objective of parity for the rural economy has been over-accomplished since long. Could these average data be taken as an indication that rural poverty – so rampant in the pre-war days, and still persistent in the early post-war years among rural repatriates and in the remote mountain and fishing villages – particularly in Tohoku – has been eliminated by a combination of off-farm employment, economic growth in the countryside and public support policies implying massive net urban–rural income transfers?

Ushiomi describes incidents of rural poverty and landlord dependency for some areas of Tohoku (the North-Eastern part of Iwate Prefecture), where families in mountain villages (former tenants) still had to rely on cash advances for all their products – especially charcoal – from the leading forestry owning families, enjoying monopoly purchasing and agricultural input dispensing facilities.[18]

But Ushiomi at the time of writing in 1963 had to conclude, that even in outlaying forestry villages – forestry land, for some mysterious reason, had been excluded from the Land Reform – of Tohoku 'such systems were "on the way out"'. Horikoshi describes a fruit growing mountain village in Northern Nagano Prefecture.

In 1971, I found no households that appeared poor. Before World War II, there was a very clear economic line between the wealthy households with large landholdings and the poor farmers with very small holdings. In the early 1970s, such a clear distinction was no longer observable. In the broad sense, almost all had achieved a fair degree of affluence.[19]

Although public rural income statistics are not sufficiently differentiated to permit a conclusive verdict on the official version of rural poverty being eradicated,[20] various other 'revisited' accounts by rural sociologists confirm this view. The income situation is probably tightest among retired people doing full-time farming without successors and other family support. They do, however, still possess farmland and housing as a saleable property. For farmers in Tokoku, southern Kyushu, Okinawa and other mountanous or small island regions, the employment opportunities necessitating long-distance commuting to metropolitan centres causing prolonged absences often for more than 6 months per year, the resulting 'family income' may be satisfactory, the conditions for family life and the women doing farm labour, however, hardly are such. Shimpo, in referring to the situation in central Iwate Prefecture, vividly described the disruptive effects which such regular prolonged absences of the adult male family member had on family life and cohesion.[21] Increasingly, however, whenever possible, poorly paid seasonal work is being replaced by steady full-time employment elsewhere.[22]

The outmigration of productive labour has led to frequently dramatic demographic and infrastructural consequences. In 1985 more than 40% of full-timers were above 60 years of age (while part-timers made up of about 5% retired people almost perfectly reflected the age structure of other industries).[23] With currently about 40% of the total 'farming population' at 60 and above, MAFF expects a further increase to 50% by 1990.[24] In the medium term, this unfavourable age structure will retard agricultural productivity gains and more efficient land use, particularly in cases in which there is no prospect of a successor taking over. Such aged farm households without succession numbered 510 000 in 1984.[25] In the long run, in the next century, this might contribute to enlarged viable farm sizes and to a reduction in the over-allocation of labour to agriculture and thus to a more rational farm economy.

Professor Hemmi reports Japanese forecasts that by the year 2000 mainly through leased transfers from retired farmers a 'fairly large number' of 10 to 15 ha grain farms and 20 to 35 ha dairy farms will come into existence.[26]

In many remote rural areas the outmigration of younger couples has reduced birthrates and social life in general, making the maintenance of public and private services a too costly affair, hence triggering the ultimate abandonment of some outlying villages.[27]

Agro-business in official statistics is much less well documented than the duality of the peasantry proper. As in all other liberal economies, companies in the agro-food sector, limited in their growth prospects by 'the natural constraints of the human stomach', seek to expand their growth and profit potential by vertical and/or horizontal integration. This applies to suppliers of inputs (feed, agricultural chemistry and machinery) as well as to food processors (millers, refiners, butchers, etc.), and to the import and retail trade. An attractive alternative to a straightforward absorption of the agricultural sector (legal obstacles apart, high land and subsequent labour costs form major deterrents, offering only very limited profit prospects for farm investment in current agricultural economies), is contract farming. Processors or traders offer contracts to farmers specifying exact quantities, qualities and dates of delivery for certain products in exchange for a pre-arranged price. The farmer is assured of his outlets and remuneration (provided he fulfils the specifications) but is deprived of entrepreneurial freedom. In Japan and elsewhere, often cooperatives' crop and livestock production schemes also may have an identical effect.

Agro-business in its narrower definition used here (a wider definition which in less protected, developed countries makes more sense refers to *all* agricultural production for commercial purposes) in Japan is most pronounced in the capital intensive greenhouse and feed–livestock sector.

The Japan Statistical Yearbook for 1980 lists under its section 'Industrial Horticulture' 509 'non-farmhousehold establishments' operating greenhouse/glassroom facilities to grow vegetables, fruit and flowers. Industrial horticulture in 1982 accounted for more than 30% of all eggplants, lettuce, pumpkins and squash, about half of all tomatoes and cucumbers, 65% of all paprika, 78% of the watermelons, 89% of the strawberries and 92% of the melons grown in the open in Japan.[28] A great many of the financers/operators/contractors should be the large supermarket chains interested in short-cut and reliable supply lines with specified amounts and qualities of produce.

Kagome, Japan's largest tomato juice producer, purchases the entire harvest of its contract farmers (some is also imported from Taiwan and Southern Europe). Its annual report describes the relationship which appears to leave little room for producer decisions:[29]

> Seeds are supplied to our farmers, and we give them advice on how to grow what we think is the perfect KAGOME tomato. We even include information on fertilizers, and stipulate when the fruit should be picked. Growing the best quality produce doesn't happen by chance. It's a carefully planned process.

In the broiler business by contrast, it is the upstream industries which dominate the sector. With shipments reaching 300 000 birds p.a., the 7 400 remaining broiler producing 'households' – with 30% of the production concentrated in the Southern Kyushu prefectures of Miyazaki and Kagoshima – have largely become dependent on the feed importing trading company (sogo shosha) subsidiaries. (Feed costs as a proportion of total production costs vary between 65 and 72%.) Jetro wrote in 1981:

> In the late 1960s, however, the sogo shosha and their affiliated feed manufacturing companies rapidly advanced into the broiler industry as comprehensive integrators. The integrated sogo shosha affiliates benefit from extremely powerful nationwide sales networks and are backed by high levels of capital, and great organizational and technological capabilities. . . . Reorganization of the business structure through comprehensive sogo shosha integration is now in progress, and in the process the oligopolistic system is becoming indisputably consolidated.[30]

As a result, chickenmeat production grew by 18.4% (1960–79), with prices remaining remarkably stable for the somehow more and more tasteless products. The same applies to laying hens. Kaminogo writes:

> The reason why eggs have become . . . models of price stabilization is that trading firms moved into farm villages and forcibly carried out an improvement of their physical constitution and rationalization on a commercial basis.[31]

Haruna, the President of Marubeni, Japan's third largest sogo shosha, describes his corporation's poultry operations:[32]

> We have worked out a broiler processing system which uses Tamnabarry Development's 'chicken harvesting' machines for picking up broilers quickly. Chicks are also imported from Britain and raised in Japan . . . (which) alone accounts for 9% of the entire Japanese broiler market.

His PR department explained their success:[33]

> Marubeni's financial strength provided for the construction of larger poultry houses and processing plants, as well as for the extensive systems needed for a stable relationship with contract farmers. On the sales side, there was a reduction of the steps in distribution thanks to the cooperation of the department stores,

supermarkets, and ham and sausage manufacturers who have long been Marubeni customers.

Pork production, with most of the production concentrated north of the main consuming Kanto area and in Southern Kyushu is similarly feed intensive. Formula feed consumption has risen to 677 kg per animal (1975/80), a level that nearly fulfils its total average nutritional requirements.[34] Longworth quotes MAFF's 1980 census, according to which apart from the 45 000 farm households who realized most gross sales from pig operations also 927 non-agricultural operations were in business[35] indicating a strong commercial orientation of the sector.

In the less competitive and more protected lucrative beef and dairy cattle business, which due to its attractiveness is more fraught with administrative barriers to commercial entrants, in 1980 681 and 508 'non-farmhouseholds' were active. The structure of both sectors is quite different – dairy herds being concentrated in Hokkaido (37% of Japan's total) in fairly large holdings – 42.4 cattle per farm – during summer on open pasture, while the beef raising operations are still largely done in small in-door holdings dispersed over Japan – with a certain regional emphasis nonetheless in Southern Kyushu, Tohoku and Hokkaido.

It was the Dai'ei Supermarket chain (Japan's largest retailer), which built the first modern 800 head large-scale feed-lot for dairy steers in Kagoshima in the early 1970s.[36] Its integrated operations cut through the extremely cumbersome and costly processing and whole-sale beef chain, and have since served as a model also for Nokyo-organized feed-lot operations.[37] Seiyu Foods, the third largest retailer, has moved into contract fattening schemes for bull calves. Farmers are to provide the cattle sheds, the rest is supplied by Seiyu which pays a minimum of Y50 per day for the farmers' labour per head of cattle fattened.[38] For obvious reasons there is strong resistance on the part of the central cooperatives association (Zenchu) against such 'cattle-sharecropping' and straight corporate livestock raising schemes, and local building permits are often impossible to obtain, due to both Zenchu's political muscles and to the environmental hazards such intensive husbandry operations pose. Increasingly, agro-business has moved abroad for greener pastures. Ito Ham Provisions, Japan's largest meat processor, for instance, owns cattle ranch operations in Brazil as a joint venture with Brazilian partners.[39]

Nippon Meat Packers, the second largest meat processor, has diversified further into both animal feeds, breeding and direct retail operations. It runs subsidiary firms to raise poultry, pork and beef for direct supplies in Japan as well as dairy beef operations in Australia and the US.[40] Overseas operations also focus on the crop products in which Japan has strong import needs. The sogo shosha (Mitsui Bussan has its origins not by accident as a privileged Tokugawa rice trader[41]) and their feed subsidiaries since the 1960s have purchased into US West Coast grain terminal and elevator facilities to guarantee reliable feedgrain supplies.[42]

The emergence of mainland China as a major corn exporter, with its superior qualities and significantly shorter transportation routes just across the East China Sea will have strong repercussions on future feed supplies and benefit feed operations near port sites in Western Japan. Since 1985 most sogo shosha and Zenno, the cooperatives' central commercial arm, are involved in the China trade.[43] The trading companies and Japan's official development authorities currently support the modernization of China's obsolete harbour export storage and rolling stock facilities.

In the Manchurian province of Heilongjang since 1980, 20 000 ha of a former prairie region in a joint venture with a sogo shosha importing US and Japanese know-how and machinery were developed into a high-yield feed grains and livestock (hay and poultry) raising and processing area. Some of the costs of this model state farm ('Hong He Farm') are to be recovered by soybean exports.[44]

Since the US soy embargo of 1973 Japan's economic diplomacy has cultivated relations with Brazil, where many of the 1 m Brazilians of Japanese origin are engaged in agriculture. Other significant sogo shosha food production in the Third World take place in Indonesia and in the Philippines where all of its banana exports to Japan are handled by Japanese trading companies.[45]

In the fishery sector, the leading fishery companies, Taiyo Fisheries, and Nissui,[46] after years of expansion face significant difficulties for their high seas/offshore operations after the world-wide extension of 'continental' water rights and the increased controls by coastal nations. Nonetheless concentration in the industry is encouraged by MAFF's structural policy to reduce the number of fishing vessels for small- and medium-scale operations.[47]

Wine production, which in most of Europe and the other growing areas is still dominated by small/medium-sized vineyards or regional cooperatives, in Japan is fully industrial. Only a fraction of Japan's

340 000-tonne grape harvest is used for wine-making (90% are more profitably sold as fresh table grapes). The four oligopolist producers of 'Chateau Lion' (Suntory), 'Mann's Wine' (Kikkoman), 'Mercian' (Sanraku Ocean), and 'Sainte Neige' (Kyowa Hakko), their wine operations all headquartered in Yamanashi Prefecture, south of Mount Fuji (the only area where the grapes can be grown in Japan's generally too humid summer climate), for almost all of their French-sounding brand names depend on blends with imported bulk wines (largely low-quality table wines from East Europe, Spain and South America).[48] With an annual demand (in 1983) of 84 m litres (about one bottle per head), only about 40 m litres could be covered by the wine fermented from home grown grapes; 17 m litres are upmarket bottled imports from Europe and California. The rest, 27 m litres, has to be made by bulk imports.[49] With as little as 5% of their contents made from domestic grapes, blends could still, until 1987, be labelled as 'made in Japan'. In the wake of the Austrian glucol scandal of 1985 it was discovered that Mann's prime 'Japanese Estate Wine', priced at around Y30 000 per bottle was largely cheap Austrian plonk. The blend and the label, however, were perfectly legal. Kikkoman, the parent company's, top management nonetheless was forced to resign.[50]

THE SOCIAL TRANSFORMATION OF JAPAN'S VILLAGES AND FARM FAMILIES

If the ideologists of Nohonshugi were right in viewing the Japanese hamlet and its social cohesion as the cornerstone of the social fabric of Japanese society, then its contemporary transformation could hardly be more complete. Most authors are fairly precise in dating the breaking point between the 'old' and the 'new' rural society and its mores. Initiated by the Land Reform of 1946 (breaking the mould of the old landlord class), but finally accomplished by the ready availability of off-farm working opportunities and the liberation of rural manual labour by mechanization, this was achieved in the late 1960s[51] with apparently only small variations allowing for regional and local particularities.

Smith observes that the mechanical rice transplanter (planting the seedlings into the flooded paddies) 'has eradicated at a stroke the part of the process of rice production most heavily involved with ritual and cooperative behaviour'.[52] In 1972 alone, 128 000 transplanters were sold.[53]

In the early 1950s only 3–4% of Japan's rural population were non-cultivators. Farmers then understandingly were ill at ease with urban ways and during visits to the cities. The rural/urban divide then appeared very pronounced: economically, socially, culturally, with the differentiation evident also in habits of dressing and speech. Rice growing households ('ie') depended for their status and livelihood on the size and quality of the land holdings inherited, and were hence vividly aware of past generations' labour and achievements which had to be transmitted to future generations. Given the labour intensity of paddy cultures the individual could only survive in a household economy. Consequently, in a normative sense family (household) needs took precedence over individual likings and aspirations, which were sanctioned and suppressed should they clash with household objectives. The households in turn depended on the hamlet (buraku) community for essentials like drainage, irrigation, flood control, public roads, labour exchange, emergency help and general information and advice.

The joint responsibility of the self-governing hamlet for taxes, crime and delinquency of the old Tokugawa system (1603–1867) belonged to the distant past. Yet, the modes of paddy culture essentially remained unchanged: 'Land management unites the household, water management unites the Community'.[54] Communal water rights were of vital importance in areas where natural supplies due to the scarcity of irrigation dams were uncertain and decided over crop success or failure. Inter-communal disputes often turned violent, individual water thieves were asked to make public apologies, or if unrepentant, could be sanctioned with cut-off water supplies or social ostracism (mura hachibu).[55]

The rice cycle determined the life of the villagers: in early May seedbeds were prepared in which the rice seeds were sown. In late May/early June, winter crops (barley/wheat, etc.) were harvested in the paddies, fertilizers (animal manure) applied, the paddies watered and the rice seedlings immediately transplanted into the soil. Later the paddies would require weeding at least 4 times as well as spraying with pesticides and insecticides (DDT until 1971). In mid-October the paddies were drained for harvesting, which implied cutting, drying, threshing, winnowing and hulling the rice. Then the winter crops were planted. The most labour intensive stages of the rice cycle – transplanting and harvesting – were done as group work by the entire household. In pre-mechanized agriculture double cropping obviously implied maximizing average yields through intensive use of human energy.

In upland fields fruit, vegetables, sweet potatoes, rice, other cereals, tea and bamboo were also grown. Animal husbandry was usually limited to draft oxen (one or two at most per household) and to some poultry.

In mountain villages forestry work and charcoal burning offered some off-season income. In coastal villages farmers pursued small scale part-time fishing. Another typical off-seasonal pursuit was sericulture as an agricultural sideline for cash income (fruit orchards and mulberry trees had taken some time to be replanted after their destruction as non-essential to food security in the war economy).

Households were almost self-sufficient in food: rice, barley, wheat, eggs, chickenmeat, beans, rape oil, fruits and vegetables were all produced on the farm. In off-coastal villages the most important additional food item was fish, usually purchased from itinerant peddlars, who also sold salt, sugar, tea, sake, sweets, noodles and basic household appliances. Rice was the highest prized food, considered indispensable for any decent meal. Yet, as a 'luxury food' when the farm households' annual stock started to run out, it had to be eked out with barley. Red meat consumption was discouraged by high prices, while the taste for milk only gradually spread through school milk programmes.

Frugality was the norm for both food and non-food consumption: the need to maintain and to transmit scarce household resources. Wasteful life styles would endanger a family's economic livelihood and social status, and were hence frowned upon in rural society. Family life was based on the individual's identification with the household ('ie'), visible at public functions when one family member was sufficient to represent the entire house, and reinforced by the pre-war constitution and civil code only recently abolished. Equally the household was held responsible in the hamlet's opinion for its members' deviant behaviour (in case of serious delinquency the hamlet assembly would pronounce social sanctions against the family in question).

The household was based on patrilineal continuity – genealogical succession through men. Household head was the father, who played a distant emotional role and decided major issues in the household economy and kept the budget. The oldest son as the heir apparent played a more placid role and was less urged to do well at school. The young wife, married into the clan, was in the weakest familial position: in her twenties/thirties she had to work her way up through fertility and hard labour: the first to wake up (at 5 a.m.), the last to go to bed (at 10.30 p.m.), closely supervised by her mother-in-law. These were no equals in the traditional farm household, a social pattern learned from early childhood: males rank before females, the elder before the young, those born in the household before those entering from the outside. The hierarchical positions were continuously reinforced by subtleties in speech, the sequence of bath use, seating arrangements during meals, etc. Succession of the household and its property followed the system of male primogeniture. Only if the oldest son was incapable, would the second assume his position. Should there be no suitable sons, one of the daughters' husbands would assume the role of an adopted son to succeed. The younger sons, should they wish to remain in farming and to reside in the village, were permitted to establish 'branch households' with some land given to them. The strong intra-communal social differentiation between the leading 'stem' ('honke') and its various hierarchical branch families ('bunke') – particularly pronounced in pre-war Tohoku – has its roots in this rule of unequal inheritance of land property. In these traditional communities, later-coming households stood in a relationship of dependency and submission to the stem family. With their meagre (and usually tenanted) land endowment these poor farmers at the edge of starvation accepted their hierarchical submission as a 'form of life insurance'[54] and internalized their status over the generations. The stem family would be consulted in cases of marriage, land purchases/sales, and could be asked for food aid; gifts would regularly be exchanged, etc. The stem families usually also had close links to the village (Shinto) deity or to the local (Buddhist) temple.

Shrine maintenance, religious festivals and prayer meetings nonetheless were communal affairs. The youth association ('Seinendan'), to which all males aged between 15 and 25 belonged, was in particular charged with festival organization, but also with quasi-policing functions, like water guard. They also formed the local fire brigade. The (married) women's association ('Fujinkai') was less active, given the labour with which the participating young women were charged. While farmwork normally was done separately, households cooperated during house construction, and in preparation of ceremonies, like marriages, funerals, etc.

The hamlets ('buraku') consisting usually of a few dozen house-holds already in the Meiji amalgamation (1899) had been merged to village ('mura') size. In 1953 administrative rationalization and increased demand for more sophisticated local public services motivated a further wave of administrative mergers to 'machi' (town) size. Already the 'mura' was considered as little more than an artificial administrative unit. Along its lines the agricultural cooperatives were organized; it was the unit in charge of the primary and middle schools, but it only gradually assumed some role in public welfare and local road and canal maintenance – traditional areas of hamlet self-help. In local elections the hamlet's entire vote would usually go for a native son to represent its local interests in the village assembly. Local offices would typically be held by elderly notables (often former landlords), leisured and better off to afford the time for public functions, politically 'independent', however conservative in their general orientation. Generally well informed about regional and national politics, farmers with their *'petit bourgeois* mentality' as small land-owners[55] nonetheless, also in national and prefectural elections, continued to show a preference to vote for native sons and their position of well-pursued local interests.

At the time, to some observers the old Japanese village with its farmers 'tied to the soil' and 'closed in a local collectivity'[56] appeared as an unattractive semi-feudal obstacle to a democratized new Japan: the rigid norms with which the hamlet would sanction dissenters and repress individualism, an enforced communalism suspected to benefit the former landlord class[57] and ultimately the conservative ruling power elite in post-war Japan.[58]

In the meantime, the Japanese hamlets have undergone a profound transformation and disintegration from communalism to contractual society (to use Tönnies in the original German terms: a change from 'Gemeinschaft' to 'Gesellschaft'). To many nostalgic observers the new suburbanized village – reflecting a change evident in almost all old rural settlements in densely populated industrialized countries and regions (Central Europe, England, US East Coast) – revealed equally unattractive elements of social disintegration, wasteful consumption, ecological abuse, and a general lack of tradition and of vitality,[59] a background before which the old hamlet turns idyllic (as it does appear in fact, when one reviews films of the 1940s and 1950s).

MAFF differentiates rural change according to four community types:[60]

1. metropolitan suburbs, in which farmers since 1955 were outnumbered by city dwellers (and got rich from the sale of their land);
2. villages around provincial cities: suburbanization occurred with some time-lag;
3. villages on plains: changes have been slower, with a larger percentage of farming households remaining; and
4. mountain villages: depopulation occurred.

With the ready availability of off-farm employment, exceeding agricultural revenue proper, in the villages land possession evidently is no longer decisive for income levels and hence social status. It is now the quality of one's own salaried employment which counts – not different from the rest of metropolitan Japan. Not only is the village's social stratification system transformed, the concept of an integrated household ('ie') loses all meaning: urban wages and salaries are paid for individual performance. Agricultural work has largely turned into a more or less profitable sideline, relegated to an occupation for housewives and those retired. Cut off from their economic significance the old rural mores were abandoned rapidly for the values of Japanese main-stream social conformity, reinforced by the ever-present norm-setting mass media: children are encouraged to reach the highest possible schooling (high school graduation being the rule) in order to be able to compete for the best possible metropolitan corporate or public employment. Young farmers will live in their own separate houses, replacing the old joint residence. First sons, once envied for their status, are now pitied – if at all, since most farmers do have problems finding a successor: usually they have to pay their prospective successor's farm labour now, build their separate housing, finance new farm machinery and promise life-time property transfers. For all their maltreatment young women once had to suffer on farms, they have now become a cherished acquisition, as most contemporary rural girls dislike the prospect of life-long farm labour and prefer marrying an urban wage earner instead.[61]

Today the average equipment of rural households is perfectly equivalent to that of urban ones. Motorization – with the second car becoming the norm for rural families (instead of the single bicycle of 35 years earlier) is superior, reflecting need to commute for work and to do long-distance shopping. The extent of capital over-investment in contemporary Japanese agriculture (with certainly the world's highest density of tractors, grain dryers, power sprayers, rice transplanters and harvesters per hectare) – which contributed to reduced net income from agricultural pursuits – is attributed to non-economic machinery purchasing decisions, such as purchases of 'consumer goods', to imitation behaviour (demonstration effects) or to attract successors to the farm, or to maximize leisure and recreation time.[62]

Such a consumerist investment orientation – which certainly is more typical for the dominant part-time sector – is a far cry from the old frugal economic rationality. Smith quotes a farm woman on the new technologies' use: 'We don't have to weed anymore. We just put herbicide in the water at transplanting time and that's that'.[63] Double cropping has disappeared and upland fields often are abandoned. Religious practices have been in continuous decline, reduced often to New Year's shrine visits and ancestral altars' upkeep. Festivals and local public traditions turned into disuse and oblivion. Hamlet meetings are no longer attended, people (understandably) find TV watching more amusing. Housewives prefer supermarket shopping to visits to the Nokyo shop. Home-made foods are reduced to pickles and relish. Road and water maintenance is done by the local government and its employees, no longer a sphere of communal self-help. Because of the lack of activities, the women's associations are moribund and the young men's clubs are frequented by the older generation. Daily neighbourhood visits are replaced by telephone conversations. Marriage partners now find themselves rather at urban work places than through elders' arrangements. Little wonder that Smith observes the appearance of a generation gap in former rural villages with different values and a lack of communication between the pre- and post-growth generations. Parents no longer feel confident (as they once were) to rely on their offspring for their old-age care.[64] The concept of 'ie', the rural household transmitting paddy land through the generations appears definitely broken. Already in 1978 Fukutake concluded that little status consciousness was left of who was descended from a former landlord, owner-farmer or tenant family before the Land Reform.[65] As most fathers have to commute long distances to their daily employment (and some still have to settle for more prolonged absences from home) even within the reduced nuclear families – as with the rest of urban Japan – their status and control power is diminished, while the position of children and women is by consequence improved, the latter aspiring to a semi-urban, 'clean, leisurely, healthful environment for her family', a life style 'that is ultimately inimical to farming'.[66]

Village amalgamations have further reduced the public functions at local level. Offices were relocated to distant townhalls, in which

villagers' proper interests were often minoritarian: farmers' representation in municipal councils has declined, with the local Chambers of
Industry and Commerce asking for municipal funds, local subsidies
being allocated to serve business interests instead of agriculture.[67]
Party politicians have replaced the rural notables as mayors. For
them, however, the endorsement by village representatives and the
Nokyo may still remain an important consideration.

Part-time farmers will attempt to preserve their political clout –
and thus the subsidy levels to make their part-time pursuits profitable
(at the expense of everyone else in the nation). But the farming
community's gradual and persistent erosion – in social, ideological,
economic and demographic terms – will accelerate the transformation of the former Japanese village. It has been abandoned in the
mountains (due to continued depopulation) and completely suburbanized elsewhere: for better or for worse transformed into commuters' suburbs, abandoned during the day, except for mainly old
people pottering around in the fields. There is a definite attraction to
residing in local areas for most Japanese having to live among
metropolitan congestion. Nonetheless, as long as technological progress in communications does not yet permit a relocation of productive
jobs, there is precious little that public policies – aiming at the 'formation of vital rural societies'[68] – can do to reverse the current trend.

Notes

1. MAFF, *Agriculture in Japan* (Tokyo, Mar. 1986) p. 20.
2. Yamaji, Susumu, 'Big Farming Is the Key to Survival', *Journal of
   Japanese Trade and Industry*, no 1. 1985, p. 37.
3. Sekiya, Shunsaku, 'Agricultural Land System in Japan', *Japanese Agricultural Review*, vols 81–4, 1981, p. 15.
4. With annual increases of 17.2% for paddies and of 19.6% for upland
   farmland (all Japan) during 1960–73; price increases for farmland in
   urban areas with 27% p.a. predictably exceeded the national average
   (Kuroda, Yoshimi, 'The Recent State of Agriculture in Japan' in Emory
   N. Castle and Kenzo Hemmi (eds), *United States – Japanese Agriculture
   Trade Relations*, Washington, D.C. : Resources for the Future, Inc.
   1982, p. 128).
5. *Japan Agrinfo Newsletter*, vol 3, Mar. 1986, p. 3.
6. MAFF, *Annual Report on Agriculture – 1984 (Excerpts)*, Tokyo Foreign
   Press Center (June 1985) p. 19.
7. Sekiya, op. cit., p. 5.
8. *Japan Statistical Yearbook* (1985) p. 150.
9. According to the OECD (1974), 'Farm households' are defined as those
   which operate farm areas of 0.1 ha, and over in the eastern part of Japan

(0.05 ha and over in the western part) or those whose annual farm sales are 50,000 Yen and over despite a farm area below that level (OECD, *Agricultural Policy in Japan*, Paris: OECD, 1974, p. 31).

10. MAFF, Annual Report, op. cit., p. 16.
11. Egaitsu, Fumio, 'Japanese Agricultural Policy' in Castle and Hemmi (eds) op. cit., p. 166.
12. By comparison, the EC 10 average dairy herd consisted of 17.8 cows and on average 58 pigs were kept in 1985. (EC Commission, *The Situation of Agriculture in the Community, Report 1986*, Luxemburg, 1987 p. 298).
13. MAFF, 'Agriculture in Japan', *Japan's Agricultural Review*, 13 & 14, 1986, p. 21.
14. *Japan Statistical Yearbook*, 1985, p. 162.
15. MAFF, 'Agriculture and Forestry White Papers FY 1974', summarized in *Focus Japan*, July 1976, p. 3.
16. Hayami, Yujiro, 'Adjustment Policies for Japan's Agriculture in a Changing World' in Castle and Hemmi (eds), op. cit., Table 10.10.
17. 'Exploitants agricoles' in *Japon économie* (Paris), no. 174, July 1984, p. 7.
18. Ushiomi, Toshitaka, *Forestry and Mountain Village Communities in Japan* (Tokyo: Kokusai Bunka Shinkokai, 1968) pp. 66–70.
19. Horikoshi, Hisamoto, 'The Changing Rural Landscape', *Japan Foundation Newsletter*, vol. 13, no. 1, 1985, p. 4.
20. Personal Communication by MAFF officials 1985/86.
21. Shimpo, Mitsuru, *Three Decades in Shiwa* (Vancouver: University of British Columbia Press, 1976) p. 57.
22. Robert J. Smith, *Kurusu. 'the Price of Progress in a Japanese Village'* (Stanford, Calif.: Stanford University Press, 1978) p. 83.
23. MAFF, *Annual Report 1985*, p. 15.
24. MAFF, *Agriculture in Japan*, 1986, p. 21.
25. MAFF, op. cit., 1985, p. 17.
26. Hemmi, Kenzo, *Agriculture in the 21st Century: A Japanese View* (New York, NY : Philip Morris Inc., 1983) p. 6.
27. Hasumi, Otohiko, 'Rural Society in Postwar Japan, Part II', *Japan Foundation Newsletter*, vol. 12, no. 6, 1985, p. 6.
28. *Japan Statistical Yearbook*, 1984, pp. 162–3.
29. Kagome Co. Ltd, *Annual Report 1986*, p. 13.
30. JETRO, *Chicken Broilers*, Access to Japan's Market, no. 7, rev. ed. 1981, p. 8.
31. Kaminogo, Toshiaki, *Bungei Shunju*, Mar. 1977.
32. *Financial Times*, 12 May 1986.
33. Marubeni Corporation, *The Unique World of the Sogo Shosha* (Tokyo, 1978) pp. 88–9.
34. William T. Coyle, *Japan's Feed–Lifestock Industry*, Foreign Agricultural Economic Report, no. 177 (Washington DC : USDA, 1983) p. 21.
35. John W. Longworth, *Beef in Japan* (St. Lucia, Queensland: University of Queensland Press, 1983) p. 39.
36. Ibid., pp. 115–16.
37. Kaminogo, op. cit., p. 00.
38. Nakao, Mitsuaki, 'Inside the Beef Industry', *Japan Echo*, vol. 11, no. 1, 1984, p. 69.

39. ASI Market Research Inc., *A Market Study of Processed Meat in Japan* (Tokyo, 1979) p. 33.
40. Ibid., p. 38.
41. Michael W. Donnelly, *Political Management of Japan's Rice Economy*, Ph.D. thesis, Columbia University, 1978, p. 66.
42. Matsuura, Tatsuo and Morio Morisaki, *The Japanese Feed Market* (Tokyo: Japan International Agricultural Council, 1985) pp. 11–12.
43. Ibid., p. 16.
44. Japan Foreign Trade Council, *The Sogo Shosha* (Tokyo, undated), p. 8.
45. Kojima, Kiyoshi and Terutomo Ozawa, *Japan's General Trading Companies* (Paris: OECD, 1984) p. 59.
46. *Japan Company Handbook* (Toyo Keizai Skimposha, 1985).
47. OECD, Doc. FI/266 of 10 June 1986, p. 18.
48. JETRO, *Wine* Access to Japan's Import Market, no. 15, Tokyo 1982, p. 4; PA International Consulting Services Ltd, *Study on EC Wine and Liquor Exports to Japan*, vol. I (Tokyo: Report for the EC Commission. 1985) p. 95.
49. 'Le Marché Japonais: Le Vin', *Tradescope*, no. 2, Mar. 1985, pp. 8–10.
50. *Financial Times*, 16 Sept. 1985; *The Economist*, 21 Sept. 1985.
51. Hasumi, op. cit., p. 5.
52. Smith, op. cit., p. 89.
53. JETRO, *Agricultural Machinery*, Access to Japan's Import Market, no. 3, 1979, p. 7.
54. Richard K. Beardsley, John W. Hall and Robert E. Ward, *Village Japan* (Chicago University Press, 1972) p. 126.
55. Shimpo, op. cit., p. 9.
53. Beardsley *et al.,*, op. cit., p. 106.
54. Ibid., p. 274.
55. Fukutake, Tadashi, *Rural Society in Japan* (Tokyo University Press, 1980) p. 201.
56. Ushiomi, Toshitaka, *La Communauté rurale au Japon* (Paris: Presses Universitaires de France, 1962) p. ix.
57. Ibid., pp. 45 and 60.
58. Fukutake, op. cit., p. 197.
59. Horikoshi, op. cit., p. 7; Smith, op. cit. p. 209.
60. MAFF, op. cit., 1985, p. 20.
61. Fukutake, op. cit., p. 45.
62. Smith, op. cit., p. 90.
63. Ibid., p. 92.
64. Ibid., p. 190.
65. Fukutake, op. cit., p. 40.
66. Gail Lee Bernstein, *Haruko's World: a Japanese Farm Woman and Her Community* (Stanford University Press, 1983) p. 169.
67. Fukutake, op. cit., p. 170.
68. Agricultural Policy Council, On the Implementation of the Basic Direction of Agricultural Policy in the 1980s', *Japan Agricultural Review*, 7 and 8, 1983, p. 30.

4 Agricultural Cooperatives: the Nokyo System

Every town or village has its cooperatives (Nokyo). In all Japanese towns two types of cooperatives exist. There are multipurpose cooperatives (4300 in 1985) providing banking, insurance, welfare services, agricultural inputs, and general household necessities to all member farm households, as well as those 'single purpose' cooperatives (about 5000) comprising producers according to their sectoral specialization (vegetables, fruits, dairying, beef cattle, pig fattening, poultry, sericulture, etc.). All are organized in about 700 prefectural federations (see Figure 4.1), the functions of which increase with the growing sophistication and diversity of members' demands (especially in non-agricultural matters) on their cooperative. At prefectural level these federations also have their proper union to facilitate coordination of activities and policies.

All prefectural federations are in turn at the national level associated in sectoral federations along either product or purpose lines. They all are linked in a Central Union (Zenchu), crowning this federative edifice; Zenchu is in charge of general coordination and political campaigning for farming and cooperatives' interests. The president of Zenchu is considered the spokesman for all cooperatives and the agricultural community's top negotiator with politics and organized business.[1] In economic terms, however, Zenno, which supervises and organizes the Nokyo system's central economic operations (warehousing, importation, processing, marketing, industrial participations, etc.), is more important (though legally Zenno is only entitled to give economic 'guidance' to prefectural and local cooperatives).[2]

Cooperative concepts were never alien to rural Japan, with the original implementation of cooperative thought culminating in Ninomiya's (1787–1856) ethical teaching and community funds, granting interest-free loans to its rural members.[3]

Japan's first legislation in 1900 determining the cooperatives' statutes and operations however was based on the more successful

45

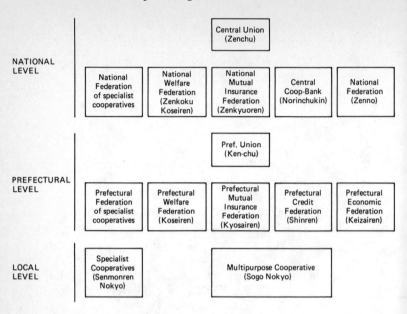

Figure 4.1   The structure of the Nokyo system[6]

German models developed by Raiffeisen and Schulze-Delitzsch. As the cooperatives remained too limited in their early expansion and local scope of operations, the government, which after the Rice Riots of 1918 became more interventionist in the food market, in the 1920s legislated national operations for cooperatives and granted certain marketing and storage privileges for rice and other cereals.

Cooperatives at the time enjoyed the support of socialists and their left-wing tenant movement and of the rightist peasantists who shared their spirit of anticommercialism, solidarity and mutual help (eliminating the pre-modern middlemen: often fraudulent merchants and usurers), in unison with the MAF bureaucrats who saw favourably their educational role in the countryside.[4] Nonetheless, Lemm's research shows conclusive evidence that the cooperatives' financial and commercial services were largely utilized by (and hence benefited) the landlord class in the early 1930s.[5]

The government's promotion of cooperatives later expanded, which with increasingly compulsory membership took an authoritarian turn. With Japan's economy being put on a wartime footing, in 1940 the cooperatives were charged with fulfilling the food production planning targets and their forced deliveries. Finally, in 1943 they were merged with all other agricultural organizations into the compulsory corporatist Nokyokai organization set up in each village and were charged with unquestioning compliance with the war economy's food control policy.

After the war, the Nokyokai was disbanded and its national leaders purged. But at the local level, after the adoption of the cooperatives' laws in 1947, the old Nokyokai was often dissolved in name only, and re-emerged with the same members, facilities and leaders as the new local Nokyo.[7] Statutes and tasks, however, were adapted to the new realities. While most statutory functions were originally removed from the new cooperatives for most farm products (except for rice, cereals and tobacco) and relatively free markets were gradually re-established in the post-war years, Nokyo – via Zenno – became the rice purchasing agent of the government's monopoly Food Agency.[8]

Later, the execution of the government's farm modernization programme and its extension services were delegated to Nokyo,[9] which receives generous public funding for these tasks.

It administers and implements with gentle persuasion 'voluntary' production adjustment schemes (i.e. *de facto* quota arrangements) for mikan oranges, dairy, poultry, eggs, several vegetables in surplus, and since 1986, also allocates the acreages to be diverted under the paddy diversion programme. Compliance is facilitated by the fact that local producer associations also distribute the public premiums and deficiency payments for the various products in question.

There are also considerable direct fiscal and budgetary benefits for Nokyo operations. Direct subsidies for the prefectural associations in 1983 alone were 1.3 bn Yen from MAFF and the prefectural governments.[10] In addition there are extensive taxbreaks for the various 'non profit' Nokyo operations, as well as interest subsidies and direct grants (from MAFF and the LIPC) for infrastructural Nokyo projects.

As a result of this semi-corporatist status and its ubiquitous local representation virtually all 5.2 m farm households are (often multiple) members of Nokyo. Increasingly also non-farm households join as associate members (usually to become eligible for cooperative banking loans). They already numbered 2.4 m in 1983.

All cooperatives in 1981 employed 6000 full-time directors and 287,000 employees – which makes about one official per 20 members. The average multipurpose Nokyo has 1300 regular and 540 associate members, 14 elected directors (mostly part-time) and 66 local employees. It annually markets products worth Y1.3 bn, supplies inputs for Y1.1 bn, and enjoys a savings' balance of 7 billion Yen, of which it has supplied Y2.7 bn as credit to its members (as of March 1983).[11]

For their supplies members are supposed to place advance orders with their local Nokyo, which are then pooled nationally for central purchasing. In 1982, the cooperatives, through Zenno, their commercial arm, supplied a total of Y4500 bn of merchandise to their member households, two-thirds of which consisted of farm input materials, such as feed (25%), oil products (20%), fertilizers (15%), other agricultural chemicals (9%), farm machinery (10%) as well as trucks, cooling equipment, and packaging, transportation and building materials. One-third of their total supplies consisted of household necessities, food mostly, but also fuel, consumer durables, clothing and sundry goods.

Nokyo earned its place as a local supplier by offering all its products on credit terms, already in the cash-tight 1950s. Also as a creditor it hardly ever used legal proceeds to collect its loans due.[12] In turn, when consigning products to Nokyo, farmers would in lieu of straight cash, be credited in their Nokyo held accounts foremost. As a result, in the 1970s 60% of a farm household's average deposits and debts would both be with the Nokyo. Given these households' strong savings' rate, average deposits would exceed debts by 140% in 1975 already.[13]

Not only as a creditor but also as a retailer Nokyo enjoys an enviable position, as Shimpo reports:[14]

'The cooperative had access to a wealth of information about its members. . . . I found the majority of its information to be very accurate and dependable. Concerning each household, . . . the cooperative held lists of the names, sex, and date of birth of all household members, information on relations between the household members, the latest data on acreage, land use, type of farm machinery and other farm implements owned, the number and kinds of animals raised, association membership, types of major consumer goods owned, . . .

I also had access to additional economic data on each household, such as savings and debt at the cooperative, sales of farm products through the cooperative, and the size and type of such purchases as farm machinery, fertilizer, pesticides, feed and other consumer goods.

Particularly for part-timers the local cooperative fulfils important functions in supplying conveniently all inputs needed, furnishing auxiliary services and contract labour (for planting, spraying, harvesting, if needed) and offering a safe outlet for all products. Its privileged role in rice marketing – equally the sector of most interest to weekend farmers – also explains why Nokyo, via Zenchu, its central union, emphasizes the annual rice price decision as its key demand for political campaigning.

Full-time farmers are more critical of the cooperatives pricing and management style, and often switch to commercial suppliers and distributors if they have a choice.[15]

Table 4.1 Nokyo share in agricultural input distribution

	Zenno share (% of farmers purchases)	Nokyo final share[a]	Year
Agricultural machinery	35	45	1977[16]
Agricultural chemicals	53	88	1982[17]
Feed	37	40	1983/84[18]

[a] Includes direct local cooperative purchases from wholesalers/producers.

Competition in the farm supplies sector is intense in general, particularly so in the feed sector – in which the sogo shosha affiliated feed compounders appear to outcompete Zenno suppliers in the more 'professional' sectors, such as dairy, pork and poultry. Zenno in turn is stronger in feeds for sectors more dominated by part-time operations like beef cattle and calf raising.[19]

Similarly, in agricultural chemicals and machinery, Zenno's strongest competition are the commercial distribution channels, in which input producers often maintain their own sales and services networks.

Nokyo asks its members to follow production plans with unified qualities and standard products and to be consigned exclusively for marketing (in exchange for a commission charged). In fact, Nokyo's marketing role appears powerful only in rice, milk and vegetable sales. In 1982, of Y5800 bn, of farm sales assigned to Nokyo, rice (both for the Food Agency, as well as 'voluntarily' marketed high quality rice), held a share of 35%, green vegetables 14%, fruits 11%, and beef cattle, fattened pigs and milk 6% each.[20] This should also help to explain Zenchu's ardent defence of the food control system maintained for rice.

In terms of farm output, Nokyo in 1975 handled 78.1% of rice, wheat and barley, 46.5% of fruits and vegetables and 45.7% of all livestock produced on Japanese farms.[21] To integrate its operations Nokyo has moved downstream into food processing. Some Y64 bn (sales value 1978) of agricultural produce it handles is processed directly, especially vegetable and fruit canning, tea, milk, and starch and fibre processing.[22] But more important is the role of its subsidiaries. Japan's largest dairy processor 'Snow Brand Milk Products' (with market shares for butter: 53%, cheese: 49%, ice cream: 19%, powdered milk: 42%, condensed milk: 24%, drinking milk: 18%) is owned by Nokyo affiliated corporations.[23] A subsidiary, *Snow Brand Food Co*, Japan's fifth largest meat processor, also produces canned food, jams, frozen food and preservatives.[24] With *Unico-op Japan*, its international trading arm, Zenno is a major importer of feeds and beef[25] in Japan. Though handsomely benefiting from these operations, Zenchu remains violently opposed to any further beef import liberalization. For storage purposes the semi-governmental LIPC uses Zenno storage facilities for its policy to purchase, hold and release import beef for domestic price maintenance. Equally, Zenno keeps the Food Agency's rice mountains in storage.

Though based on a non-capitalist ethos and tradition, and theoretically committed to a concept of 'just' prices,[26] Nokyo plays in the big league of Japan's economy. Given the Japanese farmers' propensity to save (with over-investment levels already evident in agriculture) Norinchukin, Nokyo's central bank and Shinoren, the prefectural branches, are flush with funds.

Norinchukin's total assets alone reached Y22 trillion in 1985, most of which is conservatively invested in interbank deposits and domestic public bonds. It only recently became active in international capital markets.[27] Local and prefectural Nokyo credit associations in the past often have been less prudent: they invested heavily into non-agricultural real estate developments, some of which incurred large speculative losses.[28] In fact, less than 30% of Nokyo deposits are used for agricultural investments.[29] Nokyo-owned insurances (Zenkyoren) with their reserves by far exceed the largest insurance companies in both the life and the non-life sector. Its prefectural federations in FY 1984 alone collected 2 trillion yen of insurance premiums, half of which was transferred to Zenkyoren for reinsurance. Most of the contracts are, in fact, long-term savings accounts, and concern combined life insurance/retirement pension schemes. For the compulsory disaster insurance, due to the frequency and severity of such events, the government refunds most of the premiums and the scheme's operational expenses.[30]

Zenno equally runs Japan's largest oil dealer. It is also active in health-care, works as a major real estate agent, operates cultural centres, agricultural colleges and a publishing house with its own daily newspaper, the *Nihon Nogyo Shimbun*.

While the size and multitude of Nokyo operations closely resemble that of a major business conglomerate, weaknesses in management and organizational structure have led to an expanded bureaucratization which eroded its economies of scale advantages. Its frequently monopolist position at the local level contributed to the high level of input costs and to reduced net sales revenues for Japan's farm economy. The official remedy, to encourage Nokyo mergers (33% of all local multipurpose coops still have 500 or less members, often shrinking in regular membership), has proceeded at a very slow pace: the reduction in Nokyo numbers is at around 1% p.a. since 1975.

Zenchu, with its strong Nokyo grass roots organization in each community, constitutes the farm sectors' political voice, and manages the farmers' more explicit political organizations, such as the Japan Farmers' Union and the National Chamber of Agriculture. Local and regional Nokyo heads – elected with their boards for three-year terms by their membership (general meetings, adopting 'policy lines' for the coop, are usually held only once a year) – are influential power brokers in rural areas and courted by conservative politicians, who in turn are asked to support Nokyo's political demands, such as the annual rice price campaign, its opposition to food imports (Nokyo until very recently showed precious little interest in structural improvements) and to play pork barrel politics for local farm interests. In supplying the conservative farm community's votes for LDP candidates, Nokyo according to Fukutake constitutes an 'important link in the chain of conservative Japanese politics'.[31] Yamaguchi, a Zenchu senior managing director, claims an electoral vetoing position: 'We can prevent a particular candidate from winning an election, even if we cannot bring about the election of a candidate who has our backing'.[32]

Prime Minister Nakasone's instruction in 1986 to the Management Office to begin an investigation into Nokyo business practices[33] may, however, well turn out to mark the beginning of the end of Nokyo's privileged subsidy economy (see also Chapter 7).

Notes

1. 'Fujita Saburo', *Japan Quarterly*, vol. 25, 1978, p. 299.
2. Zenchu, *Central Union of Agricultural Cooperatives* (Tokyo, 1984) p. 5.
3. Wolfgang Lemm, *Japans landwirtschaftliche Genossenschaften* (Hamburg: Institut für Asienkunde, 1977) p. 47.
4. Ogura, op. cit., p. 277.
5. Lemm, op. cit., p. 61.
6. Adopted from: 'Japan's Agricultural Coop Mainly Raises Prices', *The East*, vol. 20, no. 3, 1984, p. 30.
7. Shimpo, op. cit., p. 54.
8. *The East*, 1984, p. 28.
9. Lemm, op. cit., p. 68.
10. Zenchu, op. cit., 1984, p. 4.
11. Central Union of Agricultural Cooperatives, *Agricultural Cooperative Movement in Japan* (Tokyo, 1984) p. 20.
12. Beardsley *et al.*, op. cit., pp. 281 and 371.
13. Ogura, op. cit., p. 734.
14. Shimpo, op. cit., p. 123.
15. Mitsuaki, Nakao, 'Inside the Beef Industry', *Japan Echo*, no. 1, 1984, p. 68.
16. JETRO, *Agricultural Machinery*, Access to Japan's Import Market Series no. 3, 1979, pp. 10–11.
17. *Business Japan*, Aug. 1984, p. 86.
18. Matsuura, Tatsuo and Morisaki, Morio, *The Japanese Feed Market* (Tokyo, 1985) p. 22.
19. Ibid., p. 22.
20. *Japan Statistical Yearbook*, 1985, p. 173.
21. Ogura, op. cit., p. 735.
22. *Zenchu News*, no. 8, 1981, p. 10.
23. Asi Market Research Inc., *A Study of Dairy Products in Japan* (Tokyo, 1979) pp. 26–7, and *Japan Economic Yearbook 1981/82* (Tokyo, 1982) p. 59.
24. Asi Market Research Inc., *A Market Study of Processed Meat in Japan* (Tokyo, 1979) pp. 52–4.
25. Longworth, op. cit., p. 58.
26. Lemm, op. cit., p. 104.
27. *The Economist*, 21 Sept. 1985.
28. Ogura, op. cit., p. 293.
29. *The East*, 1984, p. 30.
30. Le Japon, *Bulletin d'information de la mutualité agricole*, no. 378, May 1986, p. 30.
31. Fututake, op. cit., p. 183.
32. *The Japan Times*, 19 Apr. 1985.
33. *Japan Agrinfo Newsletter 4*, Nov. 1986. The report was published in June 1988.

5 The Upstream and Downstream Industries

INPUT PRODUCTION AND FOOD PROCESSING

Input Industries

The process of substituting land and labour by capital (i.e. agricultural chemicals and machinery) has gone on intermittently since the 1960s. Time worked for 10 ares of paddy fields has been cut from 207 hours (1950) to 150 hours (1964), to 100 hours (1973) and more recently further reduced to 54 hours (1984). At the same time average yields have increased from 305 kg (1948) of rice for the same 10 ares to 479 kg (1984).[1] It should be noted that given the rice production structure, this tremendous gain in productivity was achieved by weekend farmers mainly, which should indicate some scope still for further improvement.

Land use has declined from 6.1 m ha cultivated in 1960 to 5.4 m ha in 1983 (even when disregarding the land idled under the paddy diversion programme), in spite of around 30,000 ha of farm land developed annually at great public expense[2] during the same period. The abandoned land was either used for residential, infrastructural and industrial purposes or as former upland fields utilized for reafforestation. Also, it should be noted that double cropping has almost completely disappeared (from 34% of usable land in 1960 to 3% in 1982).

A first glance at these costs and return figures reveals that Japanese agriculture not only faces high cash production costs, but also extremely high net and gross profit rates by any international standard (or for any commercial undertaking anywhere anyhow). As most 'labour costs' are supplied by the farm household members themselves, these represent opportunity costs rather than cash outlays. The gross profit rates calculated here, should then be very close to the genuine average cash returns. The resulting rates make crop production which uses a high share of 'labour cost' inputs particularly attractive. These rates offer a clear proof that producer prices are not the direct cause of the malaise of Japan's farming, with its insufficient income levels for most farmers at a full-time basis. Their elevated levels

53

Table 5.1 Crop production costs (FY 1982, in yen)[3]

	Rice (60 kg, unpolished glutinous)	Wheat (60 kg)	Soybeans (60 kg)	Tomatoes[a] (10 kg)	Mikan[a] (2nd grade, 10 kg)	Grapes[a] (Delaware 1st grade, 10 kg)	Sugar beets (100 kg)
1. Producers' sales value	23,960	11,490	17,090	1,681	925	4,310	21,020
2. Value of by-products	678	159	26	—	—	—	2
3. Production costs	17,071	7,296	14,433	1,057	793	3,612	14,231
4. Net profits	7,567	4,353	2,683	624	132	698	6,791
in % of total production value	30.7	37.4	15.7	37.1	14.3	16.2	32.3
Production cost factors:							
Purchases/payments	5,022	3,407	5,362	186	197	879	7,842
Own supplies	7,134	2,173	5,273	810	429	1,993	4,082
Depreciations	4,915	1,716	3,798	63	168	740	2,307
5. Real (gross) profits (net profits + own supplies)	14,701	6,526	7,956	1,434	561	2,691	10,873
in % of total production value	59.7	56.0	46.5	85.3	60.6	62.4	51.7

6. Opportunity costs						
(a) for land (rent)	3,750	1,944	3,002	34	32	188	1,959
(b) for capital (interest)	919	339	740	21	108	154	601
7. Theoretical profits (after total and opportunity cost deduction)	2,898	2,070	−1,085	569	8	356	4,229
in % of total production value	11.8	17.8	− 6.3	33.8	0.9	8.8	20.1
Production costs breakdown						
1. Seeds/seedlings	337	538	776	14	0	0	543
2. Fertilizers	1,407	1,308	2,213	83	59	193	4,704
3. Pesticides	829	254	998	42	60	206	1,002
4. Energy/fuel	549	287	547	15	18	34	375
5. Other materials	260	44	40	54	2	75	504
6. Land/water management	647	2	0	2	83	370	0
7. Charges + fees	955	1,130	176	3	11	28	368
8. Agric. buildings	498	151	329	13	11	137	264
9. Agric. machinery	4,831	1,680	4,120	55	90	395	2,458
10. Labour	6,758	1,902	5,234	777	459	2,173	3,992
Labour as % of production value	40	26	36	74	58	60	28

[a] Note that FY 1982 was a bad year for tomatoes, mikan, grape and egg production prices. By comparison to FY 1981 they had fallen by 16.3%, 39.5%, 1.6% and 16.6% respectively. Direct payments to producers (like deficiency payments for soybean producers, paddy diversion premiums and producer co-funded underwriting schemes, as for eggs) are not considered.

Table 5.2 Livestock production costs (FY 1982, in yen)[4]

	Raw milk (100 kg)	Fattening cattle (1 head, 1980) Young wagyu	dairy steer	Fattening hog (1 head, 75 kg)	Broilers (10 kg)	Eggs (100 kg)
1. Producers' sales value	9,250	715,077	538,061	33,773	2,622	24,580
2. By-products	1,017			667	14	1,129
3. Production costs	9,556	628,206	461,579	44,097	2,397	27,059
4. Net profits	1,411	86,871	76,482	-9,657	239	-1,350
in % of total production value	12.9	14.1	14.2	-28.0	9.1	-5.2
Production cost factors:						
Purchases/payments	3,986	515,859	404,276	26,855	2,161	18,039
Own supplies	4,513	97,286	44,521	16,291	167	3,179
Depreciation	1,057	15,061	12,782	951	69	5,841
5. Real (gross) profits (net profits + own supplies)	5,924	184,157	121,003	6,634	406	1,829
in % of total production value	54.9	25.8	22.5	19.8	15.4	7.1

56

6. Opportunity costs						
a) for land (rent)	340	20,037	12,434	78	9	104
b) for capital (interest)	500	3,219	2,398	460	22	593
7. Theoretical profits	571	63,615	61,650	−10,195	208	−2,047
(after total and opportunity cost deduction in % of total production value)	5.2	8.9	11.5	−29.6	7.9	−8.0
Production costs breakdown						
1. Veterinary costs	181	3,972	3,642	437	45	171
2. Energy/fuel	184	3,266	2,494	492	72	426
3. Feed/straw	5,126	231,996	213,901	16,710	1,644	16,833
4. Buildings	177	9,247	7,418	598	32	515
5. Agric. machinery	331	8,306	8,416	522	53	540
6. Charges + fees	96	997	557	56	3	12
7. Livestock purchasing costs	759[a]	301,756	191,542	21,737	372	4,997
8. Labour	2,609	68,668	33,604	3,345	176	171
Labour as % of production costs	27	11	7	8	7	13

[a] Mating charge + milk cow depreciation.

Table 5.3 Cash Costs* for Agricultural Products, 1982** (in % of non-labour production costs)

	Rice	Wheat	Soybeans	Tomatoes	Mikan	Grapes	Sugarbeet	Milk	Wagyu	D. Beef	Hogs	Broilers	Eggs
Seeds	3	10	8	5	–	–	5	–	–	–	–	–	–
Fertilizer	14	24	24	30	18	13	46	–	–	–	–	–	–
Pesticides	8	5	11	15	18	14	10	–	–	–	–	–	–
Energy/fuel	5	5	6	5	5	2	4	3	1	1	1	3	2
Other materials	3	1	–	19	1	5	5	–	–	–	–	–	–
Land/water Management	6	–	1	1	25	26	–	–	–	–	–	–	–
Charges and fees	9	21	2	1	3	2	4	1	–	–	–	–	–
Agric. buildings	5	3	4	5	3	10	3	3	2	2	1	1	2
Agric. machinery	47	31	45	20	27	27	24	5	1	2	1	2	2
Feeds/straw								74	42	50	41	74	72
Machinery costs								3	1	1	1	2	1
Livestock purchasing cost								11	54	45	53	18	21
Total industrial inputs (chemicals/energy; machinery/buildings/material)	84	69	90	94	72	71	92	85	96	95	94	92	93
Total Agric. Inputs (seeds/feeds/livestock)	3	10	8	5	–	–	5	11	4	5	3	6	6

*Excluding (farm) labour and other opportunity costs, but including depreciation and use of saleable farm produce as input costs.
**For beef: 1980

58

appear, however, as the prime reason for retarded adjustment and hence insufficient scope of operations for the core-farmers. This observation is supported by the high rent levels listed as opportunity costs (as by far most farming is still carried out on one's own land). But with annual rents of Y23 000 per 10 ares for paddies, and Y11 000 yen per 10 ares for ordinary fields in 1983, still – even after renting all one's land, decent profit levels would remain (and hence justify the amounts charged) to the tenant cultivator for almost all products – not counting the deficiency payments, taxation benefits and other direct public transfers.

Table 5.3 indicates a very clear difference in the cost structures between primary (crop) and secondary (livestock) farmers. While industrial inputs (especially machinery and fertilizers) are prime cost factors to crop producers, livestock producers' (transforming plant into animal proteins) main costs by far are high priced agricultural inputs (feeds and purchasing costs of young animals), which according to our calculation in all three categories (net, real and theoretical profits) should account for a relatively reduced profitability compared to crop products.

There is a general consensus in the literature,[6] shared by the MAFF bureaucracy[7] that contemporary Japanese agriculture is over-mechanized, with machinery making up almost 50% of rice and soybean producers' cash expenses, and forming about one-fourth of all other crop producers' production costs. A cost-rational alternative, to form joint users' groups for machinery ('Maschinenringe') has moved only slowly. They totalled 26 500 in 1976.[8] Japan's 4.5 m farm households – cultivating 5.4 m ha of arable land – in 1983 owned 4.4 m tractors (one for each 1.2 ha, a certain world record in mechanized farming intensity), two-thirds of them are low-powered pulling tractors 'typically' suited for small-sized paddy fields, the rest consisting of wheeled tractors, mostly of 15 ps or more. For the application of chemicals 1.7 m power sprayers, and 2.0 m power dusters are owned. As harvesting machinery, there are 1.7 m binders as moving machines in operation, and – more fashionably – 1.0 m combine harvesters. For the drying of the harvested cereals, 1.7 m dryers are used, largely of the solid type. Further, 2 m powered rice transplanters and 2 m farm trucks are owned. The bulk of the more sophisticated and expensive equipment – wheeled tractors, rice transplanters and harvesting machinery – was bought between 1972 and 1976, a period of growth rates of up to 150% in annual sales per type of machinery in fashion.[10]

Most of this demand was satisfied by domestic production – imported farm machinery being limited to dairy machinery (milking, cream separator and cooling facilities) and to heavy tractors (above 40 ps) with large feed harvesting equipment sold in Hokkaido mainly.[11] During the boom years Japanese producers expanded their production, only to find themselves with overcapacities and a saturated domestic and world market ever since[12] (American and European producers are in similarly dire straights since 1983 at least). Japanese producers reacted with increased diversification, export efforts (especially to S.E. Asia) and moved to a more oligopolist production structure. In rice production machinery, the top four – Kubota, Yanmar, Iseki and Mitsubishi Agricultural Machineries – managed to squeeze the market shares of the smaller local producers even further. One of the major marketing problems (especially for importers) being the cost for maintaining proper regional after-sales and repair services (inventories for the largely non-standardized parts need about 500 000 to 600 000 different spares) and on-the-spot safety training for the clients (as the great majority of accidental farm deaths and serious injuries are machinery related).[13]

The producers' problems in domestic sales are further compounded by Zenno's marketing power already mentioned, which further squeezes profit margins. By 1980 already, 32% of all power cultivators and 70% of all wheeled tractors were exported. In 1986 Kubota, the largest farm machinery-maker, moved to set up in Spain the first overseas manufacturing base for a Japanese tractor manufacturer. This will allow duty-free sales in the entire EC market (currently 9.96% import duties are charged).[14] Nevertheless, Kubota shares the problems of the sector, with essentially saturated domestic and overseas sales being depressed by the yen's appreciation since 1985. Flat sales and reduced net profits have forced the company to cut its dividend, investment volume and also management pay in 1986.[15]

Agricultural chemicals (fertilizers and pesticides) are easily the second largest cash outlay for crop farmers, counting for between 22% (for rice production) and 56% (for beet sugar) of the total.

Pesticide expenditures have risen steadily from Y4800 per farm in 1960 to Y95 000 in 1982.[16] Production grew to a relatively steady volume of 590 000 tonnes in 1982, allowing for some sectoral variation depending on the outbreak or respectively disappearance of certain plant diseases and pests. Reduced application in paddies (due to their reduced total acreage) has been compensated by growing use in vegetable and fruit farming.[17]

The manufacturing industry can be divided into producers of basic materials (produced by the big Keiretsu-affiliated chemical industry, such as Sumitomo Chemicals, Mitsui Toatsu Chemicals, Mitsubishi Chemical Industries and Nippon Soda Co.) and those specializing in finished preparations (the largest of which is Kumiai Chemical Industry).[18] Of all the agricultural chemicals used in Japan 12% are of foreign origin, three-quarters of them basic materials to be processed in Japan. Imported preparations, most of UK and German origin, have to pass painstaking toxicity testing prior to their admission for use in Japan, a great deal of which appears repetitive. Japan's agro-chemical industry exports about the same amount as its imports, a great deal being sold to China.

Room for further export expansion is limited, given the strong competitive European position particularly in the area of fine chemicals and finished preparations.

Japan has one of the world's most intensive use of fertilizers (together with West Germany, the Netherlands and Belgium). For every hectare of arable land 138 kg of nitrogen (world average: 33kg), 100 kg of phosphoric acid (world average: 16 kg), and 140 kg of potash (16 kg) were used already in 1978.[19] The Japanese authorities, however, disclaim any environmental risk from the inorganic fertilizers application, due to 'efficient water control in the paddy fields'.[20] The risk of soil and water pollution arising from manure spread from intensive husbandry is recognized.

As indicated in Chapter 4, Zenno has a very strong position in the distribution system and for this purpose also brought some preparation manufacturers under its control. Zenno also engages in annual national price negotiations with the chemical producers, insisting on freezes in supply price levels.[21]

Table 5.4   Livestock feed sources, 1980 (1000 Total Digestive Nutritives)[23]

1. Forage (grazing, hay, straw)	5,165
2. Concentrate feeds from domestic materials[a]	1,963
3. Concentrate feeds from imported materials	3,261
4. Imported concentrate feeds	15,251
5. Total Feed demand in Japan	25,640
Self-sufficiency ratio [(1) + (2)]/(5)	27.8%

[a]   Largely: rice bran, wheat bran, fish meal, food industry waste. The figure includes soymeal – the byproduct of crushed imported beans – as well.

Table 5.5 Average rations for beef production; 1979 (per head)[25]

Feed Type	Wagyu steer fattening Weight (kg)	Est. TDN (kg)	Dairy steer fattening Weight (kg)	Est. TDN (kg)
Fodders				
Green oats	31	3	–	–
Row dent corn	97	16	25	4
Italian rye grass	268	31	6	7
Other grazing grass in rice family	256	33	37	5
Lotus	14	1	–	–
Mixed grasses				
(a) mainly bean family	27	3	1	1
(b) other	71	13	–	–
Turnips	16	1	–	–
Dry grazing grass of rice family	133	61	11	5
Silage				
(a) dent corn	23	4	17	3
(b) grazing grass	37	5	–	–
(c) pulses	49	6	–	–
(d) others	–	–	10	1
Fresh grass in the field	237	41	44	8
Dry grass in the field	64	26	11	4
Kitchen & shop vegetable waste	–	–	22	3
Non-rice straw	113	40	55	19
Rice straw	779	294	365	138
Sub-Total – TDN		578		198
– % of total		(19)		(8)
Grains & concentrate feeds				
Broken rice	17	13	–	–
Barley	838	613	554	406
Other grains	64	48	195	147
Wheat bran (Government)	259	194	72	55
Wheat bran (Commercial)	126	81	48	31
Other bran	18	11	–	–
Bean curd (tofu)	26	4	–	–
Soybean meal-cake	16	13	–	–
Other plant meal-cake	22	15	24	17
Concentrate feed (adult ration)	1 951	1 404	2 131	1 535
Concentrate feed (calf ration)	55	41	40	105
Sub-Total – TDN		2 437		2 294
– % of total		(81)		(92)

Table 5.6   Formula and mixed feed use (1983 – 1000 tonne)[24]

Poultry	10,865	44.8%
Pork	6,330	26.1%
Dairy cattle	2,521	10.4%
Beef cattle	2,768	11.4%
Other animals	22	0.1%
	25,569	100%

Feed, which accounts for three-quarters of dairy and poultry production costs (Table 5.3), and for about 50% of all beef and pork production cash outlays, obviously has some remote agricultural origin. In poultry and pork production, animals are fed almost completely from purchased feeds. For dairy beef more than 97% of the feed is bought, as is 91% of Wagyu steers' feed (see Table 5.5 for details).

Due to Hokkaido's green pastures, only 63% of dairy cattle feed needs to be imported.[22] The imported feedstuffs are basically from the US, which in the field of staple feeds, like corn and soybeans, already constitutes a certain dependence. Other, however relatively minor, feed sources are Argentina (sorghum), Canada (feed barley), Australia (feed wheat), China (maize), Thailand (tapioca, manioc) and Brazil (soybeans).

With 19.5 m tonnes of imported raw materials for feed (in 1983) Japan has become the world's largest import market for feedstuffs. Japan's major nine general trading houses, the sogo shosha, later

Table 5.7   Feed imports from the US, 1984[26]

	1000 tonne	*% of total Japanese imports*
Corn/Maize	9,968	97.0
Sorghum	1,515	36.6
Wheat	616	48.5
Barley	413	27.0
Soybeans	4,181	92.6
Lucerne/alfalfa meal pellets	85	23.2
Hay (incl. bales)	471	90.1
Beet pulp	449	69.5

joined by Zenno and its subsidiary Uni-Coop, are the dominant importers, handling grains, oilseeds and concentrates directly from the major foreign producers, cooperatives or marketing boards, usually already from inland/riverside elevators, and organize maritime transport till the imported feeds reach the seaboard processing facilities of the affiliated feed compounders/processors in Japan.

There are 118 feed compounders left in Japan (1983), mostly small- to medium-sized companies with an average number of 213 workers per company (of which 89 work in the feed department). Most factories are located at coastal sites producing formula feeds which comprise all or most nutritional components to maintain animal health with linear programming techniques to produce least-cost rations from the various raw materials kept in the silos. With low value added, and keen competition in the sector, profitability is fairly low. Companies usually manufacture between 60 and 400 different feeds – suitable for each type, age and use of the livestock. They are also expected to supply advice, management and financial help to their client-farmers, and to play a supporting role in the purchase and sale of the livestock itself. As international feed grain prices are subject to volatile price and erratic exchange rate variations, compounders have to observe the short-term swings of the market. As a result, the resource-short compounders had little choice but to become integrated with either Zenno or the supplying sogo shosha.

The latter-affiliated companies now have gained a 60% total market share, a particular strength being the poultry, dairy and pork market segments. Zenno's share in turn, is stronger in beef and calf-raising feed production. Zenno has sufficient influence to set overall price standards. Every 3 or 6 months the organization in consultation with MAFF announces its adjusted new feed price levels. The Sogo shosha then usually follow the lead.

From an atomistic structure in the 1960s, and a period of concentration and 'affiliation' in the 1970s, the industry has finally reached its 'mature' oligopolist stage.

Coyle observed that as a result (and due to higher production costs and higher quality ingredients), feed price increases at times outpaced the price increase of the imported ingredients. Feed prices in 1983 were, in some instances, 60–70% higher than those for similar feeds in the US.[29]

The future of expansion of feed demand will essentially depend on the growth prospects for Japan's livestock industry with its essentially limited grazing and fodder growing land, and on the improvement in feed efficiencies.

MAFF in 1980 forecasted a total feed demand of 32.7 m tonnes (of which only 17.4 m tonnes are to be imported) for 1990.[30] Given the contemporary largely saturated domestic livestock product markets – except for beef – in Japan, with their industry's lack of competitiveness, the underlying forecast for total livestock expansion appears as widely unrealistic today. Much more moderate feed demand growth – if not stagnation in aggregate – should rather be expected.

The Food Industry

The Japanese food processing industry employs 1.2 m people (in 1982), which makes an average of only 14.5 employees for its 81 000 enterprises. Their total, however, counts for 11% of Japan's industrial production.[31] Nonetheless a tendency towards concentration is evident even from these aggregate data: in 1965 the food processing sector had still consisted of 96 000 enterprises with an average of only 11.6 employees.

The food industry reflects the typical duality of Japan's industrial structure in general. Some sectors (brewing and distilling, sugar refining, dairy marketing, grain milling, oil crushing, and to a lesser extent, baking, soft drink production and meat processing) are highly concentrated. Others, particularly those producing traditional Japanese foods (sake brewing, green tea, confectionery, fish and vegetable preparations) remain largely cottage industries. This sector is considered as 'by far one of Japan's least modernized industries'.[32]

Among the former, those corporations relying on imported commodities for processing (breweries, flour and oil millers, feed compounders and sugar refineries) for the most part belong to one of the six dominant Keiretsu conglomerates (Mitsubishi, Mitsui, Sumitomo, Dai-Ichi Kangyo, Fuyo and Sanwa) on whose trading companies (sogo shosha) they rely for imports, finance and, occasionally, for marketing as well.

Although they were never core enterprises of the Keiretsu conglomerates, whose strength and historical focus lies in heavy industry, big finance and bulk trading, food industries certainly are welcome members for their relatively recession-proof performance as well as for their function as symbols for internal cohesion due to the high visibility of their branded products.

Table 5.8 Keiretsu – affiliated agro-food corporations[33]

1. Mitsubishi	Kirin Brewery
	Nitto Flour Milling
	Nippon Meat Packers
	Nippon Nosan Kogyo (compound feed)
	Rokko Butter Co (Q.B.B)
	Chukyo Coca-Cola
	Mitsubishi Agr. Machinery
	Dainippon Sugar
	Kentucky Fried Chicken Japan
2. Mitsui	Mitsui Sugar
	Taito (sugar refining)
	Nippon Flour Mills
	Nippon Formula Feed (feed and livestock)
	Mitsui Norin K.K. (Agr. + Forestry Co)
	Hohnen Oil
	Zenchiku (meat importer/wholesaler)
	Mitsukoshi
3. Sumitomo	Asahi Breweries (controls Nikka Whisky)
	Sumitomo Forestry
	Yoshihara Oil Mill
	Marudai Food (meat)
4. Daiichi Kangyo/C. Itoh	Nippon Agr. Pesticides
	(Nippon Noyaku)
	Seibu Depaato
	Prima Meat Packers
	Fuji Oil
	Morinaga Milk Industries
	Iseki Agr. Machinery
	C. Itoh Sugar
	C. Itoh Shiryo (feeds)
	Nissan Agr. Industries
5. Fuyo (Fuji/Marubeni)	Sapporo Breweries
	Nisshin Flour Milling
	Toyo Sugar Refining
	Nippon Suizan
	Takara Shuzo
	Nippon Reizo
	Hoko Fishing
6. Sanwa	Suntory
	Ito Ham Provisions

Mitsubishi men evidently drink Kirin beer only, but Sanwa group employees had to be admonished to stick to Suntory drinks for their off-duty amusement.[34]

Figure 5.1 shows a strong Keiretsu presence in the subsectors

Figure 5.1 *Mitsui and Mitsubishi subsidiaries and affiliates in the agro-food business*

Overseas source	Import trading	Input industries	Primary production	Primary processing	Secondary processing	Distribution
Mitsui		Kanto Denko Kaisha (fertilizers)	Mitsui Norin K.K.			
United Grain	Mitsui Bussan			Mitsui Sugar	Mikuni Coca Cola Bottling	Zenchiku
Pacific Grain				Taito Sugar		Mitsukoshi
Gulf Coast Grain (US)		Nippon Formula Feed		Nippon Flour Mills		
Neptune Packing (tuna)		Fertilizantes Mitsui S.A. (Brazil)		Hohnen Oil		Sanyu Foods
Ocean Packing (tuna) (US)				K.K. Ichirei (chicken processing)		K.K. Shinsei
Mitsui Yoshioka do Brasil S.A (coffee processing & sale)						
Felda Oil Products Malaysia (palm oil refining & sale)						
Mitsubishi		Nihon Nosan		Nitto Flour Milling	Kirin Brewery	
Agrex Inc. (US)	Mitsubishi Shoji	Mitsubishi Agr. Machineries		Dai Nippon Sugar	Rokko Butter	
Mitsubishi Foods, Inc (US)				Meiji Sugar	Nippon Meat Packers	
MC Farm Sendirian Berhad, Brunei (cattle breeding)				Morinaga Milk	Chukyo Coca Cola	
				Nisshin Oil Mills	Souton Food Ind. (jams)	
				Settsu Oil Mill	Kanro Co. (confectionery)	
				Japan Maize Products	Morinaga	

Table 5.9   Market share concentration[35]

	1-firm	2-firm	3-firm	4-firm	5-firm
Sugar refining (78–82)	12.9	22.1	31.1	39.2	47.1
Edible Oils (1980)	39.4	64.4	79.5	85.9	91.6
Beer (1984)	61.3	81.3	91.3	100	–
Domestic Whisky (1984)	70.0	86.9	91.5	96.1	–
Wine (1978)	29.0	51.0	72.0	79.0	84.0
Sake (1980)	6.8	11.3	15.6	19.5	22.9
Soft Drinks (1979)	22.8	35.4	42.1	47.8	51.2
Instant Coffee (1980)	70.9	96.0	97.7		
Regular Coffee (1980)	22.1	35.1	42.6	48.1	50.8
Processed meat (1980)	25.0	43.0	59.8	75.9	82.5
Drinking milk (1979 production share)	17.8	34.7	48.2	53.3	57.2
Cheese (1979, production share)	48.6	65.1	80.0	87.4	
Butter (1979, production share)	53.2	65.3	75.4	82.2	86.2
Ice cream (1979, production share)	19.3	34.6	47.0	58.9	68.8
Biscuits & Cookies (1980)	29.2	46.4	60.0	69.2	74.0
Chocolates (1980)	22.5	40.2	58.6	76.6	88.0
Corn Flakes (1980)	18.0	36.0	48.3	56.0	63.3
Jams (1978)	15.1	28.8	40.0	49.9	59.1
Soups (1980)	61.0	66.7	72.6	77.8	80.4

which reflect classical Keiretsu strength in bulk imports and bulk (primary) processing. The presence is relatively weak in secondary transformation and the domestic distribution system, and even more so in primary production. The more concentrated a subsector is in the processing stage, the stronger usually are the Keiretsu ties (see Table 5.9).

Table 5.9 also gives strong indication for the high degree of oligopolization, sometimes bordering on monopolization, in the top tier of Japan's food/drinks industry. Monopolization is most advanced in whisky (Suntory/Nikka), instant coffee (Nestlé Japan/ Ajinomoto–General Foods) – both clear duopolies – beer (Kirin), soups (Ajinomoto), and butter and cheese production (Snow Brand Milk). All other 'modern' product sectors listed are clearly oligopolist. As a traditional industry sake production is openly competitive.

The big business orientation in the top league of Japan's food industry has not yet led to any significant overseas sales or investment orientation of the sector. The 'international outlook' is limited to licensing or cooperation agreements which almost all major corporations entertain with US and European industries, providing for processing know-how, and some limited amounts of foreign brands to be imported into Japan. Sometimes, also joint ventures have been set up for the purpose. Ajinomoto founded AGF with General Foods (US) for instant coffee marketing. Overseas investment is still the rare exception: Kikkoman, which succeeded in making Japanese soy sauce an 'all purpose international seasoning'[36] in 1972 set up a processing plant in Wisconsin, thus being able to process US soy beans on the spot. Some sake is also produced in the US with Californian rice, and since 1984 Suntory has started to brew beer in China in a joint venture.[37] Nissin Foods manufactures instant noodles abroad and so do some Japanese seafood processors, particularly in S. E. Asia.[38]

Overseas manufacturing for these producers, who largely depend on imported agricultural raw materials for processing in Japan, is the only way to remain competitive in international markets, given the high border barriers and transport costs these imports have to face in Japan.

Most companies, however, are too undercapitalized and small to capitalize on their traditional assets and use the global health food boom – to which Japanese traditional foods are rightly linked. In the ensuing battle for 'global foods', to which the current merger wave particularly among US and UK food, beverages and tobacco giants gears up, Japan's industry, though still the world's second largest measured in turnover, is left behind as a result of both a 'natural' competitive disadvantage in primary food production and of protectionist policies aggravating this handicap by excessively increasing input costs.

Also the relative share of raw material acquisition is particularly high for Japan's food industry: 69.5% of all expenditures (compared to a manufacturing average of 63.3%). In the primary transformation sector (sugar refining, oil and grain milling and feed compounding) the rate exceeds 80%.[39]

More than 50% of the industry's raw material needs are now imported – which helps to explain the sector's strong liberal policy position on imports.[40] Only 18% of the domestically produced agricultural products are actually processed, the bulk being sold largely unprocessed to consumers[41] (like most rice, vegetables, fruits, fresh milk, eggs and fish), or to a lesser extent used as inputs to the livestock sector.

The growth performance of the food industry is closely linked to developments in consumer habits and attitudes. In 1982, 54.8% (1970: 49.5%) of all food consumed at home was in processed form (the rest was either fresh [35.8%] or rice [7.4%]) Still, this percentage is below that of the US and most EC nations, offering some growth prospect for Japan's food industry even at constant caloric intake (at an admirable daily 2600 caloric level) and almost stagnant population growth.[42]

In terms of growth in sales volume, food industries of the secondary transformation (processing the basic foodstuffs produced in the first transformation – refined sugar, flour, oils, etc. – into the final consumer product) have fared better since 1975 than those basic oligopolist industries of the primary transformation stage.[43] Among them sugar refineries actually had to face a contraction of business, reflecting reduced sugar (and salt) consumption in Japan.

With annual growth rates of 'only' 4.1% (during 1980/82), and limited prospects for further domestic expansion, and through politically administered high raw material costs constrained in their export strategies, Japan's food industries perceive new technologies as their new frontier.

In the past, the food industry has been fast in adapting to new technologies; in manufacturing, continuous processing procedures and funnel freezing; in oil extracting, pressure boiling was introduced. Manual labour was increasingly replaced by automatized and computerized processing, measuring, mixing and filling operations. New preservation technologies have prolonged the shelf-life of processed food – an important quality for food as the most perishable industrial product. Food additives have been improved (and reduced), as has packaging in which various plastics and 'retortable pouched' containers (in which food is placed in laminated plastic/ metal foils, sealed and sterilized in retort) have proved superior in maintaining good quality, and are lighter as purchased items than are canned or glass packaged products (though disposal problems remain).

Sterilization technology has developed 'quick sterilization' at 149°C replacing lengthy cooking operations. Freeze drying, which affects the ingredients less, has produced higher quality instant coffees, instant noodles and soups, and other snack foods. Radiation is used to prevent germination of potatoes and onions.[44] While this method has the advantage of not raising the temperature of food during treatment, consumer acceptance of food identified as having undergone radiation treatment is another story.

Stimulated by high input prices, new products are developed offering fascinating low-priced replacements of traditional agricultural raw materials. Large segments of the sugar market (such as in the US) have been replaced by high fructose corn syrups, saccharose and aspartam; milk and meats have been substituted partially (and sometimes fully) by soy-based extracts with often more valuable nutritional qualities and minimizing the food's animal fat and hence colesterol contents (reducing heart disease and stroke causing risks).

Food processors use biotechnological research results to diversify into new production. Kirin, for instance, faced with declining net income from its beer sales, has developed bioreactors capable of continuing brewing processes (important also for sake, soy sauce and other seasoning production) which would allow replacement of the week-long tank fermentation and could cut production costs to about one-fifth of their present levels.

'Sidelines' of this bioresearch are new hybrid developments: high yielding seeds for corn, soy beans, wheat and rice developed through cloning (cell recombination). Kirin – and several other food companies – are both using biotech methods to look into disease and climatic resistant strains such as tomatoes to be grown in colder climates.[45]

As regards animal feeds, a fascinating prospect would be the artificial production of unicellular proteins through the use of microorganisms and enzymes. Other biotech research was financed by the food industry in the wide area of human and veterinary drugs.

In 1984, there were about 4000 researchers (their number growing by 12% p.a.) working in biotechnological research in Japan, who spend about 47 m yen in their R&D budgets (increasing by 20% annually) in private industry alone.[46]

Primary Transformation Industries

This sector is characterized by low growth rates, high input costs (the level of which due to world market fluctuations and government intervention is largely beyond the scope of management), low value-added, heavy public regulatory interference and strong oligopolist structures. All are perfect elements for a high-cost industry for which almost assured margins give little motivation to innovate.

Grain Milling   Sato and Ito in 1974 examined Japan's wheat flour milling industry, in which the top four makers: Nisshin Seifun, Nippon Seifun, Showa Sangyo and Nitto Seifun, continue to control

Table 5.10　The food processing industry, 1981[47]

	No. of companies	No. of employees (1 000)	Sales (Y bn)	Share
Food processing, total	82,411	1,180	24,458	100.0
Meat & dairy, total	2,971	129	3,888	16.0
Meat Processing	819	46	1,533	6.3
Dairy Products	1,088	49	1,776	7.3
Other Meat and Dairy	1,064	34	579	2.4
Marine Products, total	13,146	204	3,165	13.0
Canned and bottled fishery products	218	12	259	1.1
Kelp processing industry	1,276	18	285	1.2
Fish paste processing industry	2,620	38	441	1.8
Frozen fish industry	786	22	607	2.5
Frozen processed fish products	545	12	218	0.9
Other fishery products processing	7,701	101	1,355	5.5
Canned vegetable & fruits, total	3,074	59	646	2.7
Canned vegetables & fruits	873	25	313	1.3
Vegetable pickle	2,201	34	333	1.4
Seasoning, total	3,696	55	1,209	4.9
Soybean paste	910	10	135	0.5
Soy sauce, edible amino acid	2,032	22	283	1.2
Chemical seasoning industry	17	5	207	0.8
Sauce industry	192	5	187	0.8
Other grain condiments	545	13	398	1.6
Grain refining & milling, total	1,503	20	1,444	6.0
Rice refining	642	6	624	2.6
Wheat milling	168	9	689	2.8
Other grain refining & milling	693	6	130	0.6
Sugar Refinery, total	165	11	698	2.8
Sugar manufact. (domestic origin)	63	6	27	1.1
Sugar refinery (imported raw sugar)	102	5	427	1.7
Baking, total	17,676	293	3,321	13.5
Bread manufacturing	3,356	104	988	4.0
Fresh baking industry	8,709	93	870	3.4
Biscuits & related products	1,757	24	293	1.2
Rice crackers	1,618	28	305	1.2
Other baking industry	2,236	45	895	3.7

Beverage, total	4,019	97	4,273	17.5
Soft drinks	911	27	849	3.5
Beer brewing	34	13	1,429	5.8
Sake brewing	2,612	47	1,020	4.2
Distilled spirit	384	9	954	3.9
Feed, organic fertilizer, total	917	18	1,621	6.6
Mixed feeds	362	13	1,454	5.9
Feed (not mixed)	322	4	135	0.6
Fats and oil, total	471	13	969	4.0
Vegetable fats and oil	234	7	676	2.8
Edible fats and oil	52	5	235	1.0
Other food processing, total	34,773	281	3,224	13.1
Tea	3,721	17	335	1.4
Starch	168	3	115	0.5
Dextrose, millet jelly	70	3	206	0.8
Noodle	7,769	64	627	2.6
Soybean curd, fried soybean curd	12,261	53	250	1.0
Coffee processing	128	3	174	0.7
Frozen processed food	614	23	297	1.2
Others	10,042	114	1,222	4.9

70% of the market as its oligopolistic core.[48] Of the remaining fringe about 20 are medium-sized regional millers (with a market share of between 0.5% and 1% each), the rest of about 200 small firms served local markets. By 1981 their number – in 1967 still more than 400 – had been reduced to 150, indicating a significant extent of competitive pressure). This coexistence of oligopolist core and competitive fringe is typical also for the soy sauce, bread-making, soft drinks, and ham and sausage industries structure in Japan.

Wheat import volume and sales prices are under the governmental Food Agency's control. The Agency decides, based on production capacity and past actual production, on the mill's annual processing quotas. The firms in turn, since 1952, are free to determine to whom and at what price to sell their flour and bran. The millers which in the 1950s had re-established their pre-war Zaibatsu ties (Nippon Flour to Mitsui, and Nitto Flour to Mitsubishi) and market positions, reacted to this partial liberalization by establishing ties of vertical semi-integration to the users (bread, confectionery and noodle-makers) by financing the bakers' expanded production facilities and sales outlets (in turn relying on the sogo shosha's finance). With the larger users firmly tied to the big mills, core/fringe competition largely took the form of price rebates in the smaller users' market. In this respect, the observation of simultaneous price increases of the list prices is not necessarily indicative of the complete absence of competition.

With only limited prospects for sales growth and limited product innovation, the oligopolist core millers have, for a long time, diversified their production. Nisshin Flour Milling, Japan's largest miller, and its subsidiaries in 1983 obtained 51% of its sales from flour milling, 28% from formula feed, the rest from grocery products and fine chemicals. Other activities range from hog breeding, to granule and powder development, and frozen noodle franchising.[49] Showa Sangyo has reduced its flour milling sales share to 24% (1985), with feeds (27%) and vegetable oils (25%) making larger contributions to the turnover. Of sales 9% are dextrose products (various starch based 'artificial' sweeteners, used as syrups in soft drinks and cake production). The rest are processed foods (13%) livestock trading and warehousing operations.[50]

Sugar　The sugar refining sector processes all domestic sugar beet (Hokkaido) and cane (Okinawa, S. Kyushu) but needs to import 70% of its raw material demand, mostly from Australia, South Africa, the Philippines and Cuba, the prices of domestic and imported raw sugar being controlled by the Japan Raw Silk and Sugar Price Stabilization Cooperation. The refining industry since 1975 suffers from declining sugar consumption in Japan (her per capita consumption remains half that of the Western pattern), refining overcapacities and intense competition from an increasing number of artificial sweeteners. Since 1970, the sogo shosha – led by Mitsui, controlling 5 refineries, followed by Mitsubishi (3 refineries), Marubeni, Nissho-Iwai and C. Itoh – have moved into the indebted and stagnant sector and brought more than 80% of the market under their control. They were attracted by the guaranteed margins to be earned by selling raw sugar imports to their refineries, and then reselling the refined product domestically,[51] the principal clients being confectionery-makers, the soft drinks industry and home use. Hence the refining sector is more oligopolist in its actual organization than Tables 5.9 and 5.10 seem to indicate. Authorized by the Sugar Price Stabilization Law, repeatedly processors' cartels were arranged (e.g. during December 1976 – May 1977 and February 1978 – March 1982), fixing production shares on the basis of past performance and aiming at capacity adjustment. Most surviving independent sugar refineries such as Nisshin Seito, gave non-sugar diversification a top priority.

Edible Oil Edible oil extraction from vegetables (largely from soybeans, rape, corn, but also from cottonseed, sunflowers, olives, palm kernel, cereals, rice, etc.) has shown a continuous healthy growth of 4.2% p.a. in per capita consumption during 1977–82.[52] It is the primary processing sector with the least government interference. Price fluctuations are large, and price discounts are the rule for bulk sales (except for oil in the popular large gift packs), in spite of the fact that the market is dominated by two large makers, Nisshin Oil Mills (39.4%) and Ajinomoto (25.0%).[53] As per capita consumption is expected to level off, diversification of the industry, which so far has focused on margarine, mayonnaise, and cooking and salad oil while selling the residual meal cakes to feed compounders, is the favourite response of the sector – e.g. Fuji Oil specializes in meat and dairy substitute production. It has developed vegetable-based creams and cheeses (for processing so far). Its textured and structured soy proteins simulate meat characteristics, and are extensively used in corned beef, hamburger and sausage production.[54]

As virtually all raw materials are imported, the processing plants are located at seaside locations and they often have their own berths and direct off-loading facilities.

Dairy Total demand for dairy products has levelled off at an annual 67 kg per head (1983) with further growth expected for cheese only.[55] About 60% of all 7.4 m ton of milk produced by Japan's cows (1985) is consumed as 'drinking milk', the rest – largely the milk produced in Hokkaido and Tohoku far off the metropolitan centres of fresh milk consumption[56] – is processed to cheese, butter, milk powder, condensed milk and ice cream. Imports only take the form of butter (1% of consumption in 1983), skimmed-milk powder (7%), and more significantly, in the cheese sector, with its diversity in tastes (80%, most of this being natural cheeses imported from Australia, New Zealand and the EC and further processed in Japan). While dairies are spread all over the country, marketing of both liquid and processed dairy products is carried out on an oligopolist basis. The 'Big Three', Snow Brand (a largely coop-owned joint stock company), Meiji Milk and Morinaga Milk (affiliated with the DIK-Keiretsu) account for between 48% (for drinking milk) and 75% (for butter in 1979) of the marketed dairy products.[57] In the meantime, Nogyo also undertakes direct marketing of both liquid and processed milk. In principle, the sales price of raw milk is set by negotiations between producer cooperatives and the milk producer association.

Although cooperative officials should be represented on both sides of the table, Oshiro from past experience reported a bargaining weakness on the part of the (Tohoku) producers – be it for the 'commercial' approach of Snow Brand (Yukijirushi) or for the strength of traditional dairy farmer/milk processing plant links.[58]

Both Snow Brand, the market leader for cheeses, butter and milk powder, with its production strength in Hokkaido, Japan's dairy centre, and Kyodo Milk, the number four, are equally Zenno-affiliated (owned largely by Norinchukin, Zenno and Snow Brand). Kyodo however is limited to fresh milk and ice cream sales on Honshu. The only two corporate national competitors, Meiji Milk and Morinaga Milk, are both subsidiaries of confectionery-makers, and strong in fresh and powdered milk sales. As they are either Zenno-affiliated or subsidiary firms, Japan's dairy processors do not diversify. New products – except for some frozen food – are largely new milk/yogurt drinks.[59]

Vegetables Total vegetable consumption has levelled off at very high levels; yet consumption patterns are far from static. There is a steady shift away from traditional Japanese root vegetables and cabbages requiring cooking, towards the more convenient 'Western' vegetables, such as tomatoes, cucumbers, Spanish paprikas, lettuce and celery, which can be eaten fresh or with little preparation.[60]

Though most consumption remains fresh, the share of various processed forms is growing: precooked canned, frozen, pouched and dried packages are reducing household labour.

The tomato juice market – a monopoly between 1933 and 1965 of Kagome Co., which has introduced the product into Japan – offers an interesting example showing that monopolist rents in growth markets, in fact, attract well-capitalized competitors utilizing their established distribution systems.

In 1965 Kikkoman (the largest soy sauce maker) entered the market to create a duopoly; it lasted until 1977, when Kirin (the largest brewer) joined the fray.[61]

Today tomato products (ketchups, sauces, purées, pastes) make up one-third of Kagome's diversified sales; about one-half are various soft drinks (fruit, vegetable and coffee drinks), the rest consisting of sauces and pastas.[62]

The Secondary Transformation Sector

This sector represents all those companies processing the intermediate products (sugar, vegetable oil, flour, milk powder, etc.) supplied by the primary transformation sector into the semi-final or final consumer product. This sector should, in theory, in location and production mode be more remote from the farm areas and closer to the consuming metropolitan areas, and hence could be expected to be more concentrated and big business (Keiretsu) oriented. This, however, appears to be only partly true. Due to the persistence of regionally and individually differentiated tastes – for the satisfaction of which most consumers evidently are ready to pay a premium over standardized run-of-the-mill products – a great deal of artisanal production plants remain, particularly so in the more traditional 'Japanese food' processing (pickles, fish preparations, sweets, sake, soy beans products, etc.). The most representative of this is tofu (soybean curd) production in 12 000 plants, with an average of four employees each.[63]

In the more 'modern' sectors producing food based on originally imported Western technology – from tomato ketchup to instant coffee – production patterns are clearly industrial and the marketing situation, due to their capital intensity in production and trading, strongly oligopolist, with a tendency towards monopolization.

Processed Meat   In the meat sector since 1955 with the modernization of processing facilities, a tendency towards large-scale plants and more concentrated production has become evident.

Prior to the existence of wholesale markets, traditional village livestock dealers had bought producers' cattle and pigs, and sold them in turn to large livestock dealers on the hoof. These would then organize the slaughter in abattoirs owned by local governments. The slaughter and further distribution/processing was fully in the hands of the 'Burakumin' (also 'Dowa') butcher guild – people who are or are said to be descendants of the 'eta' outcasts of the Tokugawa era, whose Buddhist ideology considered killing of large animals and humans as impure and socially disqualifying and hence confined butchers, hangmen, tanners and undertakers to special settlements. Their underdog inhabitants, even after their formal emancipation more than a hundred years ago, are still subject to discrimination, and in response aggressively defended their traditional economic roles as an exclusively closed shop: their meat marketing system 'was characterized by non-competitive price fixing at all levels and very effective barriers preventing new entrants injecting competition into the industry'.[64]

At Nokyo pressure and with MAFF support since 1958 wholesale markets were opened, limiting the role of the village and large livestock dealers. In 1980 about half of all cattle sold in wholesale markets were under Nokyo control. Increasingly also (in Osaka since 1983) all carcasses must be auctioned publicly, enabling more efficient pricing and facilitating the entry of new firms. There are now 10 wholesale markets and 16 sub-central markets in operation, most of them owned by municipal governments and by a company set up by the major purchasing wholesaler together with Nokyo and local governments.[65] Longworth estimates that currently about 25 to 30% of all cattle are sold as carcasses at auction; 10% are still sold through traditional channels, but the bulk, 60 to 65%, pass directly to meat processing companies and wholesalers on the basis of the quotations obtained at the public carcass auctions.[66] About one-third of these are processed at meat centres, which integrate slaughtering, boning, cutting and packaging. Of the 21 largest meat centres, 13 are controlled by Nokyo, 6 are joint ventures (of traders, local and prefectural governments and Nokyo). Since 1971 also several specialized processing meat centres, located next to new abattoirs, have been set up by Nokyo (with heavy subsidization by MAFF) to prepare boxed beef and consumer packs for immediate sale in supermarkets.[67]

By far most beef is consumed as freshly cut meat. Among pork the share of processed meats (ham, bacon) is larger. Nonetheless, minor qualities of beef, pork, horse meat, mutton (and occasionally fish) are processed in various mixtures to pressed ham and sausages.

The processed meat market is dominated by 5 companies with an aggregate 78% market share in 1978 which maintain national sales networks with direct retail access for their well-established brands.[70] They are by order of magnitude: *Ito Ham Provisions* (24.4%), headquartered in Kobe, in which the managing Ito family members hold 18.7% of stock, linked to the Sanwa Keiretsu. About half of total sales are fresh meat (the rest is processed); *Nippon Meat Packers* (16.8% in 1978), headquartered in Osaka, linked to the Mitsubishi Keiretsu; 64% of sales are fresh meat. The company is integrating both upstream (into feeds and animal breeding) and downstream (restaurants); *Prima Meat Packers* (15.3%) has the US meat giant Oscar Meyer as its major share holder (25%). It is linked to the DIK Keiretsu via the C. Itoh sogo shosha. Most of its sales (58%) are in the fresh meat sector. Its particular marketing strength is the Tokyo area, where it has its headquarters. *Marudai Foods* (12.9%) of Osaka, is linked to Sumitomo, and specializes in fish, meat-based hams and sausages; 80% of its sales, however, are still

Table 5.11 Meat production, consumption and imports, 1984 (1000 tonne carcass weight equivalent)[68]

	Production	Total consumption	Consumption per head (kg)	Import sources
Beef & veal	535	757	6.3	Australia (269), US (153) NZ (23)
Pigmeat	1,430	1,708	14.2	Denmark (107), Taiwan (71), Canada (42)
Poultry meat	1,313	1,417	11.8	US (51), Thailand (30), China (12)
Sheep meat	0	150	1.2	NZ (91), Australia (56)

Table 5.12 Processed meat consumption (1000 tonne, 1978)[69]

	Production		Import sources	
Ham	59.4	(14.4%))	Netherlands	(0.1),
		(	Denmark	(0.1)
Bacon	28.7	(7.4%))		
Pressed ham	121.1	(31.4%)		
Sausages	176.6	(45.8%)	US (0.8), Denmark	(0.3),
			Germany	(0.1)
	386.0	(100)		

derived from more conventional original meat-based origins. *Snow Brand Food* (8.1%) is a subsidiary of the Nokyo-owned Snow Brand Milk Products; 43% of sales are processed meat, 4% canned meat, the rest are preservatives, jams and frozen food. The sixth largest meat manufacturer, *Hayashikane Sangyo* (2.6%) finally is a subsidiary of Taiyo Fishing Co. and to no one's surprise also processes fishery products into various sausages and meat preparations.

Chicken-processing facilities, which since 1970 have been growing rapidly in scale and efficiency, are now almost entirely controlled by the sogo shosha affiliated feed suppliers. The sogo shosha's livestock departments also handle 70% of all poultry imports.[71]

Confectionery and Bakery The sector is a major consumer of wheat flour, sugar and cocoa and in 1980 produced 815 000 tonnes of bread (19% for school lunches), 285 000 tonnes of pastries, 866 000 tonnes

of cakes (23% are 'Western cakes') 266 000 tonnes of biscuits and
cookies, 184 000 tonnes of snacks, 120 000 tonnes of chocolates,
89 000 tonnes of candies, 39 000 tonnes of chewing gums and 36 000
tonnes of toffees.[72] These delicacies are produced by 5700 bakeries,
mostly artisan in scale. The top 27 bakeries' production counts for
hardly 50% of the market. Apart from stagnant demand since the
mid-1970s, the major confectionery makers Ezaki Glico, Morinaga
and Fujiya during 1983/85 were hit by a mysterious prolonged black-
mail campaign, in which unidentified extortionists repeatedly placed
cyanide-laced sweets on supermarket shelves[73] which led to heavy
losses in both sales and profit levels.[74]

Since the mid-70s a long-term decline in confectionery consumption became evident – as the main market segment – children, the
young and women – became affected by health concerns (tooth
decay, obesity). The shift to less sugary, light sweets also reduced the
demand for traditional rice crackers and sweets which became limited
to the middle/old age group market.[75]

Given the enormous costs for advertising, promotion and new
product development, and the seasonality in consumption, a tendency to further concentration in the shrinking confectionery market
is not surprising. Companies have reacted by promoting imported
brands (still largely for the low volume/high prices – especially gift –
up-market). Import penetration is strong in the biscuit/cookie
(through Danish butter cookies) and chocolate segments. Other
strategies include diversification (Meiji Seika, the largest
confectionery-maker now obtains 40% of sales from pharmaceuticals) and joint ventures with foreign partners, like Yamazaki-
Nabisco, producing and marketing Nabisco brands in Japan.

Seasonings   The seasonings sector in which 'giants' such as Ajinomoto and Kikkoman coexist with thousands of smaller makers, in
spite of intense product innovation, grosso modo is saturated. Competition is strong particularly in the important soy sauce (shoyu)
subsector, due to the emergence of no-name products propagated by
the supermarkets. The sector in 1980 produced 1.2 m tonnes of soy
sauce, 308 000 tonnes of processed tomato products, 214 000 tonnes
of mayonnaise, 208 000 tonnes of other sauces, 88 500 tonnes of
monosodium glutamate (a synthetic chemical condiment patented
and exclusively produced by Ajinomoto), 81 000 tonnes of instant
curry, 41 000 tonnes of powdered and liquid seasonings, 33 000
tonnes of compound seasonings and 29 000 tonnes of soups.

With its limited growth prospects, the industry's response on the domestic market was to diversify. Kikkoman, a latecomer in diversification, in 1981 still had 62% of its sales in soy sauce (as the world's largest producer), the other product lines being: sauces for tonkatsu, sukiyaki (fried chicken), spaghetti, Worcester sauce, mirin (sweet rice wine), plum cake, shochu (a Vodka-like liquor), sake, fruit juices and nectars, the import marketing of Del Monte Ketchup and other brands, as well as the fateful production of Mann's wines.[76]

As prepared miso soups (which are based on soy bean pastes) as main traditional Japanese soup was not accepted by consumers favouring 'real' miso soup, Japanese makers focused on Western soups for the urban convenience market. Ajinomoto, which in the 1960s introduced pulverized instant soups to Japan, with its 'Knorr' brand licence has succeeded to near-monopolize this market segment ever since.[77]

Beverages   The beverages sector with annual average consumption of 154 litres per Japanese (except coffee and tea)[78] is the largest in Japan's food industry.

Still, compared with, e.g. a German consumption of 420 litres per head (equally disregarding tea and coffee),[79] there should be considerable room for expansion, particularly so in the fast growing soft drink, mineral water, fruit juice subsectors.

The beverage industry is characterized by the coexistence of structurally contrasting subsectors, some of which like beer, Western liquor and instant coffee belong to the most oligopolist in the Japanese economy; others like sake and shochu are competitive and small-scale in their production and marketing structure.

Alcoholic Beverages   Although the Japanese drink a large volume of soft drinks (62% of the total), a higher value added makes the alcoholic drinks' sector more significant in terms of sales and employment (see Table 5.9).[80]

The beer sector, as any visitor to Japan easily discovers, is dominated by Kirin (61% in 1984), a core member of the Mitsubishi empire. There are only three national co-competitors: Sapporo Breweries (20%), a Fuyo group member, Asahi Breweries (10%), a member of the Sumitomo group, and Suntory (8.7%), a participant in the Sanwa group. There are only two further small breweries – Hokkaido Asahi Brewery and Orion Brewery in Okinawa, which service their regional markets only. Beer brewing in Japan began in the 1870s based on imported German technology (the contemporary Sapporo Breweries called themselves 'Sapporo Dampfbierbrauerei' on occasion). The market's oligopolist structure dates back to the late Meiji era. In 1906 three major breweries merged to form the famous Dai Nippon Brewery, which in 1949, following the new anti-trust legislation due to its 70% market share (the remaining 29% were then held by Kirin), was split into Asahi Breweries and Nippon Breweries (later to be named Sapporo Breweries again). Suntory, Japan's near-monopoly distiller, became a brewer only in 1963.

The beer market, with only 2% annual growth prospects, is considered as stable and mature.[81]

Companies reacted by developing draft beers for the home market (replacing some of their pasteurized beer sales), by producing an extreme variety in packaging gimmicks (Kirin alone has 50 different beer containers, starting with a 135 ml extra-mini can, up to 3 litre kegs). They also put lighter and shandy-type beers on the market and imported limited amounts of premium-prized foreign brands as exclusive dealers. In 1983 1.3 m cases of Budweiser and 50 000 cases of Tuborg were imported by Suntory, and 55 000 cases of Guinness by Sapporo. Since 1983 Budweiser (by Suntory), Heineken (by Kirin), Löwenbräu (by Asahi) are brewed under licence in Japan to serve the young, affluent and trendy market.

Slowly, Japanese breweries are also venturing abroad. Exports to a great deal are still limited to their own restaurant chains abroad (Suntory, Sapporo) and to sales in Japanese overseas food shops. Although not relevant as share in corporate sales, exports are currently at 0.3% of domestic output (16 000 m litres in 1983), with imports still slightly higher at 21 500 m litres. Overseas expansion is highlighted as a major corporate strategy for the future. Currently this should serve more to enhance a desired cosmopolitan brand image at home, but the long-term international impact due to high R&D progress and investments in fermentation technology of these highly capitalized corporations should not be underestimated. Kirin in the fiscal year 1986 alone spent Y8.5 b on R&D. Starting out from straight product development and process innovation research in fermentation and ceramic fine filtration techniques, the move into fully fledged biotechnological research was fairly gradual. Today all four brewers present major projects investigating enzymes, tissue culture, cell fusion, gene modifications for straight commercial applications in high yielding seeds, bio-reactors and food processing, which obviously entail significant repercussions for the future of agriculture, and of the food and pharmaceutical industries.[82]

Japanese brewers – like many most brewers elsewhere – have

already diversified, largely into soft drinks. All produce a wide range of lemonade, fruit drinks, nectars, teas, vegetable juices, ciders, mineral waters and coffee drinks. They also either import and/or produce their own wines. Kirin-Seagram and Asahi (through its subsidiary Nikka-Whisky) compete with Suntory in its liquor market. In addition, Kirin produces dairy products (butter and cheese) largely for the gift market. Asahi sells dry brewers' yeast as a health food, and Suntory puts various 'health tonics' and 'sports beverages' on the markets, as well as a frozen foods service.

Diversification is slow to show tangible results in total sales. Sapporo and Kirin with 94% and 93% of sales still in beer remain largely one-product companies. Asahi has diversified further with 78% beer sales. The remainder in sales are largely soft drinks. For Suntory, essentially a distiller, beer is limited to a 20% share in turnover.[83]

Liquor production is dominated by Suntory whose Suntory Old with 6.9 m cases p.a. is the world's best-selling whisky. Its market shares in 1978 were 76% for whisky (in 1984 down to 70%), 79% for brandies, 87% for gin and 53% for liqueurs. The competitors for the whisky market are Nikka Whisky, an Asahi subsidiary (16.9% share in 1984); Sanraku Ocean (4.6%), related to Ajinomoto, and Kirin Seagram (4.6%) a joint venture of Kirin with Seagram (Canada) and Chivas (UK).[84] Apart from whisky, the only 'Western' liquor drunk in sizeable quantities is brandy, which has enjoyed strong growth over the past years. Consumption, however, still is less than 10% of that of whiskies.

Table 5.13 indicates the volatility of the Japanese liquor market: the continuous decline in sake consumption since 1972. The initial stagnation and sudden (1982–86) boom of shochu (which seems to have lost its trendyness in 1986),[86] having cut deeply into distillers' sales and profits, as whisky sales – both imported and domestic – fell by a third between 1983 and 1985 alone. Major makers – such as Suntory until 1984 – were denied production licences for shochu, which similar to sake is dominated by artisan production.[87]

Shochu, a transparent vodka-like liquor, distilled from a fermented mixture of sweet potatoes, rice, barley and molasses, which tradition-ally used to be drunk straight by labourers in the country (with an alcoholic content of between 20 and 45%), in its 'Chu-high' modern version is mixed with fruit drinks, foaming soda and lots of ice, and due to its low-alcohol content – similar to wine – enjoys high accep-tance among young women. Sake, made from rice, rice malt and

Table 5.13   The liquor market (1000 m litres)[85]

	Sake	Shochu	Beer	Whisky	Wine
1972	1,711	219	3,465	155	39 (1974)
1977	1,636	232	4,191	284	45
1982	1,543	315	4,792	361	79
1985*	1,341	632	4,794	267**	88 (1984)

* includes imports.
** of which imports = 17.

water which are later fermented and strained (alcoholic content: 15–16%), whose boom time coincided with the 1955–72 high economic growth period, perhaps due to producers' conservatism was not able to reverse its gradual decline since. Observers, however, after the 'jisake boom' – a consumer preference for local cheap, high-quality sake (graded second-class only for tax reasons) note a gradual return to better qualities (sake made from pure rice, instead of alcohol added) also among the 50 largest makers controlling more than 50% of production.[88]

Wine which, until the Austro-German glycol and the Italian ethanol scandals broke in 1985/86, had enjoyed a similar rapid expansion like shochu, benefiting from its clean, healthful, low-alcohol content image appealing to women who as the more cash-rich half of Japan's consumer society, apparently also begin to dominate the liquor market.[89] The major wine-makers and blenders, are linked to the large brewers and distillers: Suntory ('Chateau Lion', 'Delica'), Sanraku Ocean ('Mercian'), Sapporo ('Polaris'), Asahi ('My Cellar' – largely Australian imported bottled wine), but also Kikkoman the shoyu brewer, ('Mann's Wine'), and Kyowa Hakko, a chemical, fertilizer and pharmaka maker producing the tender-named 'Sainte Neige' wines. Among bottled wines, imports from France (39% of the import market in 1983) fared best (upmarket), followed by German white wines (34%) (rather downmarket), then by Californian (5%) and Italian (4.8%) and South Australian wines (3.7%), catering more for the lower end of the market: white wines that go well with Japanese seafood meals.[90]

While Japan's wine-bottlers certainly are not a fearsome threat to international markets, their parent companies appear to begin so. In January 1986 Guinness, locked in a fateful, eventually successful takeover battle with Argyll over the control of Distillers, claimed in full-page advertisements in the UK:

Suntory make the world's top-selling whisky. A similar achieve-
ment by Honda began the death knell of our motorcycle industry
twenty years ago. There is a risk Scotland's most renowned liquid
asset could suffer a similar fate. Like the motorcycle industry of
today, the international drinks business of tomorrow will be ruled
by giants. The Japanese, the Americans and the Canadians already
have towering corporations.

Made strong by thriving business in their home market, they
venture overseas with their arsenal of brands . . .[91]

Takara Shuzo, Japan's largest mirin- and shochu-maker, had just
bought the Tomatin distiller in Scotland, which Mr Sanders, then
Guinness chief executive, found indicative of an 'enormous export
drive' to come.[92] Japan's oligopolistic liquor-makers – stuck as they
are with high raw material costs and a domestic market which
appears as fairly saturated in per capita alcohol consumption (though
extremely low by developed world standards) and suffering from a
liquor tax system that discriminates heavily against the more promising up-market products – began to search for markets abroad. Their
product policies followed so far, blending imported bulk whiskies to
be drunk diluted with soda water, and venturing into expensive beer
packaging gimmicks, probably will not render them competitive in
the medium term in sophisticated markets. In the long run however,
with stepped-up overseas acquisitions, 'cooperation' and successful
bio-tech research results coming in (with both revolutionized production processes and completely new products), the picture might alter.

Soft Drinks   The soft drinks market, understandably, by nature may
appear as less exciting. Nonetheless it is in full expansion and transformation. In line with consumers' general preference for more
convenient and equally more 'natural' and healthy drinks, the share
of fresh milk, fruit juice, fruit nectars and coffee drinks (thin, sweet
café au lait, canned and heated, usually sold in vending machines)
increased. And so did vitamin-enriched 'health-drinks' (of whatever
value; at least they don't appear harmful) and protein-rich soybean
drinks. Those of colas, lemonades, lactic (made from sweetened
fermented milk) and other processed milk drinks have declined since
the 1970s.[93]

Among carbonated fruit drinks by brands, Coca Cola led with a
23% market share (in 1979), followed by Fanta (13%), Kirin Lemon
(7%), Matsuya Cider (Asahi) (6%), Sprite (3%); Kiwi Orange (3%)
Hi-C and Pepsi (2% each). New 'sports drinks' are likely to squeeze

these market shares. Among more stimulating warm drinks, green tea and coffee dominate, black tea and cocoa play minor roles.

In the coffee sector, whose raw materials – green coffee – obviously needs to be imported (from Bazil, Indonesia and Columbia mainly), 82% of the roasted and milled beans are consumed by restaurants, among them specialist 'coffee shops' (Kissaten) in particular. The remaining 18% are consumed in private households, which continue to prefer instant coffee (85% of the total produced). In particular young consumers appear attracted to instant coffees. While thin North American and *café au lait* preparations have gained ground, most of coffee-drinkers in Japan continue to favour the stronger and more flavoured Austrian and German-type blends.[94]

The instant market was founded in 1913, when Nestlé (Switzerland) made first sales in Japan. In 1933 Nestlé Japan KK was set up. It took 40 years until its current major competitor, AGF was established by Ajinomoto and General Foods (95). Today the duopoly controls 95% of the instant coffee market. The roasted coffee subsector appears more fragmented. Ueshina Coffee Co. (UCC), Key Coffee Co. and Art Coffee Co. are the three leading roaster– wholesalers, largely specializing in restaurants supply.[95] Cocoa, in contrast, proved to be a product too high in fat content, too weak as stimulator and too tedious to prepare to compete with green tea (whose share in hot beverage consumption shrank from 70% (1970) to 42% (1982) due to the popularity of coffee, while total green tea tonnage consumption remained stable at 98 000 tonnes). In 1977 Japan consumed only 3700 tonnes of cocoa powder (ground from cocoa cake, a byproduct of chocolate production left after the cocoa butter extraction), or a minimal 33y per head. An attempt to popularize and market cocoa drinks was consequently undertaken by the confectionery-makers.[96]

Non-Food Processing Industry

Tobacco

Japan's tobacco production structure is straightforward. A government monopoly buys all leaf tobacco produced from licensed producers (they are about 90 000, largely in Southern Kyushu) with acreage quotas (cut to 48 500 ha in 1985) at politically fixed prices, manufactures exclusively as a monopoly the brands it deems fit for Japan's smokers, and wholesales its output through its monopoly subsidiaries to its exclusively licensed retailers. If there are similarities to Eastern Europe, the results in terms of processing efficiency and product quality are identical.

The Japan Tobacco and Salt Public Corporation (JTS) was set up as a public monopoly in 1904 to finance Japan's victorious war against Russia, and has remained an important though gradually declining source of tax revenue ever since (originally accounting for 18%, lately down to around 2.6% of the total).[97] The monopoly was 'privatized' on 1 April 1985, with the government holding 100% of the shares and finance ministry appointees running this 'special corporation' status company in whose management MOF 'except in extreme circumstances' promised not to interfere.[98] Although no date has been set, provisions are that in any initial offering less than one-third of the shares will be sold to private stockholders. The government, however, will in any case always retain a majority stake in the equity.

The denationalization of this – the Western world's third largest – 'colossal and inefficient' tobacco manufacturer with its 36 brands produced in 35 'ramshackle factories'[99] had been demanded by the high-calibre Doko Committee on Administrative Reform in 1982. However, due to the tobacco growers' resistance – fearing cheaper and higher quality products replacing their high-priced leaf input in competitive manufacturing – and MOF's interest in a Y1.8 trillion revenue source, privatization had been watered down to the current form of a continued manufacturing and wholesaling monopoly.[100]

Currently, attempts are made to streamline the bloated sales and purchasing structure and to consolidate some manufacturing operations, with the Japan Tobacco Workers' Union promising cooperation with the proviso that there will not be any mass lay-offs for redundant workers.[101]

With about 310 billion cigarettes consumed, the Japanese with 2700 annual cigarettes per head (including babies), or 7 cigarettes per day are the world's second heaviest smokers – after health-conscious Americans. Nonetheless the global trend has caught up with Japanese cigarettes: consumption which had almost tripled in volume during 1960–77, was stagnant ever since, although sales due to repeated price/tax hikes increased. In difference to the Western pattern, the growing number of males (about 70% of them still smoke) kicking the habit has not been compensated by increased female smoking, which is levelling off at below 10% of the adult female population.[102]

As a result, an annual supply of unsold tobacco piles up in JTI's stores, with the producers in the corporatist Tobacco Cultivation Council having to accept further reductions in licensed cultivation acreage to a total of 49 000 ha (1985).[103] There are currently about 80 000 cultivators left growing tobacco in hilly sites made up of parcels of land, largely in Southern Kyushu, a labour-intensive pursuit for whose output they receive prices 3 times above world market level. For voluntary cessation of cultivation a grower is given 170 000 yen per 0.1 ha. In 1965 still 86 000 ha had been devoted to leaf tobacco. For quality reasons, the JTI still needs to import leaf tobaccos (duty free for them) which it then blends 1:2 with domestic leaves. Anybody else is free to import tobacco leaves as well, however, and unfortunately would be unable to process or to sell the stuff, due to JTI's continued monopoly. Imports of manufactured tobacco (which until 1985 had been limited to a modest 1.9% share or less) were equally liberalized. Imported cigarettes are subjected to a 20% tariff, the total of which is thereupon subjected to the domestic 85% *ad valorem* excise tax proportion (which makes for an effective tax-on-tax price differential of 37%) and a 15% specific excise tax proportion (levied on quantity), plus a varying local government levy.[104] With this tax-induced price discrimination over-priced imported brands can hardly expect to capture more than 5% of the market, being too expensive to be bought on a regular basis for most prospective customers. While JTI produces its flagship brand Marlboro under licence, Philip Morris (US) with its charcoal-filter brands Lark and Parliament holds 75% of the import market.

Philip Morris's imports and sales promotion are under the control of Nissho Iwai (for West Japan) and by Mitsui (for East Japan). They sell to Tobacco Haiso, JTI's wholesaler monopoly subsidiary, which supplies all licensed retailers. The world's other major manufacturers do the same: R. J. Reynolds (US; 'Camel', 'Winston') works with Mitsubishi; BAT (UK) and its US subsidiary Brown & Williamson ('Kool') with Sumitomo; Rothmans (UK; 'Dunhill', 'Rothmans') with Marubeni; and Ligitt's (US) with C. Itoh, attempting to get a foothold in this 3 trio yen market.[105]

Faced with a gradually declining volume market, the JTI responds by developing reduced tar and nicotine products, and also proclaims its intention to diversify. So far, its only marketable concept was to

Table 5.14 Major listed silk processing companies [109]

Total sales 1985 est. (Ym)		Share of silk (%)	Silk sales alone (Ym)
1. Katakura (Tokyo)	55,000	34	18,700
2. Gunze (Osaka)	158,000	6	9,500
3. Kobe Kito (Kobe)	17,000	52	8,800
4. Shinyei (Kobe)	63,000	10	6,300

sell flowering tobacco as an ornamental plant. JTI also set up an export subsidiary, the Japan Tobacco International Corporation, which took over the corporation's lucrative duty-free shop operations in Japan's airports. It now attempts to cater for the untapped Japanese ex-patriate market in East Asia and the US West Coast.[106]

Silk

Japan's sericulture is in continuous decline since the 1940s both in agricultural production and in its processing. In 1970 there were still 0.4 m households engaged in cocoon production. They were reduced to 139 000 by 1982. In 1970 still 112 000 tonnes of cocoons (1982: almost halved to 63 000 tonnes) were processed into 21 000 tonnes of raw silk (1982: 13 000 tonnes).[107]

Processing was dominated by small-/medium-sized enterprises with old-fashioned factories located in rural areas. Traditionally known as sweat shops for female labour, silk spinning and weaving remained a low productivity activity with apparently little technology needs. From 1926 to 1970 the number of plants declined from 78 000 to 2400, their employees from 480 000 to 27 000.

Sato in 1972 felt 'the industry is going to mark the *end* of its historical role'.[108] Once the backbone of Japan's export industry, subjected to the whims of business cycles and fashion, with inelastic supplies and furious price fluctuations, the major surviving companies diversified, thus unwittingly contributing to a further decline of the sector proper.

The major reeling manufacturers integrated downstream weaving and knitting operations, specializing in higher-value added stockings, underwear, tie and other knit fabrics and sewing threads. Some moved even further into sports wear, real estate and electrical components. The smaller traditional reeling companies went out of business.

As domestic raw material supplies became insufficient, imports of raw and thrown silk from China and Korea became unavoidable. These imports are largely handled again by the sogo shosha (C. Itoh, Mitsui Bussan, Nichimen, Mitsubishi Shoji etc.) which owe much of their current standing to their pre-war role in silk exports.

Leather and Hides

Japan's leather industry is characterized by small-scale, traditional and regionalized production. Tanners of cattle and horse hides are largely located around Osaka, those of pig hides in the Kanto area. Local producers of shoes and leather accessories are locally linked to the tanners.

The sector appears as dominated by uncompetitive Burakumin manufacturers, already mentioned above in the context of meat processing. High prices and the style of Japanese leather footwear reflect the lack of competition and design innovation only too obviously. The political and bureaucratic establishment, however, appears as almost physically terrorized and does not dare to touch these medieval economic privileges (as these socially unfortunate people appear as tightly organized in mutually hostile militant JSP and JCP camps). Production sites are still often in the separate housing areas of the former ghettos (hence the name 'Burakumin' – 'village people' stemming from the Tokugawa era separate housing ordinance), often in high-crime neighbourhoods along the rivers, where the unassimilated Korean immigrants and other underdogs also live.

Wholesale and retail margins of 20–25% and 35–40% respectively for domestic leather products – excessive even by generous Japanese standards – are equally indicative for an uncompetitive manufacturing and distribution system. These mark-ups also apply to the discretely imported leather goods, whose retail prices in Japan then, according to MITI, 'are 3 to 4 times the prices in the countries of manufacture'.[110]

Nonetheless it should be noted that also mainstream companies are engaged in leather trading (as Japan needs to import about 80% of the raw hides) and processing. One of them is Nozaki, a Y170 bn sales medium-sized trading house; 29% of turnover in 1984 was from leather – some of it also off-shore processing in Asia and third country trade – other lines of business being fruit and marine product canning ('Geisha' brand) and the exclusive imports of Cessna light aircraft and Aerospatiale helicopters into Japan.[111]

Whenever products price themselves off the market (or continue obstinately to disregard consumer preferences), substitutes become more attractive, hence hardly surprising is the attraction of synthetic footwear and accessories for casual or fashion use in Japan. Equally, synthetic leathers are used extensively in car interiors, furniture and other building and industrial applications. These substitutes are produced by affiliates of major chemical, rubber and car manufacturers. Since 1979 (with 53 m pairs), demand for leather shoes has levelled off, with a conspicuous drop in women's shoes (especially boots). A revival of demand appears to depend on more competitive pricing and design innovation which, however, in the current guild-type production structure, can hardly be expected.[112]

This chapter's analysis has shown Japan's input and food industry to be seriously affected by agricultural protection. For the input sector, inflated demand – most evident in the creation of agricultural machinery production overcapacities (1972–76) – has led to capital misallocation. The food industry's oligopolist structure and heavy government intervention favouring cartelization in the primary transformation sector, and sheltering the sector from competitive processed imports, permit excess input costs (plus margins) to be transmitted to the secondary transforming sector. Again, more often than not, in all modern sub-sectors oligopolistic (often monopolist) structures are tolerated and import protection granted. Reduced competition, which may increase production inefficiency and costs, and create oligopolist rents, permits again transmission of costs and margins to the distribution sector. As Chapter 6 will show, this sector's structure and public policies pursued serve to further add-on hefty margins until the final bill reaches the unfortunate consumer.

Notes

1. MAFF, op. cit., 1986, p. 19.
2. Sekiya, Shunsaku, 'The Agricultural Land System in Japan', *Japan Agricultural Review*, vol. 4, 1981, p. 3; *Japan Statistical Yearbook*, 1985, p. 154.
3. Author's own calculation, data taken from *Japan Statistical Yearbook*, 1985, pp. 166–8.
4. See note 3; beef figures; Longworth, John B., *Beef in Japan* (St. Lucia. 1983) p. 128, citing MAFF data; poultry and pork figures: MAFF *Monthly Statistics*, 2/1985, p. 40.
5. Adapted from *Japan Statistical Yearbook*, 1985, p. 157.
6. Smith, op. cit., p. 90; Fukutake, op. cit., p. 10.
7. MFA, *Facts about Japan: Agriculture* (Tokyo, 1984) p. 5.
8. Ogura, op. cit., p. 771.

9. *Japan Statistical Yearbook*, 1985, p. 158.
10. JETRO, *Agricultural Machinery*, Access to Japan's Import Market, no 3, 1979, pp. 8–9.
11. Ibid., pp. 12–13; Tonaka, Masatada, 'We've Contributed to the Mechanization of Japanese Agriculture', *Look Japan*, 10 Oct. 1982.
12. *Focus Japan*, Jan. 1978, pp. 14–15; *Japan Economic Yearbook*, 1981/82, p. 99.
13. 'Mechanized Farming: a Government Report', *Focus Japan*, June 1977, pp. 22–3.
14. *Financial Times*, 5 Jan. 1986.
15. *Financial Times*, 20 Oct. 1985, 23 Mar. 1986, 4 June 1986.
16. *Japan Statistical Yearbook*, p. 170.
17. *Japan Economic Yearbook*, 1981/82, p. 76.
18. *Business Japan*, Aug. 1984, p. 85.
19. MFA, op. cit., p. 5.
20. OECD, *Agricultural Policy in Japan* (Paris, 1974) p. 38.
21. *Japan Agrinfo Newsletter* 2, Jan. 1985, pp. 5–6.
22. Calculated from data given by Longworth, op. cit., p. 245.
23. Adapted, ibid., p. 240.
24. Adapted, ibid., p. 243.
25. Adapted, Matsuura, op. cit., p. 53.
26. Adapted, ibid., p. 62.
27. Ibid., p. 21.
28. Ibid., p. 22.
29. William T. Coyle, *The Feed – Livestock Sector in Japan* (Washington, DC: USDA, 1983) p. 36.
30. MAFF, 'Long-Term Prospects for the Demand and Production of Agricultural Products', *Japan Agricultural Review*, vol. 3, 1980, p. 5.
31. JETRO, *Food Processing in Japan*, rev., AG-12 (Tokyo 1984) pp. 3 and 5.
32. 'Food Processors', *Focus Japan*, Mar. 1979, p. 2.
33. Compiled from *The Oriental Economist*, various supplements, Dec. 1980 – Sept. 1982.
34. Kawakatsu, Kenji (President of Sanwa Bank) in *The Oriental Economist* (Sept. 1982) p. 14.
35. Sources: *Japan Economic Yearbook* (1981/82); MIPRO. *Survey Report on the General Market in Japan for Special Foodstuff Products* (Tokyo: 1981); IRM (wine); JETRO (beer); PA International (whisky).
36. W. Mark Fruin, *Kikkoman. Company, Clan and Community* (Cambridge, Mass.: Harvard University Press, 1983) p. 275.
37. JETRO, *Your Market in Japan: Beer*, Mini-Report no. 7, (1985) p. 6.
38. *Focus Japan*, Mar. 1979, p. 2.
39. Ishida, Akira, *Food Processing Industry in Japan* (Tokyo: Japan FAO Association, 1978) p. 17.
40. Watanabe, Bunzo (President of Ajinomoto) in *Japan Times*, 24 Feb. 1981.
41. Inubushi, Koji, 'Japan's Food Industry', *Look Japan*, 10 Mar. 1978.
42. JETRO, *Food Processing in Japan* (1984) p. 2.
43. Ibid., pp. 12–13.

44. Ishida, op. cit., p. 28.
45. *Financial Times*, 18 Dec. 1984; *The Economist*, 18 Mar. 1985.
46. JETRO, *Your Market in Japan: Biotechnology Equipment*, Mini-Report no. 3, (Sept. 1984).
47. Ibid., p. 4.
48. Sato, Yoshio, and Koichi Ito, 'A Theory of Oligopolistic Core and Competitive Fringe: Japan's Wheat Flour Milling Industry', *Keio Business Review*, no. 13, 1974, p. 18.
49. Nisshin Seifun, *A Guide to the Nisshin Flour Milling Group*, Tokyo (undated).
50. Showa Sangyo Co., *Annual Report*, 1985.
51. *Focus Japan*, Feb. 1978, pp. 14–15.
52. Fukawa, Mitsuo (Chairman, Japan Fat and Oil Association), 'Edible Oil Demand', *Business Japan*, Feb. 1984, p. 73.
53. *Japan Economic Yearbook* (1981/82) p. 61.
54. Fuji Oil Co., *Fuji* (company report) (Osaka, undated).
55. *Japan Agrinfo Newsletter*, no. 2, May 1985, p. 6; and Sept. 1984, p. 6.
56. Kenji K. Oshiro, *Dairy Policies and the Development of Dairying in Tohoku*, Ph. D. thesis, University of Washington, 1972, p. 104.
57. *Japan Economic Yearbook* (1981/82) p. 59.
58. Oshiro, op. cit., p. 108.
59. ASI Market Research Inc, *A Market Study of Dairy Products in Japan* (Tokyo, 1979) p. 47.
60. JETRO, *Vegetables* (Tokyo, 1980) p. 17.
61. JETRO, *Changing Dietary Lifestyles in Japan* (1978) p. 17.
62. Kagome Co., *Annual Report 1986*, p. 23.
63. Ishida, op. cit., p. 56.
64. Longworth, op. cit., p. 143.
65. Ibid, p. 146.
66. Ibid, p. 149.
67. Ibid, p. 153.
68. GATT, International Meat Council, *Reply to Questionnaire: Japan*, 29 Nov. 1985.
69. ASI Market Reasearch Inc., *A Market Study of Processed Meat in Japan* (1979) p. 6.
70. Ibid., p. 25.
71. JETRO, *Chicken Broilers* (1980) p. 7.
72. *Japan Economic Yearbook 1981/82*, p. 58.
73. *International Herald Tribune*, 8 Nov. 1984 and 14 Feb. 1985.
74. *Financial Times*, 24 May 1985 and 12 Nov. 1985; Dodwell Marketing Consultants, *Market Survey on Biscuits in Japan* (Tokyo, 1979) p. 29.
75. *Japan Economic Yearbook* (1981/82) p. 62.
76. Fruin, op. cit., p. 276.
77. IRM, *A Market Study of Soups* (Tokyo, 1979) p. 29.
78. 'Japanscene', *Focus Japan*, July 1981, Js-A.
79. *Agra Europe*, 29 Oct. 1984.
80. JETRO, *Your Market in Japan: Beer*, Mini-report no. 7, Feb. 1985, p. 3.
81. 'Profile: Kirin Breweries', *Financial Times*, 18 Dec. 1984.

82. Company Reports: *The World of Suntory*, *Sapporo Beer Guide*, *Asahi Beer*, *Kirin Annual Report 1986*, published in Tokyo, undated or in 1986.
83. JETRO, 'Beer', op. cit.
84. PA International Consulting Services, *EC Wine and Liquor Study* (1985) Appendix 1/13.
85. Nakajima, Tomio (Tax Administration Agency) in *Business Japan*, Aug. 1984, p. 37; Suntory Statistics quoted in *Financial Times* 28 July 1986.
86. *Japan Agrinfo* (1986).
87. *Financial Times*, 5 June 1986 and 18 Nov. 1985.
88. Mark A. Harbison, 'Sake and the Japanese', *Look Japan*, 10 Feb. 1985.
89. Kajiwara, Kazujoshi, 'Shochu Wines in Japan's "White Revolution"', *Journal of Japanese Trade and Industry*, 16 Jan. 1985, pp. 54–55.
90. *Financial Review* (Sidney) 6 Nov. 1984; William L. Davis, 'Japanese Market for U.S. Wines Is Improving with Age', *Foreign Agriculture*, May 1985, pp. 4–6.
91. *Financial Times*, 29 Jan. 1986.
92. *Financial Times*, 13 Feb. 1986; *Japan Economic Journal*, 9 Aug. 1986.
93. *Focus Japan*, July 1981, JS-B.
94. JETRO, *Comment Accéder au Marché Japonais: Le Café* (Tokyo, 1981); JETRO, 'Le Marché des produits d'importation au Japan: Le Café', *Tradescope*, no. 2, 1985, pp. 7–9.
95. 'Coffee: Trouble Brewing', *Focus Japan*, July 1977, pp. 18–19.
96. JETRO, *Cocoa. Access to Japan's Import Market*, no. 1, 1979, pp. 3–4.
97. Izumi (then President of JTS), in *Economisuto* (Tokyo, 6 Mar. 1979).
98. Naito, Satoshi, 'The Tobacco Monopoly Goes Private', *Economic Eye* (June 1985) p. 30.
99. Quotes taken from *The Economist*, 11 Sept. 1982.
100. *Japan Economic Journal*, editorial 10 Apr. 1984, *Financial Times*, 4 Apr. 1984.
101. Naito, op. cit., p. 32.
102. 'Smoking in Japan: Japanscene', *Focus Japan*, Feb. 1981, JS-A.
103. *Japan Agrinfo Newsletter*, no. 2, Mar. 1985, p. 2.
104. Guy R. Aelvoet (President of Philip Morris [Japan] K.K.) in *Journal of Japanese Trade and Industry*, 16 May 1985, p. 45.
105. *Economic Eye*, June 1985, p. 32.
106. Okubo, Shoji (President Japan Tobacco International Corporation) in *Business Japan*, June 1984, pp. 16–17.
107. *Japan Statistical Yearbook*, 1985, p. 164.
108. Sato, Yoshio, 'The Silk Reeling Industry of Japan and the Catch-up Case', *Keio Business Review* no. 11, 1972, p. 65.
109. Data from *Japan Company Handbook* (1985) p. 193.
110. MAFF, *The State of Distribution of Imported Food Products*, unpublished, Typescript, Nov. 1985, p. 2.
111. Company Report, *Nozaki & Co Ltd* (Tokyo, 1984).
112. *Japan Economic Yearbook* (1981/82) p. 130.

6 Distribution and Consumption

FOOD WHOLESALING AND RETAILING

Next to her high cost agricultural production, Japan's cumbersome distribution system with its large mark-ups charged along the way is considered as a major factor increasing retail prices and hence limiting consumption.

Japan's Engel's coefficient – the percentage of total household expenditure spent on food – is still at 25.7% (for comparison: the US: 13%, the UK and Germany: 15%, France: 18%).[1]

The particularities of Japan's distribution system and its difficulty of access to foreign importers are usually cited as a most severe single 'non-tariff barrier' inhibiting the large-scale marketing of foreign-made consumer products in Japan.

The distribution sector, the sales of which account for 15% of Japan's GNP, employs 20% of its workforce. Casual observations of employees busy polishing apples and carefully arranging small candy packages in retail shops, of elevators in department stores being manned by girls announcing the floors' sales programmes, of female representatives distributing 20 ml dairy packages individually to households, indicate significant levels of over-staffing and the sector's employment function to absorb unskilled 'reserve' labour.

Consumers pay these frills (to have a wide range of small family retail shops within walking distance, to be able to engage in lengthy shopping talks with staff also in city department stores, etc.) with extraordinary margins charged, which appear indicative of a great deal of non-price competition at the retailing level.

The results are welfare losses to the Japanese economy and a prolongation of an almost totally fragmented retail structure which is unable to participate and compete in the current global trend to 'world-wide stores plc', of big national retailers becoming multinational chains.[2]

The wholesale sector, judging from its mark-ups and multi-layered structure, operates largely on the same principle. Particularly in the traditional food industry sectors, the multiplicity of dispersed processors is reflected by a complex primary, secondary and tertiary wholesale structure collecting, storing, financing and finally delivering an assembled range of products down the chain until it reaches the retailer (who has no storage space and expects his suppliers to wait with payment until the product is sold and to take the unsold items back).

As a result, the ratio of wholesale sales to retail sales (W/R) in 1979 in Japan was 3.7, almost twice the 1.9 ratio in the US.[3]

Three factors determine essentially the structure of the distribution system for the product in question:

1. the degree of concentration/fragmentation at the manufacturing stage;
2. the degree of concentration/fragmentation at the retail stage; and
3. the frequency of consumer purchase.

The difference between traditional, multi-layered sake distribution and streamlined whisky wholesaling does illustrate the point. Sake output, which is produced in hundreds of local brands by mostly small breweries, is first collected by a regional primary wholesaler who then sells it to a secondary wholesaler in the marketing area. He in turn sells the product to a small tertiary wholesaler who assembles the varied range of bottles for the typically smallish liquor stores (there are 110 000 of them in Japan) and provides 120 days of credit for the merchandise.

The margin for the primary wholesaler is around 15% (of the retail price), that of the secondary/tertiary wholesaler about 10%. The retailer pockets another 15%.

With whisky and its oligopolist production structure and more limited domestic product range; distribution channels are understandably much shorter. A regional contract wholesaler supplies the retail level directly. In the case of major retailers, such as supermarkets (only a limited number have a liquor licence) and department stores, his major function is to provide for storage and instant delivery of the quantities wanted. Consequently, margins are much smaller: 5% for the contract wholesaler and 15% for the retailer.[4]

For imported whiskies, with smaller quantities handled and due to higher prices (and discriminatory *ad valorem* liquor taxation) and lower turnover, distribution channels are again more complex and margins higher. Exclusive importers (foreign or domestic) sell to primary wholesalers (since they usually don't have the regional network) who sell to their local secondary wholesalers. They then supply retailers, hotels, bars, restaurants, supermarkets and department stores with the fairly small quantities of this luxury-priced article.

This dual wholesale structure also applies to other processed foodstuffs: complex and expensive in the case of dispersed production (confectionery, canned fruit, sea food, seasonings), and more streamlined and less costly in the 'modern' oligopolist sector (instant coffee, soft drinks, bread products).[6]

Obviously, competing products may choose different (or several) marketing channels for their products. Also the retail structure may demand different distribution routes for the same products. Other factors determining distribution margins – apart from the multitude of handlers and turnover speed – evidently are the perishability and possible cold-storage/transport and sales promotion costs (the latter are usually borne by the producer, in the case of imported products, however, are undertaken largely by the importing agent). MAFF found that perishable or cold-storage products such as fruits and frozen vegetables had distribution margins between 50 and 70%.[7]

There are about ten different types of rebates (offered by producers to wholesalers, and then to retailers for volume of sales), which are more limited by comparison: for food they are typically 1–2%, and may, for high-priced items, increase up to 4–5%.

Other competitive instruments include payment terms (60 to 120 days after delivery; usually following the principle that the older the trading relationship, the longer the supplier credit), consignment sales (returned unsold goods are used for organizing 'bargain sales' by the primary wholesaler) and in-channel sales promotion. Wholesaler employees visit retailers regularly with marketing advice and enquire about consumer reactions. In department stores they often do the actual stocking of shelves (at hourly notice, as the stores don't keep inventories) and also often man the counters.[8] This 'detailing' function is evidently highly labour-intensive.

With an increasing retail sales share of supermarkets at the downstream end, and growing producer concentration upstream – with manufacturers beginning to invest in regional distribution centres – the squeeze on the 94 000 food wholesalers (1982) and their 800 000 employees is evident: 48% of them have less than 5 employees and handle only 5% of total sales. In contrast, the 0.7% of wholesale firms with more than 100 employees manage 42% of total turnover.[9] The largest food wholesalers (Kokubu, Meidi-Ya, Ryoshoku, Nihon Shurui Hanbei, Matsushita Suzuki, Koami) in 1985 all had sales in excess of Y200 bn, but profitability levels were considered less satisfying.[10] Pressure is increasing to rationalize operations, to cut personnel and inventories and to specialize further.

For fresh products – fruit, vegetables, fish, meats and flowers – the use of central and local wholesale markets as an intermediary is growing. In central wholesale markets in 1978 food products totalling Y44.2 bn were sold: 56% of the total were marine products, 37% fruit and vegetables, 5% meats and 0.3% flowers and plants. In local wholesale markets with a Y4 bn turnover, the dominance of fishery products and fruits and vegetables was similar.[11]

Retailers – largely supermarkets and speciality shops – usually buy these perishable products unprocessed at these markets. Also most imported fruit and vegetables pass through the wholesale markets.

While about 90% of all fishery and greenery is auctioned in these markets – exceptions being vegetables grown under contract for supermarkets or processors, direct producer marketing organized by Zenno, or fishery products imported by the sogo shosha and distributed by commissioned wholesalers – only 16% of pork and 33% of beef is sold in wholesale market auction. Still the prices achieved have a significant impact on the over-the-counter deals in the rest of the meats sector.

Livestock is typically bought up by local livestock dealers, shipped to slaughterhouses and the carcasses are then wholesaled, deboned, chilled and distributed to retailers in fairly small cuts. Reality, unfortunately, is slightly more complicated. As slaughter and meat processing is traditionally carried out by the famous 'butchers guild', the Dowa people, who understandably insist on non-competitive processing rents, and the large profit margins which accompany the resale of cheap imported beef (done by the semi-governmental LIPC) at protected domestic price levels, the meat – especially beef – processing and wholesale sector is a fairly murky affair, with allegations of 'beef mafias', and profit margins used to obtain political favours, etc. never subsiding.[12]

MAFF, which supervises the LIPC's operations, has attempted to respond to this widespread criticism by promoting the agricultural cooperatives' involvement in livestock handling (thus cutting out traditional livestock dealers), to set up integrated meat centres (which do the slaughter, deboning, cutting and packaging largely as an integrated process – whereas traditionally processing was carried out at various wholesale stages), to modernize and make meat wholesale markets more open and above board, and to auction most of LIPC's imported meats in these markets.

Longworth alleges that also in auctioning imported frozen beef, MAFF's 'administrative guidance' interferes, resulting in remarkably stable shares among the competing groups: 25% of the total goes to the five big processors, 20% to the Dowa retailers association, 5% to the supermarket chains, 4% to Zenno (1980), the rest to other processors, retailer and consumer organizations, allowing for auction prices far below true wholesale levels.[13]

In the pork sector, which with 1.5 m tonnes is about three times larger than the beef sector, the wholesale market is largely bypassed due to the sector's domination by contract farming operations organized by the sogo shosha-affiliated feed compounders. They not only supply piglets and feed but also collect the fattened hogs and trade their carcasses to the meat processors, who sell the resulting ham, bacon, sausages and cuts through their own channels. The five major meat processing companies (sometimes affiliated with the same Keiretsu, such as Prima Meat Packers through C. Itoh to the DIK group) handle about 20% of all pork distributed[14] – some of the retail meat shops being captive franchises.

These vertically integrated production/processing/marketing operations – supported by little public protection and subsidization – have resulted in relatively low consumer prices and enhanced consumption for processed pork (+ 3–5% p.a. in 1975/85).

Zenno, with its own affiliated feed cooperatives, has followed the sogo shosha's lead and established similarly fully integrated operations with its meat centres selling directly to consumer cooperatives and large users.

RETAILING

In 1982 there were 725 000 retail food shops in Japan, in which 2.3 m employees handled sales of Y29 trillion. The average store with its 3.2 employees hence caters to 165 customers only (taking all 120 m Japanese as the total clientele). With this high density of small shops, 58% of all consumers reach one food shop within 10 minutes on foot from their residence, and 84% within 20 minutes.[15] In the 1960s the small food retailers had to begin to face up to the competition of the enlarging supermarkets. By 1982 their number had expanded to 20 000 with 520 000 employees (26 per shop), a total floor space of 15 m m^2 (750 m^2 on average – in Europe a supermarket starts at 1000 m^2) and an annual total of Y9300 bn food and beverage sales.

If one assumes a 300 day/year opening schedule for both food supermarkets and retail shops, daily sales per employee are then Y800 000 and Y40 000, calculating from the above-quoted figures. Retailers have survived – though with a declining share in total sales – due to the Japanese housewife's preference to do neighbourhood shopping at least once-a-day for fresh food in small quantities (given the shortage of storage space and the small refrigerator sizes in Japanese households, and the frustration of a full-time housekeeper fenced into a rabbit-hutch).

High land prices in urban centres inhibit both the spread of supermarkets and car parks in convenient locations as do local by-laws – based on a restrictive Large Retail Store Law – which often refuse building permits, and past investment control laws prohibiting foreign investment in the retail and distribution sector.

While most general food retailers (for the lack of space and capital) appear to have changed little, others have reached to the supermarkets' competition by forming chain systems on a cooperative basis or by becoming franchisees of convenience store organizers. The Kanto-centred Seven-Eleven Japan Co. with 2700 convenience stores – often open longer than the 7 a.m./11 p.m. schedule – is the largest of these chains. A standard shop design, consolidated purchasing and a supply of 3500 fast-turnover daily need items (largely food) and advanced point of sale (POS) computer systems supervising inventories and eliminating slow moving items, and regular visits by corporate field counsellors are the typical features of this chain,[16] the franchise corporation of which is owned by Ito-Yokado, Japan's second largest supermarket operator.

Japan's biggest supermarket chains (Dai'ei, Ito-Yokado, Seiyu, Jusco, Niichi, Uny) with turnovers between 710 and Y200 bn p.a., which still are largely controlled by family management, have introduced POS systems to both monitor demand and to trim inventories, which contributed to enhanced overall profitability in recent years.[17] The share of foodstuff in these groups' total turnover varied between 29 and 43%, other significant sales categories being clothing, household utensils and sundry goods. The same cost-saving POS technology has also been introduced to Japan's leading department stores (Mitsukoshi, Takashimaya, Daimaru, Matsutakaya, Sogo), dignified institutions of pre-war origin.

Largely up-market food products – with gift packages enjoying prominence – make around 20% of total turnover which varies between Y570 bn (for Mitsukoshi) and Y220 bn (for Sogo) in 1985/86.[18] Compared to superstores (supermarkets and convenience stores) and small urban speciality shops, however, market shares of department stores have steadily declined, in spite of their convenient location at major metropolitan railroad terminals and mass commuter junctions. As more 'mature' corporations they are owned by institutions (the usual mix of banks, insurances, security companies). Mitsukoshi is closely linked to the Mitsui Keiretsu.

A higher turnover than of the two leading 'depaatos' combined is achieved by the drinks' sales of a fourth competing institution alone: the automatic vending machines, a ubiquitous feature along all Japanese roads, which in 1982 sold Y1300 bn worth of drinks, Y540 bn of cigarettes and Y90 bn yen of food. Some have heating facilities (for sake, coffee, tea, soups and cardboard tasting hamburgers), others have chilling facilities. Beer vending machines particularly offer an impressive range of different sized packages, up to 5-litre kegs for late night thirst. It is evident that these facilities are installed and maintained by the manufacturers and their distributors, though the proceeds are shared with the shopkeepers owning the sites.

CONSUMPTION

Traditionally the Japanese diet consisted of three daily meals all centring around boiled rice, to which various raw or slightly cooked side dishes of fish, vegetables and pickles would be offered. The continued dominance of rice (and other cereals) in food intake meant that per capita starch consumption, though gradually declining (1983: 48% of daily caloric supply), remained high by international standards.

Table 6.1 indicates a steady and nonetheless almost dramatic decline of rice consumption since 1960. The reduction in pulses was more erratic and certainly less consequential. Consumption of vegetables and sugar expanded only until around 1970 and declined thereafter. Consumption of fruits, fish and eggs appears as more or less static since 1970, while only dairy and meat consumption continues to expand.

Still these levels of livestock consumption remain much below the 'Western' dietary pattern of 3000 cal/day which is strong in calorie-rich fat and animal proteins and short on carbohydrates. The Japan-

Table 6.1 Annual food consumption per person (kg) [19]

	1960	1970	1975	1980	1983	1983/60 (%)
1. Cereals	149.1	128.5	122.2	114.0	110.2	73.7
Rice	114.9	95.1	88.1	78.9	75.7	65.9
Wheat	25.8	30.8	31.5	32.2	31.8	123.3
2. Beans	10.1	10.2	9.5	8.6	9.0	89.1
3. Vegetables	99.7	114.2	109.5	110.3	107.6	107.9
4. Fruits	22.3	37.9	42.4	38.7	39.2	175.8
5. Meat	5.2	13.4	17.9	22.5	23.8	457.7
6. Eggs	6.3	14.5	13.7	14.3	14.6	231.7
7. Milk & milk products	22.2	50.1	53.3	62.0	67.1	302.3
8. Fish	27.8	31.6	34.9	34.8	34.2	123.0
9. Sugar	15.1	26.9	25.1	23.3	21.4	141.7

ese daily caloric intake of 2600 calories (1983) consists of a balanced protein, fat and carbohydrates intake. Protein consumption is split equally between vegetable (52%) and animal proteins (48%), with a large proportion being provided by marine products (22%).

This nutritional pattern probably has had a strong significance in reducing the incidence of heart/coronary diseases and diabetes in the Japanese population, hence contributing to Japan having achieved the world's longest life expectancy with 80.5 years for women and 74.8 years for men (1985).

In spite of some typical 'Japanese' features in the national diet there are strong generational, social and regional differences in tastes. With respect to meat, consumers in Hokkaido, Tohoku and Kanto have a strong preference for pork, while in Kinki and South-Western Japan beef is more popular.

Chickenmeat has a more even national spread, but per capita consumption in Kyushu is strongest. The Okinawan diet with their strong liking for Danish pork luncheon meat is altogether a different story.

Even with respect to soy sauces the regional riddle is significant: in Kanto it is preferred very strong, while in Kansai the reverse is true. Equally Tokyo is judged more open, spicy and knowledgeable on foreign foods and drinks than is Osaka.[20]

The older generation (MAFF interviewed centenarians for the purpose), next to rice, likes cooked vegetables, sashimi (raw seafood), sushi (raw fish on rice), and stewed fish.[21]

Among young people the survey revealed the consumption of meats, fruit, oils and eggs to be considerably above that of older people.[22] Inhabitants of large cities consume more dairy, eggs, meat, wheat and beverages than residents of smaller towns who like a more traditional dish with a stronger share of rice, vegetables and fish. Obviously, there are also differences according to marital status. Only one third of singles still eat rice at each meal – partly because it is so time-consuming to prepare – and would rather stick to bread, instant noodles and spaghetti instead. Two-thirds of married couples, however, still have rice for all three meals.

With just over 50% of married women being employed at least part-time,[23] average Japanese households now have more disposable income and less time for household chores, and this increases the demand for convenience foods requiring less cooking and preparatory time. Already in the late 1970s more than 80% of households regularly used instant coffee, curry cubes and dried noodles; more than 60% used milk powder instant soups, while 40% fed themselves regularly with frozen food (as almost all households have refrigerators with deep freeze compartments).[24] Dining out regularly for the entire family became a socially accepted event.

Since 1965 caloric intake has stabilized in the Japanese diet. With this saturation in basic nutritional needs and regularly increasing real incomes, the consumers' preferences went for quality, new tastes, convenience and attractively packaged products. Overseas foods – Chinese, Korean, American, European – are readily accepted among the trend-setting Tokyo consumers, provided that they blend well with established eating habits and light tastes. Imported foods, for instance, should not be too sweet, too salty, too dry, too flavoured or smelling (i.e. Roquefort and mutton are out). Subjected to the whims of consumer fashion the Japanese food industry is forced to put out continuously new preparations, flavours, sizes and packaging gimmicks. At the same time, the market gets more differentiated: enlarged single men/women segments, the working housewife, men's cooking, health foods, home parties, the gift market, etc., represent diversified growth sectors.

FOOD SERVICES

Already in 1980 15% of all food expenditure was spent in the 520 000 various restaurant facilities (not counting the 230 000 bars, cabarets, night clubs, beer halls and pubs). These restaurants in 1979 employed 1.8 m persons. The latter entertainment sites add another 600 000 employees.[25] There is one eating-out facility for 21 inhabitants in Tokyo, and one for 27 in Osaka.

Total sales of restaurants and catering firms in the fiscal year 1985 totalled Y18.2 trillion[26] representing about 5% of Japan's GNP, with the share of the 100 largest companies reaching Y2.7 bn (14.7% of the total). The largest chain is McDonald's (Japan) Co., with sales of Y119 bn yen from selling 1.5 billion hamburgers in 530 downtown restaurants. Den Fujita, McDonald's Japan's President, who in 1971 opened the first establishment in the Ginza (he also wrote a remarkable best-seller titled *Those who are stupid always lose*) claims that he is 'feeding the Japanese beef hamburgers to make them physically competitive'.[27]

Most restaurant chains operate central purchasing and kitchen operations to supply precooked materials, some like McDonald's, Kentucky Fried Chicken, Lotteria, Denny's and Dustins (Mister Donut) specializing in a narrow range of American fast foods. Most, however, appear more diversified and nutritionally sounder with various either Western or Chinese dishes, and Japanese take-away lunches.

As growth rates have gradually levelled out, the sector is considered 'mature' now, with the larger chains buying smaller competitors who lack the financial resources to supply the regular refurbishings and advertising expenditure needed to follow the latest consumer fads.[28] Franchised pub chains and US ice cream parlours (Häagen-Dazs, Hobson's, etc)[29] are currently the latest favourites. They suddenly and unexplicably appear and may vanish within a few seasons similar to the shochu boom of 1983/85.

In the two-tiered structure of Japan's eating-out industry, it is only the top tier's well capitalized companies – with their share of multinationals – which are able to respond fast to changed consumer preferences. 80% of all eating-out facilities, however, still are family-managed single-shop operations, with less than four employees, largely exploiting family labour (with poor productivity due to low turnover) and burdened with expensive food procurement at retail level. These restaurants are typical of those serving traditional Japanese cuisine, noodles (soba/udon) and of most sushi shops.

The top tier is able to overcome the cost squeeze (around 45% of total expenditure are material costs, 37% personnel costs) by hiring part-timers (largely women) and employing unskilled labour through standardized manual-oriented operations.

Procurement is done through central purchasing largely in bulk from food processors or at wholesale markets level, often being able to order from producers and manufacturers direct supplies to their central kitchens according to specifications.

The large chains through public stock listing organize the capital needed to run a regular chain system with the large investments required for setting up and running their own shops (as practised by McDonald's Japan, and Seibu Restaurant).

A cost-saving alternative evidently is franchising. The franchisees under contract will supply most of the capital and labour, in order to operate under the franchiser's brand name (like Mister Donut), designs, central purchasing and instructions in exchange for a franchising fee.

Companies providing prepared food to the institutional sector (schools, hospitals, corporate canteens, welfare institutions for children and the aged) are small-to-medium sized, largely fulfilling a subcontractor role. While being able to benefit from bulk purchasing, the scope for labour rationalization remains small. Growth prospects are limited at best.

The entire eating-out industries' 1.8 m employees with an average of 8.8 hours work longer than the 7.7 hours of other service industries. With 7 days of paid leave they also take less holidays on average than other employees in services (8.4 days).

As labour productivity is much lower, wages are close to the bottom of Japan's service and industrial sector. Waiters are typically young and female, and the share of part-timers high (at 34% on

Table 6.2 Turnover in the eating-out industry, 1980 Y (trillion)[30]

All restaurant eating-out facilities		Institutional sector		Drinks/food sector	
7.1		2.7		4.2	
restaurants	3.7	business canteens	1.4	coffee shops	1.5
noodle shops	0.5	schools	0.5	pubs, beer halls	0.7
sushi shops	0.8	hospitals	0.5	bars, cabarets,	
inns/hotel	1.5	welfare	0.2	night clubs	1.7
railroad dining	0.1			ryotei (high	0.3
others	0.5			quality restaurants)	
		Total = 14.0			

average) with more than 60% in the peak-oriented noodle and fast food shops.

Skill requirements diminish gradually: the fast food chains no longer require good cooks as managers, but rather reliable machine and shop operators. Labour turnover in the entire industry is usually high, corporate welfare systems underdeveloped and unionization low at a 15% membership rate.[31] With these underdog employment conditions one cannot help associating references to Mr Fujita's cynical if appropriate best-seller title.

While the growth of the larger chains – responding to the kind of individualized tastes by setting up more segmented, trendy facilities – appears assured through acquisitions and expansions, small restaurants will survive to the extent that they are able to secure an upmarket clientele which is ready to pay a premium for quality in terms of cooking and speciality foods.

A tendency to move overseas to cater for the Japanese expatriates and to an international public gradually discovering the delights of Japanese cuisine has got underway in recent years, offering new prospects for individual businessman as well as for the chains and the foods and drinks processors. The inflow of foreign capital and management skills, which followed the liberalization of the eating-out sectors for foreign investment in March 1979, with their new and successful ideas had woken up the industry and created the foundations for its possible future international success.

Notes

1. Keizai Koho Center, *Japan 1986: an International Comparison* (Tokyo, 1986) p. 87; USDA, *Handbook of Agricultural Charts* (Washington, DC 1982) p. 31; EC Commission, *The Situation of Agriculture in the Community* (Brussels, 1986) p. 136.
2. Foreseen by *The Economist*, 28 June 1986; on US retail mergers also *Time*, 14 Oct. 1986.
3. Nakanishi, Toshio, 'Distribution Industry Must Adapt to New Reality', *Journal of Japanese Trade and Industry*, no. 1, 1985, pp. 32–3.
4. JETRO, *Planning for Distribution in Japan* (Tokyo, 1982) p. 29.
5. Yasuda, Hiroshi (President of Jardine, Matheson & Co. (Japan)) in *Cracking the Japanese Market* (Tokyo: Mainichi Newspapers, 1985) pp. 25–7.
6. JETRO, *An Outline of Food Distribution in Japan*, AG-6 (Tokyo, 1981) p. 26.
7. MAFF, 'Outline of the Results of an Inquiry concerning the Actual State

of the Distribution of Imported Food Products (unpublished typescript), Tokyo, Nov. 1985, p. 6.

8. *Frankfurter Allgemeine*, 2 Aug. 1982.
9. Nakanichi, op. cit.
10. *Japan Economical Journal*, 9 Aug. 1986.
11. JETRO, op. cit., (1981) p. 33.
12. *Le Monde*, 28 June 1977; *La Libre Belgique*, 30 Aug. 1986.
13. John W. Longworth, *Beef in Japan* (St. Lucia: University of Queensland Press, 1983) p. 192.
14. JETRO, op. cit. (1981) p. 24.
15. JETRO, *Food Processing Industry in Japan*, rev., Ag-12 (1984) pp. 14–15.
16. Seven Eleven Japan Co. Ltd, *Annual Reports* (1986 and 1984).
17. *Financial Times*, 3 May 85, 22 Oct. 85, 17 Oct. 86.
18. *Financial Times*, 30 Apr. 86.
19. MAFF, *Food Balance Sheets for Fiscal Year 1983* (Tokyo: Foreign Press Center, Jan. 1985) p. 4.
20. JETRO, *Keys to Success: Japan's "Food Lifestyle"* (Tokyo, 1983) p. 28.
21. MAFF, 'Japan's Dietary Habits', *Japan's Agricultural Review*, vol 5, 1981, p. 10.
22. 'Japanese Dietary Habits', Japanscene, *Focus Japan*, May 1981, JS-A.
23. JETRO, *The Japanese Market in Figures* (Tokyo, rev. 1983) p. 19.
24. JETRO, *Changing Dietary Lifestyles in Japan* (Tokyo, 1978) p. 9.
25. *Japan Economic Yearbook* (1981/82) p. 154.
26. *Japan Economic Journal* 10 May 1986.
27. Fujita, Den, 'Golden Arches on the Ginza', *Speaking of Japan* 7, June 1986, p. 25.
28. Yagai, Akinobu, 'Restaurants and Catering', *Japan Economic Almanac* (1986) p. 215.
29. *Japan Economic Journal*, 5 Apr. 1986.
30. JETRO, *Dine-Out Industry in Japan*, AG-7 (Tokyo, 1982), p. 9.
31. Ibid., p. 19.

7 Farm Politics

Japan's post-war political system centred around an uneasy coalition of the ruling LDP, organized business interests, and the central government bureaucracy, whose policies were supported by an essentially conservative electorate. In agricultural policies this basic equation becomes troubled through the inclusion of the agricultural lobby, as organized by Zenchu, whose protectionist policies are opposed by big business – voiced by Keidanren, Japan's industrial federation.

The LDP, a great deal of whose legislators (and hence faction leaders) need to rely on Nokyo endorsement to secure their re-election (the districts are heavily skewed in favour of rural representation) especially around election time, loudly espouses Zenchu views. The government ministries concerned, on price issues (MOF, MAFF) usually endorse policies more in line with economic common sense and budgetary prudence, but on export disputes MAFF defends its farm constituency, with MFA and MITI being more accommodating to liberalization requests.

Zenchu's highly visible lobbying style (of which the media are mildly critical) and the persistent disagreement in the ruling coalition makes for an easily charged and politicized decision-making on the most significant agricultural policy decisions: the annual rice price setting and the US beef, orange and (more recently) rice import demands.

This chapter will demonstrate the operations of the agricultural policy system, first by describing each participant's structure and rationale, then by analysing their interactions on the major price and import issues.

JIMINTO, THE LIBERAL–DEMOCRATIC PARTY

With its predecessor parties ruling Japan almost without interruption since 1898 (the longest break having been the military's dictatorship 1940–45), the LDP undisputedly is the world's most successful conservative party. Its landslide victory in the Lower House election of July 1986 (with 49.4% of the total vote, and an absolute majority of 300 out of 512 seats), showed that the LDP has reversed its gradual

demise forecasted frequently in the 1970s, when the party's share –
following various environmental and financial scandals – had fallen to
a low of 41.8% (1976) and was maintained in power apparently
largely due to big business support and rural and traditional voters'
over-representation in gerrymandered election districts. In the meantime the party has regained ground particularly among the younger,
better educated white-collar and suburban voters which in the past
had expressed socialist preferences in elections.

The party's formal organization is almost non-existent – paying
members are only local and regional office-holders. The party is
effectively rather more structured along factional lines and on the
local level relies on the MP's personal support network (Koenkai) or
his (rural) local followers' inherited loyalties (Jiban). Currently there
are two mainstream factions (successors of the dominant post-war
Yoshida faction) – still led by Tanaka and Suzuki – and three
'side-stream' factions (formerly opposed to Yoshida's policies) of
Nakasone, Fukuda and Komoto. Membership (by July 1986) varies
between 141 PMs (Tanaka) and 34 MPs (Komoto)[1]. Factions are
hierarchically organized, with individual rank depending on loyalty,
merits and length of service to the faction chief and his lieutenants.
They maintain central secretariats, their own funding systems and
regular member meetings. Faction leaders, their key aides, and the
small group of the party's semi-retired elder statesmen in elaborate
intrigues and in-fighting, decide on who becomes prime minister (and
by which continuously changing rules).

Similar to the Italian Christian Democrats, faction chiefs also
propose their candidates for ministerial and senior party posts. The
Prime Minister's final choices then usually reflect a carefully balanced
coalition government of factions. The party's Secretary-General –
usually from a different faction than the president (and concurrent
PM) in a similar delicate fashion – has to select candidates (other
than incumbents) to run for the LDP in the multi-member districts.
Too many candidates from a particular faction could rock the boat
and fuel simmering inter-factional feuds. In these districts during
elections LDP candidates rather campaign against each other (as,
most prominently, Nakasone and Fukuda did regularly in 14 elections in their Gumma prefecture constituency) for the same sym-
pathetic electorate rather than fighting for the more hostile clientele
of the opposition parties. As it is in the vital interest of each faction
chief to see as many of his men returned to the Diet, he is expected to
finance with his funds his followers' election campaigns.

Programmatic differences are only of minor importance between the LDP factions (although Fukuda and Nakasone men are generally considered more 'right-wing', Suzuki and Tanaka more 'centrist', and Komoto more 'centre-left'). Consequently, LDP-leaning voters' choices between the competing candidates (multi-member districts elect 3 to 5 candidates as MPs and depending on the size of the district and the LDP electorate, the party fields 2 to 3 officially endorsed LDP candidates in each district) are strongly influenced through personal ties and recommendations, and through straight pork-barrel politics.

Sitting and would-be LEP MPs usually build up their own personal followers' network in their district (or inherit it from their retired mentor or close relative). This implies relying on and espousing a wide range of local politicians, notables, associations, etc. These political and personal 'friends' are organized in personal support associations ('Koenkai'). The MP is meant to help these persons' careers and public interests. It also requires organizing social events, trips to Tokyo, supplying jobs, to set up youth, women, old folk's associations, doing public good, and supporting the constituency's economic interests. In return, the 'Koenkai' and its affiliated local politicians (with their own little Koenkais) will work untiringly for their man's re-election. They will expect their campaign expenditure to be reimbursed from the MP, who in turn rarely spends his own money, but uses the cash handed over to him from his faction chief for maintaining his expensive Koenkai and to run his election campaign. A more traditional – and probably cheaper – version of the 'modern' (voluntarist) Koenkai-concept is 'Jiban': the rural Japanese version of US metropolitan 'machine politics': MPs and prefectural assemblymen rely on the fact of being the local boss (often a hereditary status) for re-election and for domination of local politics. Increased mobility, urbanization and voter sophistication, however, has led to a gradual withdrawal of 'Jiban' to only the most conservative areas in Japan's countryside.

A faction leaders' influence (and prime ministerial changes) depend largely on faction size (i.e. the number of member MPs). Contributions from industry and finance to the ever needy faction fund will vary accordingly.

These insatiable finance needs – both of the LDP faction leaders and of the MPs directly – has led to the phenomenon of 'structural corruption' in Japanese politics.

In this situation the pursuit of local agricultural interests is privileged: the local cooperatives – and their leaders as local 'bosses' – are usually key members in an MPs Koenkai (and subject to competing politicians' recruitment attempts), as their personal recommendation can often swing a village's vote. Nokyo thus is able to perform its already quoted role as an 'important link in the chain of conservative Japanese politics'.[2] The vigorous pursuit of regional agricultural interests further enhances the native MP's local standing. The subsequent Table 7.1 shows a list of 'political brands' as effective in 1982.

Farmers in Japan – like in most industrial countries elsewhere – are 'naturally' conservative in way of life and politics. As small and independent land-owners they share a desire to maintain their family's status and property which is reflected in an interest to see traditional order and the status quo maintained. As small businessmen at the receiving end of possible price manipulations of their products or inputs needed, at the same time, there is a latent distrust also among Japanese farmers against big business, and the LDP government's suspected inclination towards it.

Though relatively successful in the pre-and post-war days in the militant tenants' movement, socialists and communists have soon lost their rural organizational and electoral base after the land reform. The JCP's brief Maoist revolutionary experiments – which involved calls (and some initiatives) for rural uprisings in the early 1950s – imitating the Chinese Great March[4] – and their subsequent collapse – did little to endear this party to the rural electorate. The same effect was reached by the socialists' theoretical enthusiasm for socialist cooperatives and its various implementations in East Europe, North Korea and China.

Despite recurrent 'workers and farmers' slogans, farmers still identify the parties of the left as representing the interests of unpropertied industrial workers.

Strong JSP and JCP party support for various Zenchu demands – such as those for higher rice prices – did little to alter this perception (a handful of left-wing MPs do, in fact, collect rural votes, e.g. some socialists in Hokkaido, though apparently rather on the strength of their personal merits).

The more 'centrist' opposition parties, Minsanto (Social-democratic), Komeito (Buddhist), and the New Liberal Club (an LDP faction, independent during 1974–86) are largely urban and have apparently few rural votes and no organizational network there.

The LDP's notables and power brokers' local strength apart, farmers when reviewing their families' and communities' economic

Table 7.1 List of political brands[3]

Influential LDP Diet member	Native Prefecture	Import-restrictions concerned
Prime Minister Zenko SUZUKI*	Iwate	Herring, cod, yellowtail, scallops, cuttlefish, and scallop eyes
Former Prime Minister Takeo FUKUDA	Gumma	Devil's-tongue roots, laver, etc.
Secretary-General Susumo NIKAIDO	Kagoshima	Grape sugar and starch
MITI Minister Shintaro ABE	Yamaguchi	Oranges, tomato juice, herring, scallops, cuttlefish, and scallop eyes
Science and Technology Agency Director-General Ichiro NAKAGAWA	Hokkaido	Beef, milk-cream, grape sugar, starch, and beans and peas
Administrative Management Agency Director-General Yasuhiro NAKASONE:	Gumma	Devil's-tongue roots (Konyaku)
Chief Cabinet Secretary Kiichi MIYAZAWA	Hiroshima	Oranges, fruit juice, tomato juice, and processed pineapple products
Agriculture-Forestry-Fisheries Minister Kichiro TAZAWA	Aomori	Oranges, fruit juice, tomato juice, herring, cod, and yellowtail

Taxation System Research Council Chairman Sadanori YAMANAKA	Kagoshima	Beef, processed pork products, milk-cream, and processed cheese
Former Agriculture-Forestry Fisheries Minister Takao KAMEOKA	Fukushima	Oranges, tomato juice, tomato ketchup, purée, etc.
Former Agriculture-Forestry Department Chief Takami ETO	Miyazaki	Beef, processed pork products, milk-cream, and processed cheese
Lower House Communications Committee Chairman Kiyoshi MIZUNO	Chiba	Peanuts
Fisheries Department Chief Fumio OKABE	Hokkaido	Herring, cod, yellowtail, scallops, cuttlefish, and scallop eyes
Former Agriculture-Forestry-Fisheries Minister Tokuro ADACHI	Shizuoka	Oranges, tomato juice, tomato ketchup, purée, etc.
Upper House Steering Committee Chairman Tokutaro HIGAKI	Ehime	Oranges, tomato juice, tomato ketchup, purée, etc.

* Political function as of March 1982.

progress during the past decades of continuous LDP rule, probably cannot fail but to conclude that on the whole they did pretty well under a party that proved so amenable to the sectoral interests of organized agriculture.

The farm lobbies' demands, however, do not go entirely unopposed even in the LDP's structure. In local politics, in the fights over municipal funds Nokyo's subsidy interests are opposed by the Chambers of Industry and Commerce[5]. With increased urbanization, parliamentary and mayoral representation of farmers proper declined steadily, making the long-term outcome of such confrontation only too certain. At the national level, Keidanren spearheads the (still timid) movement against agricultural protection.

The LDP at the national level maintains a series of policy deliberation councils whose work is coordinated by its Political Affairs Research Council (PARC). Here interested LDP politicians and MPs discuss politics, and invite the interest groups and ministries concerned to give their views on issues under deliberation.

PARC discusses agricultural issues in its powerful Sogo Nosei Chosa Kai (Comprehensive Farm Policy Committee), in which future and former agricultural ministers serve. It maintains various permanent and ad hoc subcommittees. With the LDP's continued rule it is evident that this body's deliberations should have considerable impact to shape public policies. Yet, factional differences apart, one major schism splits LDP agricultural legislators: the hard core of the Beika Tairaku Giin Kondankai, the non-partisan Rice Price Caucus of Diet members (to which nominally up to 300 MPs belong), who appear to support fervently Nokyo's price demands, is opposed by the LDP's Sogo Noseiha group, MPs who are close to the MAFF line (and hence are favoured by the bureaucrats on discretionary pork barrel issues) in advocating structural adjustment policies instead of hand-outs to affluent part-timers.

During most of Japan's post-war history, the LDP's parliamentary majority was big enough to secure its chairmanship in the Diet's Standing Committees such as the one on agriculture, fisheries and forestry. Hence the administration's agricultural draft bills – subject to intensive prior consultation in the PARC structure – usually face a safe passage in the committee and later in the plenary reading. In order to avoid the impression of disharmonious steamrollering the LDP's leadership and the MAFF administration will, however, use the occasion or negotiate behind the scenes to achieve some accommodation of opposition demands.

THE FARM LOBBY

Chapter 4 already outlined the Nokyo system's pervasive economic and political significance in the Japanese countryside with its 'virtually inseparable ties with the local . . . communities', and its leadership 'coinciding exactly with the hierarchy of political power within local society'.[6] The cooperatives' policy preference to insist on (adjustment inhibiting) price increases over structural improvement policies is noted: it reflects its business emphasis to service part-time farmers and the bureaucratic organizational interest of its apparatus of 236 000 full-time officials and employees (1982)[7] to keep these part-timers in business, to continue receiving rents and subsidies, and to enable organizational growth through continued corporatist high support policies. With politics being the main provider of its continued profitability and expansion, Nokyo's political investments and dynamism should not be surprising.

Zenchu, its central federation, coordinates all political activities, defines priorities and mobilizes Noseiren, the Japan Farmers' Union, whose positions are usually occupied by Nokyo local chiefs in personal union.

As such, the president of Zenchu is considered as the authoritative spokesman not only of the cooperative movement and its institutions, but also as the agricultural community's top negotiator with the political and business establishment.[8] Zenchu makes sure, e.g. in case of sectoral import liberalization demands, that *all* prefectural associations rally behind in its rejection, in order to avoid the isolation of those few – given the strong regional diversity in product structures – whose economic interest appears at stake.[9]

Nokyo in its rice price demands may go as far as to threaten to withdraw electoral support from the LDP. This was done in 1974 – with the LDP in dire straights following the disclosure of Lookheed bribes and Japan in its first oil crisis and suffering from an inflationary upsurge. Then the government to a producer request of rice increases by 64.7% had responded with an offer of 25.5% (after the election it settled for 32.2%).[10]

Although the farm vote rests solidly conservative, Zenchu regularly solicits support for its demand from all political parties and candidates running for office. On its annual rice price demand – in 1986 after some 'discussions' Zenchu for the first time had asked for a freeze (with reduced production costs and zero inflation, the rice price formula would have stipulated a 6.6% cut) – in June 1986 it received vaguely supportive notions from the LDP and DSP. Socialists, Communists and Komeito, however, asked for *higher* producer prices, the socialists with the curious reasoning that 'appropriate interest rates on owned capital' (i.e inflated land prices!) should enter into the farm cost equation. The JCP claimed since farm implements were 'mostly the products of monopoly enterprises' their 'high prices were unilaterally forced on the farming population'.[11] The New Liberal Club (which has returned to the LDP since November 1986) however, expressed 'hope that Zenchu will make a new dynamic move towards greater farmland fluidity and improvement of the nation's agricultural structure'.[12]

When asked to further elaborate on their rice policies (i.e. on the paddy field conversion programme), and on Zenchu's demand for larger conversion acreage, all parties were in favour of maintaining the current food control system (with government monopoly purchases of rice). LDP, Komeito, DSP and Communists 'hoped' for expanded rice consumption, but thought a continued acreage reduction programme necessary. The socialists, true to form, promised to expand rice demand and paddy acreage, and to finance these miracles by cutting the defence budget. Only the NLC, again, was open in its fight for structural policies favouring core farm households.[13]

On import liberalization demands, Socialists, Communists and Komeito, declared themselves vigorously opposed to any 'reckless' further reductions in import protection. The DSP was opposed only with respect to 'principal foodstuffs'.

The LDP was vaguely in support of continued protection, while the NLC joined, but at the same time insisted: 'Japan ought to refrain from assuming a negative attitude every time when sitting at the negotiation table, since our country can suffer more from the onslaught of protectionism.' Structural strengthening of Japan's agriculture should enable it to withstand foreign competition in the future.[14]

While all parties made the obsequious references to food security, the JCP was more explicit. A further liberalization would make Japan's food supply 'extremely unstable' and 'leave us at the mercy of the US, thus resulting in the loss of Japan's economic independence'.

Zenchu does not limit itself to sending out questionnaires. As with all well-organized lobbies it carefully keeps track of MP's (and MAFF bureaucrats') voting and support records, and decides on whose re-election bid to sponsor and whom to oppose. It is only too well known, that obviously, in close races this may make the difference.

The farmer unions, as Nokyo's lobbying arm, are not shy with their perceived institutional adversaries either. Hokkaido's Noseiren in 1984 threatened to call for a boycott of Daiei supermarkets, and of Sony and Ajinomoto products.[15] The companies were selected because senior executives had publicly advocated import liberalization concessions, and in the case of Ajinomoto, simply because its senior adviser happened to be chairman of Keidanren's food industry sub-committee, which mildly had expressed its doubts about the wisdom to continue the subsidization of agricultural cooperatives.

The Boycott initiative was called off only after the Farmer Union had received proper apologies and after the Ajinomoto executive had resigned his Keidanren function.

KEIDANREN

Japan's organized business interests practise a sensible division of labour: *Keidanren*, the Federation of Economic Organizations, is the representative largely of big business and takes care of political tasks. This ranges from organizing business associations' annual contributions to the LDP, its factions and – though to a lesser degree – to the centrist opposition parties, to drafting policy memoranda and exercising behind-the-scenes influence in the government party on various policy and personnel decisions, and to conduct 'private' diplomatic missions and foreign economic policy representations of Japan.

Nikkeiren, the 'Federation of Employers' Associations', is in charge of industrial relations and the labour unions' national counterpart. *Nissho*, the Japan Chamber of Industry and Commerce, articulates also small and medium business interests. Its Osaka chapter is renowned for being opposed to Keidanren's export and free trade interests. *Keizai Doyukai*, the 'Committee for Economic Development' has individual memberships, often overlapping with Keidanren, but usually takes more long-term and less operational political views.

Leaders and key figures in the four business associations are said to belong to a grouping, labelled as 'Zaikai' by the media: Japan's financial and industrial elite, which maintains strong ties with the LDP's leadership (occasionally also through 'Keibatsu' – suitable marriage alliances), and are invited by faction leaders to attend their monthly 'club' meetings for mutual information and benefit.

With respect to agriculture, Keidanren regularly issues recommendations to reform agricultural policies towards market-oriented adjustment and gradual import liberalization. In 1982, compelled by the increase in US–Japan agricultural trade tensions, Keidanren argued that Japan's food security was better served by a more competitive farm sector rather than by current policies:[16]

> Japan's agricultural policy is geared toward protecting farmers, while it ignores industrial users and individual consumers of farm products. In fiscal 1982 farm subsidies totalled yen 2.3 trillion, or about 4.6% of the government's general account budget. But agricultural productivity has not risen in proportion to the huge amounts of government assistance, and farm product prices remain high. This situation not only makes the people's lives more difficult but also hinders Japan's food industry from becoming as competitive as its foreign counterparts.

and:

> The contradiction in the Japanese government's farm policy present themselves most glaringly in the sorry plight of the rice production-distribution management system.

Four symptoms of this crisis are listed: the rising deficit of the Food Agency (which buys rice at higher prices that it resells) – Y140 bn in 1982, the surplus disposal and storage costs for the unsold rice mountains – another Y140 bn in 1982, the need to pay premiums for paddy field conversion – Y350 bn – and to pay deficiency payments and other support for the non-rice crops produced. One of the paper's authors, Bunzo Watanabe, president of Ajinomoto (later a victim of Hokkaido Noseiren's boycott threat) asked for the reduction of 'hyperprotection' in border protection and in public support for Nokyo. Core farmers, through deficiency payments exposable to market mechanisms, should rather gradually turn into efficient producers, thus improving Japan's food security.[17]

Later, Keidanren asked that food security should no longer be equated with current self-supply ratios, but rather operationalized with a stockpiling programme for emergencies (financed through cuts in the agricultural budget) and high self-supply capacity through agricultural productivity gains.[18] MAFF appeared to be in mild disagreement with this criticism of its policies, while Nokyo's rejection was more outright.

On the prolonged agricultural trade disputes with the US, Keidanren advocated enlarged Japanese import quotas on beef and oranges, leading to a gradual liberalization of the sector. Deficiency payments should then compensate the Japanese producers.[19] But when the US Rice Millers Association in 1986 asked that rice be added to the US list of immediate import liberalization demands, even Keidanren made known that this request was in breach of an 'understanding' between the US and Japan 'that rice is considered a special item and (be) treated separately from other agricultural products'.[20]

With her demands for structural adjustment policies Keidanren – which evidently spearheads the campaign for agricultural policy reform – appears largely in line with the NLC, and the LDP's Sogo Noseiha groups of MPs, as well as with EPA, MOF and MAFF policy ideas. Its requests for gradual import liberalization, are tacitly shared by MFA and MITI as well as by some national dailies (Nihon Keizai Shimbun, Sankei Shimbun, *et al*).

OTHER INTEREST GROUPS

Among unions, the moderate *Domei*, a federation of blue-collar company unions, is critical of Japan's agricultural support policies, which it sees as driving up food prices and threatening the export-oriented jobs, on which its members depend. As Domei provides the organizational backbone to the DSP (Minsanto), the party's gradually changing line should soon reflect the unionists' rank-and-file view. The more radical and (still) larger *Sohyo*, a federation largely of white-collar and government-employee unions, plays a similar crucial role to the Socialist Party (Shakaito). It appears a question of time until the 'workers and farmers' revolutionary romanticism (which fuels the party's current protectionist opportunism) gives way to a more rational assessment more in line with voters' economic interests.

In quoting numerous opinion polls (all asking biased questions such as: 'Are you in favour of food security, even if that costs you a bit more than unreliable foreign imports would'), MAFF officials and Zenchu claim wide consumer support for their policies. Mr Sadao Nakabayashi, head of the Japanese Consumers' Cooperative Union repeatedly claimed that the defence of agriculture against import liberalization was also in the interest of the consumer public.[21] His consumer cooperatives are good Nokyo business partners and privileged clients of the LIPC's import beef.

Poorly organized in Japan as elsewhere, consumer organizations' concerns rather relate to health and safety issues than to prices, which they can hardly hope to affect by their political means. Consumers' economic interests find a vocal response only in Japan's media.[22] It is only recent that the fear of being publicly criticized as being over-zealous in the pursuit of producers' one-sided interests and hence of alienating Japan's urban voters, put a lid on politicians' compliance with Zenchu demands. This was probably the most effective single factor to cause the rice price struggles' decline since 1977/78.[23]

NORINSHO (MAFF)

MAFF may not rival MOF or MITI in their rank as 'elite of the elite', but still as part of Japan's prestigious central administration is able to attract its share of the best and brightest among the graduates of the top ranking universities. A great many recruits passing the entrance examinations had graduated in the faculties of law and economics (most at Todai, the University of Tokyo), and only about half of them had either studied agriculture or had enjoyed practical exposure having grown up in farm families. The subsequent training period, however, alleviates some of this empirical shortcoming. Officials in MAFF, like their colleagues in the other ministries, rotate their professional assignments about every three years, and are promoted in the early stages of their career largely according to seniority, although later for more senior positions merit and luck is more decisive. Positions and posts held vary considerably according to job contents and prestige (among the more desirable ones are, e.g. assignments as agricultural counsellors in Europe, Oceania and North America), Likely future high-flyers can easily be identified when a generation's promotion for division chief (Kacho) are decided.

Ministers habitually change about every 10 months (in order to enable the satisfaction of LDP backbenchers' ministerial ambitions). The post carries great clout in LDP faction politics: MAFF's budget with its numerous infrastructural projects offers attractive possibilities to endear oneself in one's own constituency and with political friends. Although usually knowledgeable in agricultural policies and having served prior in the LDP's comprehensive agricultural policy committee, the ministers (some exceptions, like Ichiro Kono, apart, who are held in horrific memory for decades) except for some 'political projects', are not expected to intervene in the bureaucratic decision procedures (usually emanating at the section/division chief levels) and in personnel appointments, but rather to represent the ministry's consensus to the cabinet, to the lobby and to the public at large. The administrative vice-minister, and his deputy as the highest ranking career officials, are in office for 2 to 3 years and, in fact, should be regarded conjointly with the 5 bureau chiefs as the true masters of the house.

As Japanese ministries usually draft the laws submitted to the Diet, these are kept in fairly vague terms and offer the administration wide discretionary powers for subsequent regulations and implementation. Even without a firm legislative basis it is often more prudent for a major company or key economic actor to follow 'its' ministry's more or less firm advice or guidance on certain issues. However, this dependence again is a two-way street: as 55 is the mandatory retirement age for Japan's bureaucrats, they join the job market at that date. The range of choice usually depends on their last ministerial ranks and postings, and on the contacts established during their administrative careers. MAFF officials' second careers are typically advisory positions in the food and feed processing and importing industry, but more frequently as 'amakudari' ('descendants from heaven' – the French equivalent would be 'parachutage') in management and consultant functions in the range of public and semi-public institutions which the Ministry supervises: the associated research, inspection and training institutes, the Livestock Industry Promotion Council, etc. but also appointments within the Nokyo system (although presumably only a few will return to farming). Political careers within Jiminto are probably a more attractive option for senior administrators. Particularly the mainstream factions (Tanaka, Suzuki) are still dominated by former bureaucrats. Former MAFF officials are strongly represented in the LDP's Agricultural Policy Committees, a position in which they can easily contact their former colleagues (subordinates) in the ministry.

Former administrative vice ministers, e.g. served in extremely influential functions: Tokutaro Higaki as chairman of the LDP's Overall Agricultural Policy Research Council, and Tomoyoshi Kamenaga (an Upper House member) as head of the Japan Fisheries Association.[24] The influence of 'retirees' however can work both ways: MAFF through its old boys can also attempt to influence the party's or an association's orientation. This corporatist structure, the LDP/MAFF/NOKYO trinity, with big spending programmes and privileged business opportunities for institutional and party power maintenance at consumer and taxpayer expense, probably explains most of 'excess protection' policies. But it was not Japan, if ultimate checks and balances were not built into the 'consensus' system.

MOF since 1983 succeeded in cutting MAFF's budget successively from Y3.7 bn (1982) to Y2.6 trillion (1988)[25] in a period in which public budgets for agriculture in almost all other OECD countries expanded to the limits of manageability. MOF predictably is also opposed to Nokyo's rice demands which annually surface at inter-ministry and cabinet meetings. On trade issues, MAFF's protection-ist line is opposed by MITI, MFA and the EPA, which take a wider view of Japan's trading interests. Under an assertive Prime Minister such as Mr Nakasone, the Prime Minister's Office may also intervene in agricultural policy. In September 1986, Nakasone, in an unprece-dented step, instructed the Management Agency 'to investigate the activities of agricultural cooperatives for posible reform',[26] threaten-ing to disrupt some of the cosy MAFF/Nokyo arrangements. It is thus too simple if professors Talbot and Kihl conclude:

> A few dozen senior bureaucrats in the ministry exercise an inordi-nate amount of influence in developing Japan's food and agricul-tural policies. They wield almost absolute power in the formulation and implementation of agricultural policies.[27]

As with all ministries, MAFF maintains a range of advisory coun-cils (shingikai) whose members are selected by the ministry and generally represent producer, processor, consumer and general public interests in equal parts. Their deliberations and final consensus are likely to also reflect the collaborating ministry's views, and have a strong chance of political acceptance. Most prominent among MAFF's advisory councils is the Rice Price Council, set up in 1949, which since 1969 consists equally of representatives of producers, consumers and 'men of learning and experience' (operationalized as: professors of agricultural economics, former senior MAFF officials and agricultural journalists).[28] It is supposed to examine the rice price formula for the season's price setting and make a well-reasoned and mutually acceptable proposal to the Ministry. When they found themselves in a minority position, producer interests, however, chose not to play according to the corporatist script book, and repeatedly vetoed and prevented a consensus proposal of the Council.

MAFF as a separate ministry was set up in 1925, when the former

Table 7.2 Organization of MAFF[29]

Minister
    Parl. Vice-Minister
    Admin. Vice-Minister
    Minister's Secretariat
    Economic Affairs Bureau
    International Affairs Department
    Statistics and Information Department
    Agricultural Cooperative Division

    Agricultural Structure Improvement Bureau
    Agricultural Administrative Department
    Planning Department
    Construction Department

    Agricultural Production Bureau
    Various Crops Divisions
    Fertilizers and Machinery Division
    Extension Department

    Livestock Bureau
    Various Livestock Product Divisions
    Feed Divisions

    Food & Marketing Bureau
    Various Crop Products Divisions
    Wholesale Division
    Consumer Economy Division

    Agriculture Forestry and Fisheries Research Council
    Secretariat – various R&D divisions
    Various research and training institutes,
    Inspection stations, seed and breeding farms.

Food Agency

Forestry Agency

Fisheries Agency

ministry of Agriculture and Commerce (founded in 1881) was split
into MAF and the Ministry of Commerce and Manufacture (the
pre-war MITI predecessor).

The *Ministry's Secretariat* as the 'brain' of the ministry is a department charged with overall policy planning and formulation. It coordinates the bureaux, supervises the regional offices, carries out
budgeting and auditing, handles personnel affairs, legal matters and
PR. Its office of Pollution Control spent Y3 bn (1981) as subsidies for
the construction of non-polluting farm facilities.

The *Economic Affairs Bureau* handles Japan's international agricultural relations, including agricultural development aid. It supervises the cooperatives and their financial and insurance empire. The
bureau also deals with agricultural taxation, and runs MAFF's concessional loans (Y88 bn of subsidies in 1981) and disaster compensation scheme (Y64 bn in 1981). It also compiles Japan's excellent
agricultural statistics.

The *Agricultural Structure Improvement Bureau* with a large
budget tries to rectify what price policies have messed up. It aims to
expand scales and efficiency of farming operations and to build vital
rural communities through large-scale land and water development
(Tochikairyo), offering subsidies for the construction of dams, can-
als, drains and roads (Y684 bn in 1981), and medium-scale projects
(Y73 bn), through land reclamation from forests or wetlands (Y95
bn), 'rearranged' farm villages with subsidies for improved houses,
roads, water supplies, drainage, public parks (Y110 bn), and support
for farmland management and acquisition (Y15 bn). The Bureau also
contributes to farmers' pensions (Y63 bn) hoping to induce their
early retirement.

When creating new farmland, 'late' priority is given for dryland use
so as to avoid allocating a paddy diversion premium instantly to the
surplus producing fields.

The *Agricultural Production Bureau* deals with policies for rice,
wheat, barley, fruits, flowers and silk. In 1981 Y18 bn were spent in
direct subsidization of non-rice crops (including sugar beet and cane).
The bureau administers the rice control and paddy conversion programme (Y332 bn in 1981, Y238 bn in 1985). It supervises farm-input
production, distribution and 'price stabilization' and sponsors phytosanitary measures (Y7 bn) and extension services (Y65 bn).

The *Livestock Industry Bureau* administers beef, dairy, pork,
poultry and egg policies and supervises the functioning of the LIPC.
Most of the money it directly spends, goes for farmland development

(Y14 bn), forage promotion (Y13 bn), feed grain price stabilization (Y11 bn), breed improvement (Y8 bn), animal health measures (Y4 bn) and direct support for various livestock productions: dairy (Y5 bn), beef (Y14 bn), pork and poultry (Y1 bn) – which top the LIPC's more generous goodies (Y170 bn – total expenditure minus purchasing costs of imported beef in 1984) – and the general price support schemes. The Bureau also supervises horse racing which apparently does well without public subsidization.

The *Food and Marketing Bureau* oversees the food processing, distribution and eating-out sectors. It developed the Japanese Agricultural Standard (JAS) quality labelling system and watches over wholesale market operations. The Bureau is also in charge of the sugar, oil and fat, and vegetables policies and gives good advice to consumers on nutrition deemed proper by the Ministry.

The *Agricultural, Forestry and Fisheries Research Council* coordinates and plans the research projects of the 30 MAFF research institutes. There appears to be a strong emphasis on applied biotechnology with cell fusion, biomass conversion and other green energy projects in the fore. Other research promoted concerns coastal marine ranching. Subsidies are also given for university and private sector research work.

The *Food Agency* is the government's monopoly purchaser, importer and distributer of rice and wheat. It also supervises all further downstream activities, which include grain milling, sake and soy sauce brewing, etc. These activities require the establishment of local offices in all prefectures, with grading, purchasing, storing, and finally rice consumption promotion activities. As a result, the position 'handling costs' made a Y288 bn contribution to the Agency's consolidated loss of Y461 bn in 1985,[30] and per capita rice consumption declines at rates of 1.6% to 1.9% p.a., likely to reach 63–66 kg in 1990.[31]

The *Forestry Agency* manages the national forests (one-third of Japan's total) and gives guidance and subsidies to private forests for afforestation and forest road construction. It also oversees timber and 'Shiitake' mushroom production and marketing, controls forest pests and diseases, and works on forest taxation issues.

The *Fisheries Agency* supervises Japan's offshore and coastal fisheries operations, fishing ports, fishing cooperatives, and fish processing and marketing. Following the worldwide introduction of 200 mile fishery zones it conducts negotiations for continued Japanese access to the major fishing grounds. The Agency also sponsors coastal fish farming with man-made fish shelters and salmon hatching for Japan's rivers. It also administers subsidized credits and tax breaks for the depressed fishing sector.

With this plurality in institutional interests and clienteles, MAFF is far from being a monolithic farm interest fortress, e.g. on import issues, one could expect the Economic Affairs and the Food and Marketing Bureaux to be relatively more accommodating, with the Product Bureaux taking a more intransigent line. Japan, no doubt, is a country in which the assumptions of universal bureaucratic politics ('where you stand depends on where you sit') also hold true.

POLICY DECISION-MAKING: THE AGRICULTURAL BASIC LAW OF 1961

The policy targets of the immediate post-war period – sufficient food supply and democratized rural life (through land reform) – had been achieved in the mid-1950s. Politicians gradually became aware that they had to address the issue of agricultural productivity and incomes lagging behind the industrial sector whose dynamic expansion began to unfold after 1955. Visiting Dietmen touring Europe came to learn about the German agricultural basic law (of 1955) and were instantly fascinated by its provisions triggering automatic spending increases. Back home, they asked for something similar. MAFF (in 1959) set up a high level 'Agricultural, Forestry and Fisheries Basic Problems Research Committee', reporting to the Prime Minister, which investigated French and German farm legislation and its transferability to Japan. MAFF's draft then followed the Committee's recommendations.[32] They essentially asked for increased agricultural productivity through more effective land utilization and improved agricultural technology. Farm structures and product marketing were to be rationalized, and agricultural product and import prices to be stabilized in order to provide adequate farm incomes in parity to industrial wages. The law further asked for annual reports on the situation of Japan's agriculture. Against MAFF objections, LDP MPs then inserted the 'augmentation of gross agricultural production' into the draft as a further policy goal. With strong JSP and JCP resistance – who charged that the law's structural objectives would lead to 'mass dismissals of farmers' – the law was enacted in 1961 and was to lay the legal foundation of Japan's agricultural protection policies implemented thereafter. Ogura, vice minister at the time of drafting, observed that subsequently farm ministers, politicians and the lobby were more interested in the income parity objectives than in the structural improvement aspects of the law, a shift in preferences which clearly went against MAFF's original intentions.[33]

THE RICE PRICE DECISIONS 1984–86

In principle, rice price decisions should follow a complicated formula which aims at compensating farmers for input costs and providing income parity. To no one's surprise, however, the rice price decisions are taken 'politically' (rice still counts for 30% of Japan's agricultural output value, but only for 6% of agricultural households' total income). The annual price setting rituals follow a regular schedule.

Zenchu in May decides on its price demand for the next fiscal year (beginning in April). The local Nokyo organizations arrange meetings in all municipalities and prefectures to which all local politicians are invited and expected to attend and to endorse publicly Zenchu's demand. By the end of June a national rally with 10 000 farmers and Nokyo employees is held at the Budokan in Tokyo. About 40% of all Dietmembers attend, including almost all prominent in LDP which are also asked to pledge their support.

In July, Zenchu sets up campaign headquarters in Nokyo's insurance (Zenkyoren) HQ in Nagatacho, which is conveniently close to the Diet and to the ministerial Kasumigaseki area, to obtain further LDP MP commitments (and to monitor them actually carrying out their promises) and to try and persuade Rice Price Council members (8 of the 24 are already institutionally in Nokyo's camp). The Rice Price Council then looks at the rice price formula and comes up with a recommendation (provided that its Nokyo minority does not block a consensus) which is usually much below the lobby's demand. The proposal is endorsed by MAFF (in case of persistent disagreement in the Council, the Ministry makes its own price proposal) and submitted to the Cabinet.

The cabinet then in August after some Zenchu/LDP/MAFF warfare (so much for coalition politics) – involving confrontations between the comprehensive agricultural policy and the rice price LDP groups – decides more often than not to add a political premium on top of MAFF's austere proposal. In the final stages of these negotiations, the Prime Minister, his Chief Cabinet Secretary and the LDP's General Secretary are actively involved.[34] This early decision is

Table 7.3 Rice price decisions[35]

	Formula	MAFF proposal	Zenchu demand	Result
1986	– 6.6%	– 3.8%	0*	0
1985	– 4.0%	– 0	'increase'	0**
1984	0	1.45%	7.7%	2.2%

* Zenchu arrived at this 'moderate' demand only after 'repeated discussion' in its Standing Committee on Rice Measures, noting 'what is really needed is a 6.2% increase', which however after 2 straight bumper harvests was not feasible politically.[36]

** The premiums for high quality rice (whose reduction MAFF had advocated) remained equally frozen.

needed to give some estimate for the resulting deficit in the Food Agency's Food Control Account which is to be balanced by the general budget and has to be provided for in MOF's draft budget (which is finalized in December and formally voted for by the Diet in March for the fiscal year beginning in April).

The cabinet's 1986 final price decision (taken in August) has to be seen in the light of the LDP's 60% parliamentary majority after the July 1986 elections. Support price cuts had been made earlier for other agricultural products. This new emphasis on more 'political' price setting will hence reverse the incentives for farmers to continue the needed diversification of rice production.

A second decision to be taken concerns the government setting the sales price of rice to consumers (which in 1986 is 0.4% below the purchasing price of the Food Agency).[37] While MOF wants the difference to be as small as possible (in order to reduce the Food Agency's deficit), EPA, watching over monetary stability, insists on minimal consumer price increases. Repeated increases in rice prices for the consumer in the early 1980s have reduced the Food Control Account's deficit, and represent a further shift of the subsidy burden from taxpayers to consumers.

The decisions made on the Agricultural Basic Law and the annual rice price setting (also evident on trade issues discussed in Chapter 9) show that they are arrived at only after considerable deliberation and intensive searches for consensus among the three major participants: Nokyo, MAFF and the LDP (as well as, on occasion, with other ministries concerned). It is equally evident that in case of disagreement, the party's political leadership will ultimately make a political decision (with the clear intent not to antagonize any of the key players). MAFF's influence is probably stronger on more technical issues. However, in Japan, as many other countries with a strong ministerial bureaucracy, on political issues it is the elected leaders which, for better or for worse, make the ultimate decisions. The close involvement of vested interests in the decision process and the integration of Nokyo interests into the LDP's fractionalized power structure at the same time, in spite of mounting macroeconomic and political costs, makes agricultural policy reform difficult to be implemented if only in the most gradual incremental fashion. Even more decisive than the ministry's corporatist approach for the lobby's influence appears the LDP's intense inter-factional competition for power and votes, as the party's structural weakness (caused by the multiple member districts of the electoral system) requires contenders in rural districts to continue to rely on the Nokyo organization's network.

Notes

1. *Financial Times*, 9 July 1986.
2. Fukutake, op. cit., p. 183.
3. Translated from *Rentaku*, Mar. 1982.
4. Manfred Pöhl, *Die Kommunistische Partei Japans* (Hamburg: Institut für Asienkunde, 1976) pp. 79.
5. Fukutake, op. cit., p. 170.
6. Kenzo Hemmi, 'Agriculture and Politics in Japan', in E. M. Castle and K. Hemmi (eds), *US–Japanese Agricultural Trade Relations* (Washington DC.: Resources for the Future, 1982) p. 229.
7. *Zenchu News*, no. 13, 1983, p. 7.
8. 'Fujita Saburo', *Japan Quarterly*, vol. 25, 1978, p. 299.
9. Hemmi, op. cit., p. 234.
10. Ibid., p. 239.
11. *Zenchu Farm News*, no. 2, 1986, p. 8.
12. Ibid., p. 8.
13. After their disastrous showing in the July 1986 national elections – losing more than 25% of their Lower House seats – in particular in the metropolitan districts, both JSP and DSP have begun painful soul-searching with respect to their agricultural policies as well. Takako Doi, the JSP's new chairwoman, was quoted as saying: 'Our party should place greater importance on the standpoint of the consumers', and DSP chairman Saburo Tsukamoto announced they would face the food control system 'head on' and 'discuss it'. (*Japan Agrinfo Newsletter*, 4, Nov. 1986, pp. 2–3; *Asahi Shimbun*, 8 Oct. 1986).
14. *Zenchu Farm News*, no. 2, 1986, p. 9.

15. Y. Tachibana, 'Are Farmers Really Victims?', *The Oriental Economist* (June 1984) p. 6.
16. Keizai Koho Center, 'Cost Reduction by Productivity Increase Is Imperative', *KKC Brief*, no. 11, 1983.
17. *Japan Times*, 24 Feb. 1981.
18. *Japan Agrinfo Newsletter*, 3, Aug. 1986, p. 2.
19. Keizai Koho Center, 'Domestic Adjustment Measures for Japanese Agriculture', *KKC Brief*, no. 19, May 1984.
20. *Japan Agrinfo Newsletter*, no. 4, Sept. 1986, p. 2.
21. *Zenchu News*, no. 14, 1983, p. 2–4.
22. Yukata Yoshioka, 'The Personal View of Japanese Negotiator', in Castle/Hemmi (eds), op. cit., p. 353.
23. Hemmi, op. cit., p. 241.
24. *Japan Economic Journal*, 5 Sept. 1978.
25. It must, however, be noted that 50% of this cut is caused by a reduction in the deficit of the 'Food Control Special Account' which fell to Y460 bn in 1985 largely due to higher revenues levied from increased cereal imports in marking up the low world market prices. The LIPC's budget does not appear at all. Some miracles happen through creative accounting (Tsubota, Kunio, 'Agricultural Policy in Japan', *Journal of Agricultural Economics*, vol. 36, 1985, p. 369).
26. *Japan Agrinfo Newsletter*, no. 4, Nov. 1986; *Nihon Keizai Shimbun* 28 Sept. 1986.
27. Ross B. Talbot and Young W. Kihl, 'The Politics of Domestic and Foreign Policy Linkages in US–Japanese Agricultural Policy Making' in Castle and Hemmi, op. cit., p. 316.
28. Ogura, 1979 op. cit., p. 211.
29. MAFF, *The Ministry of Agriculture, Forestry and Fisheries* (Tokyo, 1986?).
30. OECD, *Ministerial Trade Mandate, Part II - Country Report Japan*, Statistical Annex, Table 22 (1986).
31. Agricultural Policy Council, 'On the Implementation of the 'Basic Direction of Agricultural Policy in the 1980's!', *Japan's Agricultural Review*, vols. 7 and 8, 1983, p. 15.
32. Ogura, 1979, op. cit., p. 442.
33. Ibid., p. 97.
34. *Japan Agrinfo Newsletter*, no. 3, Aug. 1985; *Japan Agrinfo Newsletter*, no. 4, Sept. 1986.
35. *Le Monde*, 12 Aug. 1986. *Nihon Keizai Shimbun*, 10 Aug. 86, *Zenkoku Nogyo Shimbun*, 3 July 1985, *Nihon Keizai Shimbun*, 28 July 84, *Japan Agrinfo Newsletter*, no. 2, Aug. 1984.
36. *Zenchu Farm News*, no. 2, July 1986.
37. *Japan Agrinfo Newsletter*, no. 3, Feb. 1986.

8 Agricultural Markets and Product Policies

GENERAL SUPPORT POLICIES

According to OECD estimates for 1979–81, which are based on extrapolations of the products covering 60% of total production, Japanese agriculture was subsidized by taxpayers at 10.2 bn ECU p.a. (41.4% of the total) and by consumers at 14.4. bn ECU p.a. (58.6%).[1]

Taxpayers' contributions in the Y3300 bn (1985) annual MAFF budget (to which agricultural expenditure of municipalities, prefectures, separate agency accounts and the LIPC projects ought to be at least partly added) go at 80% (Y2646 m) to agriculture (the rest to forestry and fisheries presumably – although a great many fishery and forestry workers and owners are farmers as well. (Out of 2.5 m 'forestry households', 78% were also engaged in farming, owning 77% of Japan's forest acreage. Among the 216 000 fishery organizations, 88 000 were run by part-time operators, partly engaged in farming.) Of the agricultural budget, 17% is used to cover the Food Control Accounts' deficit (hence essentially go for rice price support); the bulk is spent on direct and indirect production and income subsidization for farmers (and indirectly for rural dwellers in general): 33% for public works on infrastructural improvements (kiban seihi), 9% each for the Paddy Field Conversion programme, and for the promotion, production and marketing of agricultural products, 7% for agricultural structural investments; 6% for farmers' insurances and concessional loans, and 3% for research and extension services.[2]

While these public aids and investments serve to reduce agricultural production costs, the largest share of public support is price support, which due to Japan's low overall self-sufficiency levels is largely budget neutral (except for rice) and paid by consumers.

The following price and income policy mechanisms apply:

1. *price and production control* due to Government-controlled monopoly purchases on rice and tobacco;
2. *guaranteed minimum prices* (but no maximum prices) on wheat,

131

barley, potatoes and starch, and sugar (beet and cane);
3. *guaranteed price bands* (with minimum *and* maximum prices) on beef, pork and raw silk (cocoons);
4. *public deficiency payments* for producers of soybeans, rapeseed and milk for processing;
5. *producer co-funded deficiency payments* for veal, piglets, eggs, vegetables and fruit for processing.

Tax concessions for farmers are yet a further, albeit difficult to assess, subsidization of agriculture. The average farm household in FY 1980 had an annual gross income of Y4.5 m – about 80% of it from off-farm sources – out of the total Y410 000 (9%) were paid as taxes; e.g. farmers are exempt from inheritance taxes, and from petrol taxes for heavy fuel oil. Agricultural cooperatives' tax breaks in 1983 were estimated by MOF to value Y3 bn.[3]

CROP PRODUCT POLICIES

Rice

Based on the Food Control Law of 1942 rice marketing and price setting are still controlled by a governmental monopoly, the Food Agency. The producer prices, according to the legal norm (for the political practice see Chapter 7), are set on the basis of 'production costs, commodity prices and the economic conditions'. In the production cost component the farmer's own labour is valued as equivalent to wages paid to workers in the manufacturing industry. This indexation based on industrial productivity gains (a false parity, as they are not reflected in an analogous agricultural labour or capital input development) is a major reason for excess protection and surplus production in the rice sector.

The wholesale price for rice – the sales price of the Food Agency – which is almost as political, is set in order to 'stabilize the consumers' household economy', by taking into account household expenditure, commodity prices and general economic conditions.[5] In 1980 the Government's consumer rice prices were 10% below producer prices. In the meantime the gap has successively been narrowed to 0.4% (1986), hence contributing to a reduction in the Food Account's deficit. Authorities will, however, insist on a continued price gap with higher producer prices in order to prevent farmers from trading

Table 8.1   Subsidies received and taxes paid by farmers[4]
(household average; FY 1981)

Prefectures	Subsidies received* (A) (Y)	National taxes paid (B) (Y)	(B) + Local taxes paid (C) (Y)	(A) / (C) (%)
Hokkaido	747,300	188,300	544,700	137.2
Miyazaki	136,700	89,000	304,800	44.8
Aomori	114,900	83,900	314,400	36.5
Akita	156,600	123,800	382,100	51.0
Iwate	143,600	135,200	399,700	35.9
National average	79,600	183,200	457,300	17.4

*   Includes local and prefectural subsidies.

directly with consumers and to forestall a loss in bureaucratic control.

In order to cope with the mounting rice mountain in face of steadily declining demand in 1969 a parallel 'voluntary marketing' for high quality rice was permitted. The Food Agency's rice collecting agents (i.e. the rice departments of Zenno) negotiate the quantities to be marketed for each local brand with the Government and then negotiate the up-market sales price with the wholesalers. The market share of these brands, priced 25% higher at wholesale level and 35% higher at retail level than the long-stored Government rice, has reached 50% now, indicating the quality premiums Japanese consumers are prepared to pay.[6] Although voluntary marketing gets 116 billion yen in subsidies (in 1983), it remains the less costly marketing channel. A third marketing avenue is top quality 'free rice', sold at no cost to the Government and at zero profits to Zenno – directly (and illegally) from producers to consumers.

As total demand for rice has declined from its all-time peak of 13.4% m tonnes in 1963 to 11 m tonnes twenty years later (with ever-increasing production prices nota bene), it is evident that production control policies had to be initiated. Since 1971 these take the form of 'soft' production quotas (producers had to notify their rice sales to the Food Agency which would only buy those 'booked' amounts), and of various more or less voluntary paddy diversion programmes: during 1971–75 the Government paid to leave land fallow; until 1978 the alternative land use for strategic crops (especially feed crops) was subsidized; since then diversion was put into a more long-term comprehensive perspective. In 1983 among the

630 000 ha (reflecting a MOF demand this acreage has been increased to 700 000 ha in 1986) converted paddy fields[7] – counting for nearly one-fourth of Japan's wet rice fields and reducing Japan's rice crops by 2.9 m tonnes – 25% was utilized for forage, 18% for wheat and barley, 14% for soybeans, 2% for buckwheat, 17% for vegetables (especially eggplant, cucumbers, tomatoes), and 2–3% for perennial crops. Some of the alternative crops have attained over-supply problems of their own. The diversion programme, however, was successful in reducing Japan's rice mountain off its peak of 6.7 m tonnes (1980) (at cumulative disposal costs of Y3 trillion to a targeted, more manageable level of around 1.5 m tonnes (14% of Japan's annual consumption of 11 m tonnes).

Importing and exporting of rice is only undertaken by licensed dealers; both transactions are strongly discouraged by the Government. In 1983 only 18 000 tonnes were imported (for specific needs only) and 380 000 tonnes exported, largely as food aid (to Pakistan and Indonesia) of long-stored products.

Beneficiaries of Japan's rice support system are largely part-time farmers for their favourite crop, the Food Agency's bureaucracy, and Zenno, the Government's privileged cooperative rice-dealers.

Rice growing is done on a small-scale – although 26% of the crop is produced by 6% of the farmers.[8] Rice is grown in all Japanese villages on land suitable for wet field cultivation, but there is a clear regional focus of production in the North and North West, with Hokkaido, Tohoku and Niigata prefecture accounting for 42% of Japan's output.[9]

Wheat and Barley

Wheat and barley are also covered by the Food Control Act of 1942. The Government's Food Agency offers to buy all domestically-produced wheat and barley at a purchasing price which multiplies their 1950/51 average price with a 'parity index', indicating the development of farmers' costs for production and living since. The Food Agency's sales price is a blend of the Government's purchasing price of imported cereals (authorized importers – largely the sogo shosha and Zenno's Uni-coop – are allocated specified import quotas) – plus governmental handling costs of Y33 bn in 1983 which probably arise at the moment the grains leave the sogo shosha's chartered bulk carriers and jump on the elevator belts of the millers' coastal silos – and its purchasing price for domestic grain (plus again handling charges of Y25 bn in 1983). As 88% of Japan's 6.3 m tonnes wheat consumption (1984) and 85% of her 2.7 m tonnes barley consumption are imported, the Food Agency can afford a domestic wheat purchasing price 2.7 times higher than its blended sales price. Its perennial – small – deficit in the wheat account is entirely accounted for by handling costs.[10]

The Food Agency offers cereal quantities to the millers at its uniform sales prices. The mills' production quota depends on flour production capacity and their past actual flour production. The mills' sales price of flour and bran to bakeries, confectioners and other consumers is then left to the market.[11]

Aggregate growth prospects in quantitative terms are still positive with 4.6% p.a. for wheat and 9.2% p.a. for barley milling and compounding. Human and feed consumption of wheat (which is used not only for bread and confectionery-making, but also for traditional Japanese noodles such as udon and soba) and barley is projected to reach 6.4 m and 3.5 m tonnes respectively by 1990.[12]

Wheat and barley for feed use are equally bought by the Food Agency, but sold on the basis of competitive tenders to feed compounders. While theoretically the Agency insists on a 'minimum sales price in tenders', feed grain prices apparently have remained relatively close to international levels. In some years the Government's 'imported feed account', charged to mitigate price fluctuations, made losses which necessitated transfers from the general account (Y2.2 bn in 1982). For feed barley producers compensatory deficiency payments are made. Imports of barley for brewing (150 000 tonnes p.a.) and malt (430 000 tonnes p.a.) have been liberalized since 1974 and imported freely by the Japan Brewers' Association subject to a tariff quota only.[13]

While cereals are produced in most parts of central Japan, there is a regional concentration in Hokkaido (31% of Japan's cereal planted area), in the Northern Kanto prefectures (Ibaraki, Tochigi, Gumma): 17.5%, and in North Western Kyushu (Saga and Fukuoka prefectures) : 13%. Domestic production of wheat (740 000 tonnes in 1984) and barley (400 000 tonnes) has remained remarkably stable since 1980, in spite of continued paddy diversification incentives. But recent producer price decisions – freezing rice prices and cutting wheat and barley prices by 1.2% and 1.5% respectively in July 1986[14] – after a freeze since 1982 have contributed to reducing producer incentives for such production shifts.

Fats, Oils and Feeds

Soybeans and rapeseed were liberalized in 1961 and producers were compensated by a deficiency payment, which covers the difference between the markets' average selling price and the desired target 'base' price which is fixed each fiscal year on the basis of a parity index by the Government. Although the crops also benefit from paddy diversion premiums, domestic production of soybeans has declined from 390 000 tonnes in 1961 to 217 000 tonnes in 1983 (4.5% of consumption) and even more drastically for rapeseed from 270 000 tonnes to a minimal 3000 tonnes (0.3% of consumption) during the same period,[15] the bulk of imports coming from the US and Canada respectively. In 1983 deficiency payments for soybean producers totalled Y23 bn, and for rapeseed Y300 m.[16] Both target 'base prices' were reduced by 1.7% in October 1986 for the first time, reflecting a decline in the agricultural parity index due to reduced rural living and production costs.[17] The US soybean export embargo of 1973 (lasting only one week with no discernible impact on Japan's imports) and the subsequent policy redefinition in terms of food security objectives (interpreted in self-sufficiency rates) therefore apparently did not have a lasting impact on protein feed production.

Area diverted to pulse production (275 000 ha) is concentrated in Hokkaido (40%) and Eastern Kanto – Ibaraki and Chiba prefectures – (11%).

Consumption for soybeans is projected to increase further both in feed and human consumption (to a total of 5.4 m tonnes in 1990). As the Japanese major source of vegetable protein, it is not only consumed in the traditional foods like tofu (curd), miso (paste) and shoyu (sauce), but also plays a major role in new product development in milk and meat substitutes. Rapeseed demand is likely to remain fairly stable at the current level of 1.2 m tonnes, the seeds being crushed for their edible oils, and the residual meal used for feed.

Other Feeds

For other feeds produced in Japan – rice bran and straw, fish meal, beet pulp, hay, brewery wastes and similar delights – no particular support schemes exist. Among the 1 m ha lesser quality farmland to be used for forage and feed crop production, 57% are located in Hokkaido, 11% in South Kyushu (Kumamoto, Miyazaki, Kagoshima prefectures) and 7% in northern Tohoku (Iwate, Aomori).[18] On 80% of the forage area grain is grown, on 12% green maize, and on the fairly residual rest area oats, sorghum, beets and turnips for feed.

Essentially, however, coarse grains other than barley, i.e. maize, sorghum, oats, luzerne (alfalfa) are not produced to any significant extent in Japan and hence are imported freely – except for maize for processing (in order to protect sugar beet and cane producers from corn syrups).

Other vegetable oil plants – palm, corn, cotton seed, sunflower, etc. – are used primarily for oil extraction, but some are made into cakes for use in feed mixes and compounds; these are also little protected and imported in still growing quantities.[19]

Feed manufacturers and livestock farms both participate in an underwriting scheme against sudden feed cost increases. From its funds collected through premiums raised from both sides (35% of the livestock farmers contribute voluntarily and are hence eligible for support) producers receive compensations in a case of sudden price increases. Should prices rise above 8% p.a. extraordinary compensations will be paid – from a fund to which the Government (through MAFF's Livestock Bureau) and the feed manufacturers contribute at equal rates. A special semi-Governmental 'Compound Feed Supply Stabilization Organization' administers the scheme as well as the acquisition and management of feed buffer stocks in Japan. Transfers from the budget's General Account to the organization's 'Imported Feed Account' since 1974 varied strongly between Y80 bn and nil.[21]

Sugar

Japan's sugar producers and refiners are protected through the operation of a price band on imported sugar (1.7 m tonnes in 1982) and through guaranteed basic prices for domestic sugar crops (0.9 m tonnes in 1982).

Sugar importers are required to sell their raw sugar to the Government's monopoly purchasing agency, the Japan Raw Silk and Sugar Price Stabilization Corporation. Should the average export price fall below the price band's floor price, when re-selling the imported sugar the Corporation will add on levies to lift the resale price to within the band. Even when inside the price band, a levy will raise the resale price upwards towards a target price in the upper range of the band. Should the import price in fact exceed the band's upper ceiling price – which happened in 1974 and 1980 – the Corporation will buy at this price and resell the raw sugar at the ceiling price, hence refunding the importer. On top of the Corporation's price stabilizing activity a fairly high tariff of 41 500 yen per tonne has to be paid.[22]

For domestically-produced sugar crops, refiners, which – as described in Chapter 5 – are largely sogo shosha affiliated and often organized in production cartels, pay a minimum producer price (based on the same parity index as wheat and barley). In return they are able to sell the refined sugar to the Corporation at cost prices and repurchase it at much lower resale prices (at the levels of import sugar). The Corporation's resulting deficit is covered by Government grants and from the funds accumulated through sugar import levies.

Both the import sugar's price band and the domestic producers' minimum price are set by the Government each year. Since 1982 a major substitute, high fructose corn syrup (having replaced sugar in most soft drinks), is also incorporated into the sugar regime: a levy is charged to prevent further inroads into the sugar market. A tariff quota for imports of maize for processing has also been introduced.

Sugar consumption went down from 2.9 m tonnes (1979) to 2.5 m tonnes (1982), its current levels having stabilized after the introduction of price-enhancing measures for HFCS of which 0.6 tonnes (dry weight) are consumed.

The production of sugar cane at a level of 230 000 tonnes has remained stable (grown on Okinawa and in Kagoshima prefecture), while sugar-beet increased to 610 000 tonnes (in Hokkaido), as beets are more cost-efficient crops in Japan with producers responding more strongly to enhanced support prices. In fiscal 1984 the Raw Silk and Sugar Price Stabilizing Corporation for its sugar operations received Y31 bn subsidies.[23] Some subsidized glucose refining is done from the starch of sweet potatoes, for which there are few other uses. As a result of reduced consumption and enhanced production Japan's imports in raw sugar terms were reduced to 1.9 m tonnes (1983).

Silk

Although not really contributing to food security, raw silk prices are under a stabilizing price band system since 1951. Since then the above mentioned corporation buys and sells raw silk in order to keep its price within MAFF-decided price band (after having considered production costs and other factors). Zenno is also paid a storage subsidy for cocoons if their floor price risks being undercut. Subjected to the unforeseeable whims of fashion, silk production – the fattening of worms with mulberry leaves, the subsequent drying of the cocoons, their processing in reeling mills into silk yarn, later woven into fabric – was considered a very traditional, low grade, small-scale rural industry, victimized and starved of capital through its high speculative risks.[24]

In order to stabilize prices the Corporation may proceed to purchase and re-sell raw silk and dried cocoons to approximate prices towards a MAFF determined standard sales price within the price band. It is also the only authorized importer of raw silk: imports in principle only take place if ceiling prices for certain qualities are exceeded.

In 1984 180 000 bales (one bale is equivalent to 60 kg) of raw silk were produced in Japan. During that year[25] 190 000 bales were held in storage (106% of annual production). Silk is still produced as a sideline activity close to the upland mulberry fields of northern and western Kanto, on land unsuitable for paddies. The Raw Silk and Sugar Price Stabilization Corporation, though theoretically self-financing in its silk operations, receives an undisclosed Government grant to finance the storage reimbursements.

Tobacco

Since 1904, when the Russo-Japanese war required urgent public finance, Japan's tobacco processing has been controlled by a Government monopoly. Although formally privatized on 1 April 1985, the Japan Tobacco Inc. (JTI) is fully Government-owned, runs a manufacturing monopoly, purchases all domestically-produced leaf tobacco, *de facto* also imports all of it, controls the distribution system and still authorizes all retail outlets.

In 1985 after having paid about Y1.8 trillion in taxes, the JTI still made an after-tax profit of Y24.6 bn on a Y2.7 trillion turnover.[26] MOF continues to supervise its favourite revenue earner, and although some streamlining and modification of the monopoly with its 37 000 employees has begun, major management decisions – such as branding and retail price-setting – still require MOF approval.[27]

JTI is also required to put all (currently 80 000) Japanese tobacco growers under contract, and to purchase all leaf tobacco output, the contracts having specified acreages, varieties and grades. In 1984, 135 000 tonnes of domestic tobacco were processed and blended with cheaper (and higher quality) 70 000 tonnes of foreign leaf tobacco for 310 bn cigarettes. Production-cost oriented administrative price setting applies to the home-growns. As currently the equivalent of one annual leaf crop is in JTI storage (contributing to the supply security of Japan's chain smokers), the price fixing Leaf Tobacco Council insists on acreage cuts in return for frozen producer prices. For 1987 the acreage authorized was cut by 4100 ha to 39 500 ha. Farmers agreeing to leave voluntarily tobacco fields uncultivated receive Y170 000 per 0.1 ha.[28] There is an evident readiness among tobacco farmers – situated primarily in Southern Kyushu but also in Tochigi and Fukushima prefectures – to abandon production, as work is dirty and difficult to mechanize: fields are mostly on parcellized sloped hill sites.[29] Still, Nokyo charges the Finance Ministry in its tobacco policy of being interested in tax revenue rather than in the welfare of leaf tobacco farmers and reneging the former 'very strong relationship of trust between the growers and the company'.[30]

However, smoking is decreasing among Japanese adults from a share of 45% (1975) to 39% (1983), and US pressure forced tariffs on overseas cigarette imports to be dropped in 1987, enabling US and UK brands to capture more than their traditional 2% up-market share.[31]

Fruits

Policies in the fruit sector consist of supply control policies in the fresh fruit sector and of a price stabilization scheme through underwriting (producer associations' and Government contributions) for fruits for processing. In the 1960s farmers planting orchards received low interest credits and other public support.[32] As a result, unshu orange production multiplied by 3.3 during 1960–72, when it reached 3.6 m tonnes far in excess of effective demand. When support measures (such as the promotion of orange juice processing, diversion to other fruit trees) did not show effects, producer associations received subsidies to cut unshu orchards from a total of 142 000 ha (1977) to 121 000 ha (1983). Additional clearings are planned to cope with future declining demand, estimated to reach 2.5 m tonnes by 1995 (corresponding to 95 000 ha).[33]

In 1980 Japan's Y740 bn fruit production (6.7 m tonnes) consisted by value of the – overproduced – unshu oranges (26%), apples (21%), grapes (14%), pears (10%), peaches (6%), persimmons (5%), and summer mandarins (3%). All these fruits enjoy considerable border protection, through either tight seasonal import quotas or import prohibitions on phytosanitary grounds, as Japan has a 'policy to sustain the self-sufficiency of fruit to the greatest extent possible'[34] – although during the war orchards had been cleared in the name of food security. Imported fruits (largely bananas, lemons, limes and grapefruit) are fairly stable at 1.2 m tonnes (1980). Though juice processing plays a significant role in adjusting inevitable seasonal price fluctuations – with orange juice counting for 65% of Japan's juice production – considerable unshu stockpiles continue to accumulate.

Japan's fruit production is strongly varied regionally: citrus fruits are concentrated on the hillsides of West Japan: in Saga (W. Kyushu) 9%; in Ehime (on Shikoku) 16%; in Shizuoka 12%, Wakayama 9%. Citrus orchards are all located in the more protected prefectures of Pacific coast with their warm climate and heavy summer rain. Grapes are grown in the dry air of Yamanashi prefecture, south of Fuji-san. Apples are cultivated in the harsher climates of North-Western Tohoku : Aomori (47%), Yamagata (7%), and Nagano (21%) in the Japanese Alps with its cool summers, cold winters and light summer rain. Orchards in Japan are quite small with a 0.4 ha average and strongly sloped. Strawberries finally grow in the vinyl-houses of Tochigi (20%) and Saitama (20%) in the Kanto plain.

Vegetables

Similar to fruits, vegetables due to their seasonality and short shelf life in unprocessed form are subjected to strong price fluctuations. A statutory body, the Vegetable Supply Stabilization Fund, covers 14 major products (cabbage, onions, tomatoes, carrots, etc.) and with the contributions collected from central Government (65%), prefectural governments (17.5%) and co-operatives (17.5%), compensates the producer cooperatives if market prices fall below 'guaranteed base prices'. Public expenditure for the Stabilization Fund in 1985 was Y9.1 bn.[35]

With around 110 kg/person annual vegetable consumption is high in Japan, and fairly stable at that level since 1974. Contract farming for supermarkets and processors is widespread. The largest single vegetable growing prefecture is Hokkaido (renowed for 'daikon', Japanese raddish), but even larger areas – upland fields formerly used for sericulture – are used in northern and western Kanto: Chiba and Ibaraki prefectures (Chinese cabbage, burdocks) as well as Nagano, Gumma and Saitama prefectures (cucumbers, eggplant, spinach, onions), all within close range of the Tokyo markets. Only Aichi prefecture is a major growing area further South.

Although foreign produced vegetables due to their transportation costs are relatively less competitive, import barriers persist, especially in the processed tomato market, in which two processors, Kagome and Kikkoman, enjoy a near duopoly.

Potatoes

Should prices for sweet and fresh potatoes fall below certain levels, the Government offers to purchase all starch manufactured from these potatoes at the request of the producers' marketing association. The purchases – last made in 1977 – are effected at a starch market price plus transport and processing margins. This guaranteed price is fixed according to the developments in the parity index, production costs and the market situation. Like the other commodities following the same formula (soybeans, sugar), it was lowered by 1.7% in 1986 following a four-year freeze. Stocks of starch – at 100 000 tonnes in 1981 – have all but disappeared, as importers of potatoes and of maize for processing (the latter in order to qualify for the duty-free tariff quota) have to purchase certain amounts of domestic starch at the same time.

In 1983, 25% of all starch consumed in Japan was imported, with prices kept up also due to buoyant demand for fresh potatoes.[36]

Both white and sweet potatoes were introduced by the Tokugawa shogunate to combat famines in case of rice crop failures. They proved life-savers last in the 1945/46 famines.

Sweet potatoes (1.4 m tonnes in 1984) are grown largely in the volcanic soil of Southern Kyushu (Kagoshima, Miyazaki) – mostly processed for starch, and in Northern Kanto (Ibaraka, Chiba), where they are used as hog feed. Few are still eaten as a stone roasted traditional winter 'snack' ('ishi-yakiimo'). White potatoes (3.8 m tonnes in 1984) which have the equal advantage of growing on poorer soil than rice, used to be the traditional food of Hokkaido colonists in the Meiji days. Today still most white potatoes (70%) are grown in Hokkaido, with the remainder largely in Tokoku, mainly for starch products.

Livestock Product Policies

Dairy

As raw milk is used alternatively for direct consumption and for processing, MAFF through the LIPC subsidizes producers' returns through support for processing outlets only. Directly consumed fresh milk hence finds its markets with a premium above the competing manufacturing milk price. Suppliers of the milk for processing purposes obtain a deficiency payment between a guaranteed target price (which is based on the production costs in the more efficient Hokkaido dairy sector) and the standard transaction price paid by the dairy (the price is in fact calculated as the dairies' sales prices minus transport and processing costs). Both prices are fixed by MAFF, and remained stable during 1977 to 1981. After a marginal increase, since 1983 the guarantee price is frozen at Y90/kg, while the standard transaction price was further increased from Y64.8/kg (1982) to Y70.2/kg, thus by reducing the deficiency payment shifting further price support costs from taxpayers to consumers. These deficiency payments were made up to a national maximum quantity of 2.3 m tonnes of raw milk (1985), and paid by the LIPC (Y46.4 bn in 1984) with funds from Government grants and profits from dairy monopoly import sales.[37]

In addition, for processed dairy a price band with supportive LIPC intervention applies. Should prices of butter, condensed milk and milk powder fall to below 90% of a MAFF decided 'indicative stabilization price', the LIPC is supposed to purchase into intervention storage. In case prices exceed the desired price band at 104%, the LIPC will release its stocks in question, or, in their absence, import suitable quantities. The only dairy imports exempted from LIPC's state trading monopoly are natural (unprocessed) cheese (70 000 tonnes p.a.) and SMP for feed and school lunches (100 000 tonnes p.a.). Fresh milk can theoretically be imported free of duties and quotas; transportation costs and sanitary provisions, however, prevented any such imports. The LIPC's surplus stocks in 1980 were at tender levels (by EC standards), with 7500 tonnes of butter and 15 000 tonnes of SMP. Price freezes and 'voluntary' production plans then were introduced. As the deficiency payments are oriented towards the cost structure of the more competitive farms, it was claimed that 7000 farms (Japan's dairy farms totalled 93 000 in 1984) annually have to give up dairying as a result.[38]

By 1982, all stocks had been absorbed by the market and even some butter was imported by the LIPC in 1982 as its only recent dairy import business. Although annual dairy consumption with 67 kg/person is still fairly low, total consumption of dairy in raw milk equivalents has levelled off at 8.7 m tonnes in 1983 (of which 1.6 m tonnes were imported raw milk equivalents) as consumer preferences shifted to competitive drinks and to dairy substitutes (margarine, etc.). Zenno whose dairy cooperatives handle all the producer sales to the dairies (for Zenno's further downstream market power, see Chapter 5) in 1986 decided on a total raw milk output 'target' not exceeding 7.06 m tonnes.[39] Similar to their monopsonic role in rice and orange management, Zenno's departments for manufacturing milk also collect the processors' payments, and after deducting their commission, hand them on to their members once a month. The LIPC's deficiency payments are also made to Zenno for redistribution.[40]

Fresh milk which counts for two-thirds of all milk output in principle only benefits from the manufacturing milk's support. But, in addition, use in school lunches is Government sponsored at a cost of Y13.5 bn (in 1985). The LIPC also distributes milk for various other socially worthy causes (maternity homes and homes for the elderly, etc.).

Dairy farming in Japan has experienced considerable concentration in recent years. In 1983 the average dairy herd was at 22.7 cows, compared to a 15.7 average in the EC. Of Japan's dairy herd 37% is located in Hokkaido with an average herd size of 42.4. Hokkaido also receives 80% of the LIPC's deficiency payments.[41] In Northern Tokoku with their long distances to major consumption areas, North Japanese dairymen produce manufacturing milk mainly. As more grazing land is available, cows in summer are fed on pasture, which reduces both production costs and yields (2.8 tonnes/cow in Hokkaido and Iwate in 1983). The holdings in northern and western Kanto and other areas in West Japan near metropolitan areas specialize more in higher priced drinking milk production due to shorter transport routes.

Most dairy cattle here are fed on concentrates, leading to yields of 3.3 tonnes (Chiba) to 3.7 tonnes (Nagano) milk per cow.

Beef

For beef a price stabilization scheme applies. If wholesale prices are about to fall below a certain minimum floor price, the LIPC will intervene and purchase suitable quantities for storage. In return, when an upper ceiling price is reached, the LIPC will release stored and imported beef largely by public tender on the wholesale markets. It will also subsidize Zenno stockholding for the purpose. After 1975 beef supplies were kept so skilfully scarce, that wholesale prices in fact never fell below the floor price.

Both ends of the price band are fixed by MAFF after consultation with the LIPC. In 1986, for the first time, the average minimum beef prices were cut by 2.7% to Y1090/kg, reflecting reduced production costs due to declining feed and energy expenditure.

LIPC management costs of the stabilization scheme were only Y98 m in 1983.[42] Overall profits in the fiscal year 1985 are estimated at Y38 bn, and in 1986 are likely to exceed Y60 bn, reflecting the revalued yen and the benefits of cheaper meat import prices which are largely pocketed by the LIPC.[43]

For veal production, of which only 2,300 tonnes (corresponding to 0.4% of the 550 000 tonnes beef production) were put on the market in 1985, an 'underwriting' deficiency payment system applies: organized at prefectural level, payments funded from local governments, coops and the LIPC, are made if market prices fall below certain levels.

Two basic types of beef are produced in Japan: Wagyu beef (160 000 tonnes in 1983), a strongly marbled beef (i.e. with strong intramuscular fat), suitable for thinly sliced restaurant specialities (sukiyaki, shabu-shabu), priced about 35/40% above average whole-sale price levels of the ordinary lean dairy beef,[44] which counts for the bulk (330 000 tonnes, i.e. 68% of the total in 1983) of Japan's domestic beef output. Gradually, however, according to housewives' surveys,[45] consumer preferences shift towards the leaner meat and may erode the Wagyu's top grade premium in the long run.

A dual structure has emerged amongst the total of 300 000 beef producers (with an 8.7 average beef herd size in 1985).[46] Dairy beef is produced to a great deal in large modern feed lot operations (based in Hokkaido, and to a lesser extent in Southern Kyushu) often in contract farming for supermarkets (like Daiei and Seiyu) and meat processors. Wagyu is raised in labour and feed intensive small-scale operations spread nationwide, but with some emphasis in Southern Kyushu, Eastern Tohoku and Hokkaido, usually by former draught animal holders which count for the bulk (73%) of Japan's beef farmers, keeping only between one and two head of cattle.[47] In order to achieve the desired top grade marbling, Wagyu cattle are fattened with concentrates beyond the normal period of optimum feed efficiency, which obviously pushes up production costs. According to folklore, they are on occasion fed with beer, and some stables are reported to have stereo-music facilities. More reliable, however, is the information that the cattle receive regular massages to facilitate marbling.

Following a 1984 agreement with Australia and the US, Japan has enlarged its import quota from 141 000 tonnes (fiscal 1984) by an annual 9000 tonnes to 168 000 tonnes (fiscal 1987). The LIPC which directly controls 80–90% of imports, specifies the amounts and qualities of beef it wishes to import (and hereby determines its origins), pays the tariffs (25% of the cif value), then levies its 'procurement costs' and puts most of the meat up for tender at a minimum bidding price at wholesale level.[48] In August 1986, following the yen's appreciation towards the US dollar, the LIPC at MAFF pressure for the first time cut its minimum bidding price by 10%.[49]

The 'special quota' imports (10–20% of the total) not directly controlled by the LIPC, are handled by LIPC authorized dealers which exclusively supply specific 'user associations', i.e. suppliers of school lunches, international hotels, and for consumption in Okinawa.

Still, as Hayami observed, LIPC sales prices are close to the bottom of the wholesale price band, thus allowing purchasing meat dealers (see Table 8.1) to pocket handsome rents,[51] as wholesale price levels are generally pegged towards the upper ceiling price. This arrangement generates a strong vested interest in all participants – Government, producers, cooperatives, meat traders, processors, retailers, etc. in the system, all at the expense of consumer welfare.[52] The LIPC's total revenues in 1982 were at Y332 bn, of which Y133 bn accrued from imported beef sales, the rest being dairy sales (Y31 bn), Government grants (Y63 bn), loans (Y42 bn), and carryovers from the 1981 account (Y65 bn).

Total LIPC expenditure in 1984 was Y286 bn, of which Y112 bn were spent on beef imports (cif prices plus tariffs for MOF), Y17 bn laudably for school milk, Y47 bn as a contribution to the deficiency payment for processing milk, Y33 bn for loan repayment, and Y66 bn for project grants.[53] The latter cash is spent on livestock (especially dairy and beef) production, processing and marketing rationalization projects, undertaken by cooperatives, their federations or corporations controlled by either of them.[54]

It is hence probably an exaggeration to suspect, like Kaminogo, that a great deal of the LIPC's budget is spent on LDP farm Dietmen,[55] or as *Le Monde* assured its readers, that a 'meat mafia', a racket of Osaka-based DOWA butchers, headed by the shadowy right-wing 'wheeler-dealer' Sasakawa, is being sponsored.[56] Nonetheless, also in Japan, there is no smoke without fire, especially when monopoly rents are to be distributed. Demand for beef is bouyant in Japan – with annual consumption per capita having grown from 5.6

Figure 8.1   Imported beef sales by the LIPC, 1982[50]

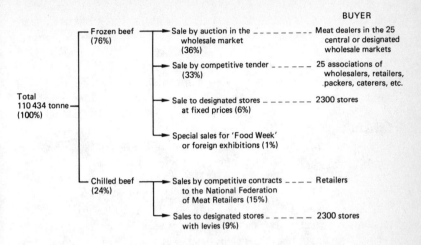

kg in 1982 to 6.5 kg in 1985.[57] With strong income elasticities of demand, it is apparent that it is only high prices that prevent a further expansion in consumption (US annual per capita beef and veal consumption, for instance, stands at 53.2 kg).

Pork

As with beef a stabilization price band applies to pork – with MAFF after consultation with the LIPC deciding annually on the ceiling and floor prices for carcases at wholesale markets. Since 1977 the price band in nominal terms has been practically frozen.

As pork prices tend to fluctuate strongly in 'pig cycles', pork carcases are either bought by the LIPC (last in 1980), or, preferably, stored by the producer cooperatives or meat packers – with storage subsidies from the LIPC. There was a rapid expansion and tendency towards concentration (from 2.4 animals per farm in 1960 to more than 100 now) in pig fattening operations in the 1960s and 1970s. Since 1980 demand has levelled off at a 15 kg/person annual consumption level. Since then, producer associations operate voluntary supply adjustment schemes.

The LIPC has no direct role in pork imports, which were liberalized in 1971 when quantitative import controls were replaced by a system of either a 5% duty or a variable levy ('differential duty') lifting the price of imported pork to a level above the centre price of the stabilization band.[58] This variable levy ensures that imported pork cuts are of high quality and are largely used for processing. Imported pig meat (ham and bacon) is also of up-market quality to minimize the differential duty's effect. If wholesale market prices exceed the price band, MAFF has few other means than lowering the levy or exempting imports from customs duty.

In 1985 270 000 tonnes of pork were imported, of which 110 000 tonnes were from Denmark and 96 000 tonnes from Taiwan. Domestic production was stable at 1.8 m tonnes, with production concentrated in the Kanto plains near the Tokyo metropolitan region, the main consumption area. Of Japan's 10.2 m pigs 16.1% are raised in Northern Kanto (Ibaraki, Gumma, Tochigi prefectures), 9.2% in Southern Kanto (Chiba, Saitama, Kanagawa), 16.4% in the Southern Kyushu prefectures of Kagoshima, Miyazaki and Kumamoto, 6.9% in central Tokai (Shizuoka and Aichi) and 5.9% in Hokkaido. These concentrated pork facilities, some of which are near the metropolitan agglomerations, now give rise to environmental concern due to their massive waste output in form of sludge and smell.

Poultry and Eggs

On poultry meat no significant public support applies except an *ad valorem* tariff of 20% – with its effective rate being lower due to tariff cuts for bone-in meat.[59] Japan's broiler producers (145 000 farm households are left to specialize in egg and broiler production) are closely linked to agro-business: with an average of above 20 000 birds per broiler flock, they are firmly tied to (imported) feed suppliers and/or poultrymeat processors. In 1982 the broiler/egg sector alone consumed 6 m tonnes of maize and 1 m tonnes of sorghum. Japan's 135 m broilers (1984) to a great extent are raised in Southern Kyushu: 16% of the total spent their short lives in Kagoshima and 14% in Miyazaki. The rest is pretty evenly spread nationally with some focus on Iwate (8%), Hyogo and Tokushima prefectures (5% each). Poultry imports (100 000 tonnes in 1985) are largely from the US (47 000 tonnes) and Thailand (35 000 tonnes).Thailand – 95% of its output is Japan-bound – specializes in deboned chicken[60] which evidently requires labour-intensive processing, a competitive advantage for sales in a chopstick culture with little liking for the 'finger-licking good' approach. In general, imported poultry (i.e. broiler meat largely) suffers from freezing – while Japanese meats are considered fresher and tastier. Hence they are used mostly for processing – with the US supplying a great deal of CCM ('comminuted chicken meat') for use in (pure beef) hamburger steaks, sausages, etc. – and for restaurant use, which usually require fairly uniform drumsticks. Prepared chicken meat is also in demand for entertainment bars and fast food restaurants selling yakitori and other fried chicken. Kentucky Fried Chicken Japan actually prays – as a 'cultural concession' – for the 20 m chicken souls they slay each year.[61] Japan's poultry consumption with 12.2 kg per person per year (1.5 m tonnes total consumption 1985) is fairly high by international standards.

Eggs, overproduced since 1972, from 1975 have benefited from a price stabilization system. If market prices fall below a certain standard price, 90% of the difference from the market price will be paid to producers who have entered into a contract to participate in production control. This 'underwriting' fund is paid in by producers, the cooperatives, and the Government, which via the LIPC and prefectural governments contributed Y1.3 bn (in 1985).[62]

Layer hen flocks (930 birds per farm on average) appear to be distributed fairly evenly nationwide, with Aichi prefecture producing relatively the most eggs (6.5%).

EVIDENCE AND CONSEQUENCES OF EXCESS PROTECTION

The types and specifications of public support for agriculture are virtually limitless, ranging from the constitutional right of Swiss mountain farmers to cost price guarantees for bread-making cereals, to production, price and sales allocation for licensed Queensland sugar growers, to guarantees for grain rail transport at tariffs frozen at 1898 levels for the Canadian prairie farmers, and finally to a range of invisible and unquantifiable tax breaks for farmers in the entire OECD world.

Among the more quantifiable data the following two major categories can be distinguished: *budgetary outlays*: direct payments to producers (deficiency payments, premiums and diversion incentives), and public schemes to subsidize production such as field rearrangements, crop insurance, extension and veterinary services, irrigation, drainage works, rural road building, subsidies for fuel, and farm investment credits, etc.) paid by the taxpayer; and *border protection*, the nominal rates of protection, paid in the form of domestic price levels pegged above average import (international cif) prices, the differential obviously paid by consumers. Table 8.2 which attempts to quantify this protection for 57% of Japan's agricultural production for the year 1981 clearly indicates the preference of Japan's policymakers for the second less visible type of subsidization: Y3060 bn were transferred from consumers, while 'only' Y1070 bn were thrown in from the budget.

Extrapolating these data to the entire agricutural production (100%), budgetary transfers for product support in 1981 could be estimated as Y1880 bn (out of a total MAFF budget of Y3690 bn) and consumer transfers as Y5370 bn. This corresponds to Y15 700 and Y1 580 000 from both forms of support combined. Compared with farm income data (Table 3.2), it is clear that all agricultural income is currently entirely dependent on public support. Further, as public support per farm exceeds its (declared) agricultural income proper, it is equally evident that reliance of product price support (through consumer transfers) is an inefficient and costly instrument of farm income support.

In industrial commodities, it is ideal only if a fairly marginal tariff (averaging around 3–5% among major OECD traders) which raises wholesale prices above comparable international levels. In agricultural products, distortion is more endemic and world markets often turned residual in consequence, hence protection rates of up to 50% above unassisted world market price levels could still be considered as indications of light assistance. 'Medium assistance' could probably still go up to 120%. 'Strong assistance', with significant subsidy rates and serious resource distortions in consequence, would be constituted by protection rates up to 250%. Any support rate above this level, could safely be considered as *'excess protection'*. Producer prices have lost all reference to market prices. Production and consumption patterns, depending on their elasticities, follow subsidization levels and administered prices for supply and demand. Investment and production decisions are divorced from market realities domestically and even more so globally as, except for feed import costs, world market signals are fully prevented from reaching producers. The result of excess protection is gross misallocations of resources.

Welfare losses are no longer theoretical (Table 8.3). Excess protection causes a structural crippling of the sector, that will take decades to be remedied. Agriculture proper becomes a thoroughly maladjusted client and supplier for upstream and downstream industries. There is a loss of dynamism in the sector through permanent frustration of entrepreneurial talent (which will ultimately move out, while retired people, part-time operators and bureaucrats move in) and the creation of parasitic networks of guaranteed rent operators (Nokyo, Dowa, etc.) enjoying exclusive revenue access and collusive relations with semi-statal monopoly agencies (the Food Agency, the LIPC etc.). Everybody else in the system (traders, processors, 'consumer organizations') gets their share of the cake – as evident in the allocation of imported beef quotas. Politicians and bureaucrats have similar vested interests. Such cosy arrangements, once exposed by the media, lead to an erosion of political trust and to a crisis of political legitimacy, given the enormous difficulty of disentangling the thoroughly mis-structured sector. Rather than reducing assistance, an excess protection sector, not unlike drug addiction, will call for and requires more assistance for survival (see Figure 8.2).

Table 8.2 shows the following assistance levels in Japan for 1981:

1. Light assistance (up to 50% support rates) for 12.5% of her agricultural production (pork, poultry). Eggs probably are also only lightly assisted.
2. Medium levels of assistance (up to 120%) for 1.2% of production (beet sugar).
3. Strong assistance (up to 250%) granted to 12% of agricultural production (dairy, beef).
4. Excess assistance (above 250%) given to 31.3% of production (rice, wheat, barley, soy beans and cane sugar). Starch, fruits, vegetables, tobacco and milk probably are also strongly assisted to excess.

Rice policies appear as the key to the excess protection development: the need for a paddy diversion programme as a 'second best policy' had to lift protection levels for alternative crops. Support rates (via pricing arrangements or direct payments) for grain, soy beans, fruit and vegetables had to be raised to similar levels: excess protection is clearly contaminating. The rice price formula introduced in 1961 already contained all the necessary ingredients for excess protection (though at the time rice with import prices at less than 20% below producer prices (1960)[64] was only lightly assisted):

Table 8.2 Product policies and nominal rates of support, 1981[63]

Products	Volume of production (in tonnes)	Value of production (domestic prices) (Ybn)	Share in total production (%)	Support policies	Self-sufficiency rate 1984 (%)	Budget support 1. direct payments (Ybn)	Budget support 2. production subsidization (Ybn)	Consumer support (domestic price–import price) multiplied by production (Ybn)	Production at world price value (cif) (Ybn)	Support rate (%) (Budget +consumer support divided by prod. value at world prices)
Rice	10.3	3047.8	28.8	price + prod. control paddy diversion import prohibition	99	323.0	322.0	2003.0	1046.5	253.1
Wheat	0.6	108.1	1.0	guarantee prices state trading	12	25.4	44.1	80.6	27.5	545.8
Barley	0.4	68.3	0.6	guarantee prices state trading	15	10.6	25.0	52.0	16.3	537.4
Soybeans	0.2	15.1	0.1	deficiency payments	4	47.1	19.8	–	15.1	443.0
Beet sugar (refined)	0.5	125.7	1.2	price band	31	4.6	12.8	58.1	67.6	111.7
Cane sugar (raw)	0.2	82.1	0.8			1.3	6.7	51.4	16.3	364.4
Fresh milk	4.3	470.2	4.4	deficiency payments interv. purchases	100	–	67.1	262.5	207.7	158.2
Processed dairy	2.3	147.5	1.4		76	47.4	37.8	91.2	98.8	178.5
Beef	0.5	655.6	6.2	price band import monopoly	71	–	87.3	320.3*	262.3	155.4
Pork	1.4	963.2	9.1	price band	83	–	21.3	79.6	869.7	11.6
Poultry	1.1	364.5	3.4	tariff	92	–	9.9	60.8	303.8	23.3
			57.0			417.0	653.8	3059.5		

* Includes a 40% quality premium pro rata for the Wagyu share in production.

152

(a) production costs were based on marginal producers;
(b) family labour valued at urban wage levels; and
(c) rent and interest costs were imputed for land and equipment.

As a result, with low productive farm labour growing in renumeration – index linked to high productive industrial labour – and subsidy rents capitalized in paddy land prices (and rent 'costs' growing in response), rice prices skyrocketed: output increased and demand contracted. Nine years later (in 1970) the Government sat on 7.2 m tonnes of unsold rice stock, 3.5 m tonnes of which had to be disposed of as (little suitable) animal feed.[65] In 1971 the Food Control Account's deficit with Y463 bn had grown to 50% of MAFF's budget. With formula-bound growing guarantee prices (to which political premiums would be added periodically), a permanent paddy diversion programme – with equally growing diversion incentives had to be installed (until these alternative crops, like mikan oranges, also priced themselves out of the market). At the same time budgetary costs had to be shifted to consumers by increasing the rice monopoly consumer price, which in spite of low demand elasticities, further contracted demand. The rice-based excess protection spiral has not reached its peak yet.

Almost all industrial countries at some historical juncture – continental Europe in the late 19th century, Japan after 1904, the US with the New Deal of the 1930s, Korea and Taiwan in the late 1960s – reversed policies which in their early industrialization period had held food prices down in order to benefit the urban sector, to agricultural support policies increasing farmers' returns at consumers' expense. In Japan's period of overall light assistance (1904–61), according to Hayami, rice had been the principal wage good: until World War II 60% of all calorific intake was supplied from rice, dropping only in the late 1960s to below 40%. Urban blue-collar workers until 1938 spent 15% of their consumption expenditure on rice alone. For white-collar workers this share was 11%. Only after 1959 did urban workers' rice spending fall below 10%.[66] Prior to 1960 labour intensive light industries held a prominent position in the Japanese economy and for her export earnings. These industries evidently needed low rice prices to contain workers' living costs and wage demands. Ag policies then aimed at preventing producer incomes from falling while keeping rice cheap and plentiful, and at the same time producer prices slightly above subsistence levels in order to maintain incentives to increase ag productivity and to forestall rural social unrest.

Figure 8.2   Nominal rates of protection estimates[69] (rates of Japanese prices to world prices*)

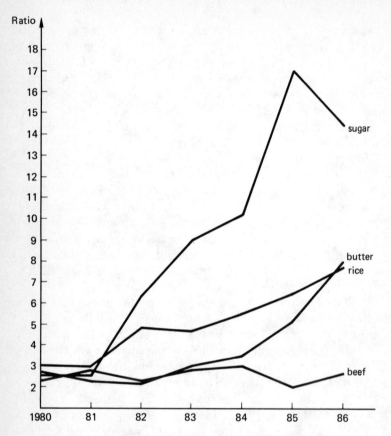

*   For rice   : Japanese producer prices to Thai white, milled fob Bangkok.
     For sugar : Japanese target price to fob Caribbean ports.
     For butter : Japanese stabilization indicative price to indicative NZ.
                   price
     For beef   : Japanese dairy beef wholesale price to import price.

Japan's restructuring and rapid economic growth since has led to a speedy decline in the rice wage role and made the policy reversal of 1961 possible, as consumers remained unorganized and industrialists gave up their pressure for cheap food availability.

Declining relative agricultural employment and production also made agricultural protection politically less costly to support. The shift to a net importing situation in most non-rice commodities in densely populated Japan also permitted the introduction of more covert policy instruments, such as import quotas and monopoly importing agencies, which provided 'invisible' assistance and funds for discretionary spending. In 1960 Japan's political establishment was shaken (and PM Kishi forced to resign), by the widespread unrest following the US-Japanese Alliance Treaty renewal. Increased ag support then may have appeared as a suitable means to enhance social stability in a turbulent high-growth period in which metropolitan infrastructures were heavily strained through unrelenting rural – urban migration and to keep the embattled LDP in power.

The producer support rate for rice then rapidly increased to exceed 100% in 1968;[67] in 1981, according to Table 8.2, its support rate (including also budgetary support) stood at 253%. In Miller's estimate (Figure 8.2) this rate (for consumer support alone) has increased to 700% in 1986. Even MAFF's own 'provisional estimates' admit average Japanese rice producer prices to be four times higher than in the US.[68]

It is evident that this degree of protection can no longer be absorbed by the downstream processing and distribution sectors. Rather, excess protection also bred Government intervention in subsequent handling (processing quotas for millers, Government controlled meat trading, rice monopoly marketing, supermarket licensing, etc.) and stifled competition. Table 8.3, reproducing USDA samples of retail food prices clearly shows Tokyo – irrespective even of exchange rate fluctuations (whether at Y228 to 1$ in May 1984, or revalued at Y185 to 1$ in November 1986) – to be by far the most expensive place to shop for food, followed only by Switzerland, which maintains similar excess protectionist policies, but where the food processing sector, due to its traditional export orientation and efficient distribution system, is more competitive.

Table 8.3 is equally striking in its evidence, that European agricultural protection has done little empirical harm to consumers, as Canberra, Ottawa and Washington DC prices are mostly higher than those of London or Paris. All, however, (including Seoul) evidently play in a different retail price league from Tokyo or Bern.

Table 8.3 *World food retail price comparison November 1986 (in US $ per kg or units as indicated converted at current exchange rates: 1 ECU = US $ 1.02 = Y166)*[70]

Item	Bern	Canberra	London	Ottawa	Paris	Seoul	Tokyo	Washington DC
Steak, sirloin, boneless	27.37	6.64	10.11	7.36	11.23	7.00	39.57	10.10
Roast, pork, boneless	10.29	3.47	3.43	4.96	6.01	4.24	11.74	6.17
Broilers, whole	3.83	2.90	2.03	3.33	2.94	1.75	4.97	2.27
Eggs, large (dozen)	3.44	1.69	1.47	0.84	0.85	1.12	1.74	0.77
Butter	10.59	3.15	2.79	4.46	4.54	4.64	8.03	5.46
Cheese, Cheddar, Emmental	10.99	4.49	3.71	7.95	6.06	9.29	6.70	7.05
Milk, whole (litre)	1.01	0.60	0.56	0.84	0.69	0.84	1.18	0.46
Oil, cooking (litre)	3.05	2.34	1.13	1.51	1.70	1.43	1.93	2.03
Potatoes	0.71	1.05	0.49	0.40	0.58	0.37	1.49	0.95
Apples	1.78	1.94	1.22	2.16	1.02	1.17	3.34	2.16
Oranges	1.77	0.71	1.19	1.58	1.17	0.97	1.98	1.35
Flour	1.21	0.87	0.46	0.82	0.89	0.32	1.24	0.44
Rice	1.95	0.92	1.16	1.57	1.66	1.14	2.42	1.04
Sugar	0.81	0.61	0.66	0.33	0.95	0.70	1.48	0.73
Coffee	11.57	12.31	9.80	9.77	6.95	15.67	19.96	7.67
TOTAL	90.37	43.69	40.21	47.88	47.24	50.65	107.77	48.56

157

9 May 1986

(current exchange rates: 1 ECU = US $ 0.81 = Y185)

Item	Bern	Canberra	London	Ottawa	Paris	Seoul	Tokyo	Washington DC
Steak, sirloin, boneless	20.46	7.36	11.26	6.76	7.03	10.85	30.70	7.69
Roast, pork, boneless	10.30	4.75	4.80	5.51	4.87	3.76	7.63	5.48
Broilers, whole	2.99	3.25	2.44	1.68	3.35	2.38	3.52	1.52
Eggs, large (dozen)	2.43	1.66	1.41	0.76	1.09	1.48	1.06	1.05
Butter	7.58	3.23	2.72	4.23	3.65	4.98	6.04	4.74
Cheese, Cheddar, Emmental	8.07	4.75	3.53	6.97	4.18	NA	4.06	6.59
Milk, whole (litre)	0.69	0.62	0.54	0.82	0.44	0.88	0.76	0.52
Oil, cooking (litre)	2.45	2.19	1.18	1.59	1.64	1.67	1.32	2.10
Potatoes	0.54	0.89	0.63	0.48	0.40	1.07	1.74	0.56
Apples	1.14	2.16	1.60	1.29	0.81	1.93	1.18	1.74
Oranges	0.98	1.72	0.67	1.32	0.58	1.44	2.45	0.88
Flour	0.83	0.82	0.34	0.93	0.64	0.32	0.78	0.49
Rice	1.47	0.91	0.91	1.94	1.30	1.09	1.57	1.06
Sugar	0.67	0.63	0.73	0.73	0.65	1.04	1.21	0.99
Coffee	7.65	13.69	6.46	7.32	5.38	12.66	14.30	7.45
TOTAL	68.28	48.62	39.22	42.33	36.02	45.54	78.33	42.86

Notes

1. OECD, Ministerial Mandate on Agricultural Trade, *Draft Report to the Council* (AGR/TC/WP (86)21) p. 66.
2. OECD, Ministerial Mandate on Agric. Trade, *Country Report on Japan* (1986), Statistical Annex, Table 17.
3. OECD, Ministerial Mandate on Agric. Trade, *Country Report on Japan* (1986) pp. 90–1.
4. MAFF, Report on Economic Survey of Farms, quoted in *Oriental Economist*, June 1984, p. 9.
5. GATT, Japan, Subsidies: notifications pursuant to Article XVI:1, L/5603/Add 25, 23.11.1984.
6. OECD, Ministerial Mandate on Agric. Trade, *Country Report on Japan*, p. 31.
7. MAFF, *Agriculture in Japan*, Mar. 1986, p. 15.
8. *Mainichi Shimbun*, 5 Nov. 1985, *Japan Agrinfo Newsletter*, 3 Dec. 1985.
9. Calculated from *Japan Statistical Yearbook*, p. 159.
10. OECD, *Country Report on Japan*, p. 35, Statistical Annex, Table 22.
11. Sato Yoshio, and Koichi Ito, 'A Theory of Oligopolistic Core and Competitive Fringe: Japan's Wheat Flour Milling Industry', *Keio Business Review*, no. 13, 1974, pp. 18–19.
12. Agricultural Policy Council, 'Report on the Implementation of the 'Basic Direction of Agricultural Policy in the 1980s', *Japan's Agricultural Review*, 788, 1983, p. 23.
13. *Japan Economic Journal*, 13 Sept. 1986, *Financial Times*, 9 Sept. 1986.
14. *Japan Agrinfo Newsletter*, 4 Sept. 1986.
15. GATT, Notifications . . . L/5003, 23 Nov. 1984, p. 7.
16. OECD, Ministerial Mandate on Agric. Trade, *Country Report on Japan*, p. 56/57.
17. *Japan Agrinfo Newsletter*, 4 Nov. 1986.
18. *Japan Statistical Yearbook*, p. 159.
19. Fukawa, Mitsuo,'Edible Oil Demand', *Business Japan*, Feb. 1984, pp. 72–4.
20. Longworth, *op. cit.*, p. 263.
21. OECD, *Country Report Japan*, Statistical Annex, Table 23.
22. OECD, *Country Report Japan*, p. 52.
23. GATT, L/5063/Add.25, p. 5.
24. Sato, Yoshio, 'The Silk Reeling Industry of Japan and the Catch-up Case', *Keio Business Review*, no. 11, 1972, p. 64.
25. GATT, State Trading, Notifications pursuant to Article XVII: 4(a). Japan, L/5937/Add.2. 20.3 1986, p. 10.
26. *Financial Times*, 17 July 1986.
27. Naito, Satoshi, 'The Tobacco Monopoly goes Private', *Economic Eye* June 1985, p. 30.
28. *Japan Agrinfo Newsletter*, 2 Mar. 1985.
29. Interview with Minomatsu Izumi, then JTS president, in *Economisto* (Tokyo), 6 Mar. 1979.
30. *Nihon Nogyo Shimbun*, 3 Sept. 84, *Japan Agrinfo Newsletter*, 2 Oct. 1984.

31. *Financial Times*, 13 Nov. 1986.
32. Motoki, Ryo, 'Pomiculture Promotion Deliberation Council', *Kankai*, May 1982.
33. *Japan Agrinfo Newsletter*, no. 3, Mar. 1986.
34. Nozaki, Hiroyuki (then Director General of the Agricultural Production Bureau, MAFF), 'Fruit Farming in Japan', *Look Japan*, 10 Mar. 1978.
35. OECD, MTM, *Country Report Japan,* p. 57.
36. GATT, Subsidies. Notifications L/5603/Add.25, 23.11.1984, p. 4.
37. GATT, International Dairy Arrangement, Reply to Questionnaire 5 DPC/INN/3/Add.2, 7.2.1986, p. 3.
38. *Japan Agrinfo Newsletter*, No. 2, Oct. 1984.
39. *Agra Europe*, 18 Apr. 1986.
40. GATT; IDA, *op. cit.*, p. 4.
41. Calculation based on *Japan Statistical Yearbook*, 1985, p. 165.
42. GATT, Subsidies, 23 Nov. 1984.
43. *Japan Economic Journal*, 7 June 86.
44. Agricultural Policy Research Committee, *Beef Situation in Japan* (Tokyo, 'undated 1986 ?'), p. 8.
45. *Mainichi Shimbun*, 23–4 May 1984.
46. *Agra Europe*, 10 Jan. 1986.
47. Mitsuaki, Nakao, 'Inside the Beef Industry', *Japan Echo*, no.1. 1984, p. 72.
48. GATT, State Trading. Notifications conforming to Art. 17: 4(a) Japan L/5937/Add.2/Suppl.1, 18.11.1986.
49. *Japan Agrinfo Newsletter* no.4, Sept. 1986.
50. OECD, *Country Report Japan*, Statistical Annex, Table 25.
51. Hayami, Yujiro, 'Trade Benefits to All: Design of the Beef Import Stabilization in Japan', *American Journal of Agricultural Economics*, vol.61, no.1, p. 344.
52. Quantified by Kym Anderson, 'The Peculiar Rationality of Beef Import Quotas in Japan and Korea', in K. Anderson and Y. Hayami (eds), *The Political Economy of Agricultural Protection* (Sydney: Allen & Unwin (1986) p. 87.
53. OECD, *Country Report Japan.*, Statistical Annex, Table 30.
54. *Livestock Industry Promotion Corporation* (Tokyo, LIPC, Aug. 1975) p. 8.
55. Kaminogo, Toshiaki (Tokyo Shimbun reporter) in *Bungei Shunju*, Mar. 1977.
56. *Le Monde*, 28 June 1977.
57. GATT, Arrangement regarding Bovine Meat, International Meat Council. Reply to Questionnaire, Japan, IMC/STAT/10/Add.13, 5.11.1986.
58. OECD, *Country Report Japan*, p. 49.
59. Ibid.,p. 112.
60. Import item: Broilers, *Focus Japan*, July 1979, p. 32.
61. *Journal of Japanese Trade and Industry*, no. 4, 1984, p. 46.
62. OECD, *Country Report Japan*, p. 58.
63. Basic data (budgetary figures, their product allocations, domestic and comparable import prices, etc.) are taken from OECD. Ministerial Trade Mandate, *Country Report Japan.*, Calculation of Producer and

Consumer Subsidy Equivalents, DAA/1950. 22 Sept. 1986. The calculations here, however, are my own.

64. Hayami, Yujiro, 'Rice Policy in Japan's Economic Development', *American Journal of Agricultural Economics*, vol. 54, no. 1, 1972, p.27.

65. Quoted in Otsuka, Keijro and Yujiro Hayami, 'Revealed Preference in Japan's Rice Policy' in Anderson and Hayami (eds), *The Political Economy of Agricultural Protection* (Sydney: Allen & Unwin, 1986) p. 66.

66. Hayami, *op. cit.*, 1972 p. 21.

67. *Ibid.*, p. 27.

68. *Japan Times*, 8 Oct. 1986.

69. Synthesized from Geoff Miller, *The Political Economy of International Agricultural Policy Reform* (Canberra: Australian Government Publishing Service, 1986,) p. 28. In my opinion, his comparison of Japanese target prices on sugar with Caribbean prices is not entirely justified.

70. FAS, *Survey of Average Retail Food Prices in Selected World Capitals*.

9 International Implications

Agricultural protection which reduces import demand effectively depresses world commodity prices. Though Japan does not subsidize her agricultural exports, her ever-growing trade surplus due to competitive industrial production enhances political pressure on the part of all major agricultural exporters – the US, the EC, Australia, Canada, New Zealand, Thailand, etc. – which demand liberalized import access on foodstuffs on which they happen to enjoy greater competitive advantages.

This chapter attempts to identify major areas of friction: beef, oranges, timber and rice with the US, liquor, wine and processed foods with the EC, sugar, beef and horticultural products with Australia, etc. It seeks to find patterns in these conflicts, especially in the Japanese responses, with key domestic actors' conflicting interests and policies, and to outline the fairly inevitable future development in the agricultural trade sector for which Japan's agriculture and food industries currently still appear ill prepared.

LEGITIMIZING PROTECTION

Japanese officials and policy-makers legitimize their protectionist policies with a set of standard justifications, which with little variation are repeated *ad nauseam*. This reflects the traditional Japanese tenet if only her perfectly reasonable positions were properly 'understood' by her foreign partners, then these countries would drop their 'unreasonable' demands. The official standard reasoning runs as follows:[1]

1. Japan's agriculture with its 1.2 ha farms would be 'wiped out' by import liberalization.
2. Japan without agriculture would no longer be Japan.
3. Japan is already the world's largest food importer.
4. Liberalization would!contribute only marginally to balance Japan's visible trade surplus.
5. On those products liberalized in the 1960s – feeds, cereals and some citrus fruits – domestic production declined drastically.
6. Japan caloric intake is saturated at daily 2 500 cal./head. Cheaper imported food would not increase consumption.

7. Global food shortages are around the corner. Improved self-sufficiency ratios are the best food security policy in response.
8. Overseas food supplies are not reliable (e.g. US soybean embargo of 1973), be it for reasons of war, labour disputes, crop failures, etc.
9. Japanese consumers remembering the post World War II famine are willing to pay a premium for safe domestic food supplies.
10. Japan's agricultural organizations are violently opposed to liberalization. Antagonizing them would risk losing the farm vote for the LDP, hence put political stability and the US alliance at risk.
11. Liberalization would counteract regional social and environmental policy objectives: lead to soil erosion, depopulation, unemployment, etc.
12. It would also put the structural objectives of the paddy diversification programme at jeopardy.
13. Almost all countries – including the EC and the US – protect agriculture. Japan is not an exception, neither in principle nor in degree of protection.
14. Agriculture is specific, as it satisfies primary needs (inelastic demand) with atomistic production (i.e. delayed cyclical supply responses) and is dependent on external factors (i.e. the weather), resulting in strong cyclical price fluctuations. It is hence a sector to which the theory of comparative advantages and the GATT rules of free trade should not be applicable.

Nonetheless, should 'unreasonable' external pressure become too strong upon the small Japanese islands, then on political grounds Japan might make symbolic concessions on items which are either insignificant or on which she has improved her sectoral competitiveness.

Zenchu, moreover, has radicalized its intransigence by proposals for 'new' principles for agricultural trade:[2]

(a) Nations should give priority to domestic food autarchy, and mutually respect such policies.
(b) Imports should only be undertaken to make up for inevitable structural or temporary shortfalls in domestic production.

In fact, Japan has always pursued a less doctrinaire trade policy. With the 1961 Agricultural Basic Law stipulating the selective expansion of certain crops and livestock production, imported products fall into three categories:[3]

Table 9.1 Imported Products[6]

Products	1975	1980	1982 ($bn)	1982 (m tonnes)
Maize	1.1	2.0	1.8	13.6
Cotton	0.8	1.4	1.3	0.9
Soybeans	0.9	1.3	1.2	4.3
Wheat	1.1	1.2	1.1	5.7
Wool	0.6	0.7	0.7	0.2
Pork	0.3	0.4	0.5	0.1
Coffee beans	0.2	0.7	0.5	0.2
Raw sugar	1.7	1.2	0.5	2.2
Sorghum	0.5	0.6	0.4	3.4
Leaf tobacco	0.3	0.4	0.4	0.1
Beef	1.1	0.4	0.4	0.1
Vegetables			0.4	1.2
Natural rubber	0.2	0.6	0.4	0.4
Cow hides	0.3	0.3	0.3	0.2
Subtotal agr. products	11.2	17.6	16.2	
Logs	2.3	5.7	3.6	30.4
Sawn lumber	0.3	1.2	0.9	5.0
Pulp wood	0.4	0.9	0.6	5.8
Subtotal forestry	3.1	8.1	5.3	
Shrimps and prawns	0.5	1.1	1.4	0.2
Tuna, skipjack	0.1	0.2	0.3	0.1
Squid	0.1	0.2		
Salmon		0.1	0.4	0.1
Subtotal fisheries	1.3	3.4	4.2	
Total agr./fish/for.	15.6	29.1	25.8	
Total imports	57.9	140.5	131.9	

1. Items for which Japan insists on full self-sufficiency (rice and dairy), or which due to their perishability are not suitable for long distance transportation (fresh vegetables, drinking milk): imports should not take place.
2. Items, which are essential to the development of Japan's feed-livestock economy and cannot be produced domestically in sufficient quantities (soybeans, feed grains). Imports are liberalized for this category (which also includes most tropical fruits and beverages).

3. Items on which imports are necessary to make up for quantity or quality shortfalls in domestic production and/or to manage stabilization price bands mechanisms (beef, pork, poultry, sugar, tabacco, wine, etc.)

Since 1983, under the firm premiership of Mr Nakasone, the MAFF has also through the Agricultural Policy Council (a great deal of its members being gradually former MAFF senior officials) and its policy recommendations, accepted the inevitability of 'internationalization' for its clientele industries. Current policy reform attempts to strengthen productivity and to increase farm sizes to enhance viable farm operations able to withstand import competition and to be protected only by tariffs in the long run.[4]

All post-war Japanese trade policies reflect the strategy: to liberalize only if and when domestic production is strong enough to withstand foreign competition unharmed. The weeding out of inefficient producers is done preferably by domestic competition; if immediate adjustment proved too painful domestic crisis cartels would cushion the process.

Recent developments in biotechnology have made Japan's bureaucrats aware that some agricultural and food production in fact are 'future industries' in which Japan might gain competitive advantages. Evidently, it will take some time to shift gear from the corrupting price policies keeping part-timers and Nokyo apparatchiks in business, to developing a new, vital and competitive core farming structure. Until that date Japan will continue vigorous protectionist rearguard defences.

AGRICULTURAL TRADE DEVELOPMENT

Japan's imports, reflecting largely the development of her livestock industry grew strongly from \$4.2 bn (1970) to \$18.5 bn (1981), but levelled off thereafter (see Figure 9.1), partly reflecting the depression in world market prices since.

With the spread of 200 miles fishing zones, fishing imports grew from \$1.3 bn (1975) to \$4.0 bn (1981). Forestry products – logs largely – developed from \$3.7 bn to \$5.4 bn during the same period.

Though the share of agricultural, forestry and marine products in Japan's total imports has declined from 27% (1975) to 20% (1982), they still represent a considerable proportion in her import trade.

Figure 9.1 Development of agriculture, fishery and forestry imports[5]

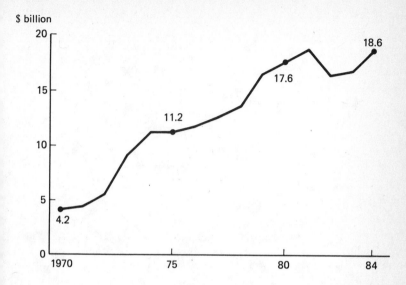

This reflects the basic pattern of Japan's external economy: to import the lacking raw materials and to export the processed value-added final products. With respect to food, it is the processed industrial products that pay the import bill.

Agricultural suppliers are clearly concentrated around the Pacific Basin, with the US continuing to play a major role, particularly due to its dominance in the soy bean and feed grain sector. Other significant US AFF exports to Japan are logs, lumber, cotton, tobacco, hides, beef, citrus fruits and fishery products. ASEAN countries export mainly logs, natural rubber, palm oil (Malaysia), poultry (Thailand), bananas (Philippines), tropical timber, coffee, spices and shrimps (Indonesia). China supplies maize, soy beans, tea, canned foods and animal by-products. Taiwan exports shrimp and pork.

Australia is strong in beef, wool, wheat, barley and raw sugar; New Zealand with equal predictability excels in dairy, wool, mutton and kiwis; Brazil in coffee and oranges; Canada exports mainly sawn lumber, rapeseed, barley, wheat, herring, cod and pork. The EC which covers a great geographical distance exports higher value-added food and drinks; liquor, wine, malt, SMP, instant coffee, natural cheese, pork, confectionery, tomato products and marmalades.

Table 9.2   Supplier countries of agricultural, fish and forestry products to Japan ($bn)[7]

	1981	(%)	1985	(%)
1. US	7.6	39.0	6.4	34.2
2. ASEAN	1.5	7.8	1.6	8.3
3. Canada	1.5	7.6	1.4	7.4
4. Australia	1.4	7.5	1.2	6.2
5. EC–10	1.1	5.5	1.1	5.7
6. China	0.8	4.0	1.2	6.6
7. New Zealand	0.3	1.7	0.4	1.9
World total	20.0	100.0	18.6	100.0

IMPORT RESTRICTIONS

The Japanese government takes great pride in having reduced agricultural/forestry/fishery (AFF) import quotas from a total of 103 (1962) progressively to 22 (1985). Items currently under quota (IQ) are: milk cream, condensed milk, processed cheese, beef, beef and pork preparations, rice, wheat flour, fresh and frozen oranges, fruit and tomato juice, fruit purée and paste, pineapple preparations and pulp, tomato ketchup and sauce, glucose, lactose, starch, pulses, peanuts, konnyaku (devil's tongue), herrings, cod, yellow tail, cod roes, scallop, squid, adductors of shell fish, other prepared foodstuffs, and hides and leather.[8] The products protected by import quota (IQ) account for about 52% of total agricultural production. It must be noted, however, that mainly due to foreign pressure, IQ AFF imports increased from $530 m in 1976 (3% of the AFF import total) to $1.4 bn in 1984 (4.9% of the AFF total).[9] This largely reflects the repeated enlargements of the beef and orange quotas – after the agreements in the GATT in December 1978, and with the US in January 1978 and April 1983 – to annual targets of 58 400 tonnes for beef and 126 000 tonnes for oranges by FY 1987.[10]

Average tariff rates on AFF imports after the conclusion of the Tokyo Round (1979) have declined from a weighted 9.7% to 8.6%. Tariffs on soy bean imports were zero-bound. In its subsequent various 'action programmes for improved market access', the Japanese Government announced further tariff cuts, such as for instance, for plywood imports and in Japan's GSP scheme (for the benefit of developing countries), and a readiness to cut tariffs by 20% across-

Table 9.3 Japan's agricultural exports

Japan's AFF exports		(fob, Ybn)
	1982	1984
Agricultural products	198	202
crop products	177	176
livestock products	20	23
silk	1	4
Forestry products	27	27
Fishery products	263	303
AFF exports	487	533
AFF exports as % of total exports	1.4%	1.3%

Source: *MAFF Monthly Statistics*, 3 Mar. 1985.

the-board in the new Uruguay GATT Round was made public.

Non-tariff barriers, ranging from 'administrative guidance' to importers to cancel import contracts, to veterinary/phytosanitary barriers, and to discriminatory excise duties, will be dealt with in the subsequent section.

AGRICULTURAL EXPORTS

While together a minor item in Japan's total exports, fisheries remain a salient feature in her AFF exports, with agricultural products being stagnant at best. They largely appear to consist of speciality processed products for the Japanese expatriate community abroad; fresh and preserved fruits, i.e. mostly unshu oranges and pears (Y10 bn 1984), fresh and dried vegetables – largely dried Shiitake mushrooms – (Y22 bn), confectionery (Y14 bn), seasonings (soy sauce, sodium glutamate, etc.) (Y10 bn), sake and beer (Y8 bn), tobacco (Y3 bn), milk powder for infants (Y7 bn), and vegetable seeds (Y4 bn). Some of these exports in turn face problems of market access, on phytosanitary grounds. Japanese orange exports to the US are permitted to only 5 non-producing West-Coast states.

Among fishery exports most prominent were canned products (Y92 bn in 1984): skipjack, sardines, mackerel and tuna; but also fresh, chilled and frozen fish (Y60 bn), largely consisting of skipjack, tuna and shrimps; further fish oil (Y23 bn); and pearls (Y83 bn), also a traditional Japanese export. Almost half of all fishery exports (by value) are sold to the US, the rest to the European Community, Hong Kong, Canada, New Zealand and Singapore.

BILATERAL ISSUES

The US

It is not by accident that economic relations with the US enjoy a certain priority among policy-makers, bureaucrats, business leaders and the general public in Japan. 'High politics', i.e. security considerations, are closely linked to the more 'low politics' trade and technology issues, in which the US again are Japan's most important single foreign partner.

This observation also holds true in agricultural trade, with 37% of total imports originating in the US, their feedstuffs constituting a veritable lifeline for Japan's intensive livestock industries. The public discussion of farm import liberalization in Japan is consequently dominated by the consideration of issues (be it beef, oranges, tobacco or lumber) which the US administration, for domestic purposes, has largely chosen as targets for priority 'treatment'.

Other partners' often more considerate requests are discussed rather in passing.

In public pronouncements in Japan, US policy-makers in turn do not fail to stress the importance of Japan as their second largest export market (1982: $5.5 bn) after the European Community ($8.3 bn), taking about 15% of total US farm exports. John Block (US Secretary of Agriculture 1981–86) stressed that 17 m acres (6.8 m ha) are planted annually for Japan-bound export crops in the US, which represented a 'long term commitment to produce for the Japanese market',[11] with the US respecting 'the responsibility it shares for the food security of the Japanese people'. Earl Butz (US Secretary of Agriculture 1971–76) was apologetic for the US's 'horrendous embargo of soybean shipments'[12] undertaken in 1973, and assured his audience the US was now 'Japan's Farm'.

Sato and Curran have analysed the dispute settlement pattern in phases I and II of the US–Japan beef and orange conflict,[13] with its roots in the respective domestic politics of 1977/78: the US Special Trade Representative had felt that he needed agricultural support for the safe passage of his MTN results in Congress and hence sought additional concessions for the benefit of citrus and beef export interests largely concentrated in California, Florida and Texas. The US administration, farm and Congress leaders rallied behind the demand, while the Japanese political establishment's response was more divided: MAFF and the Zenchu-managed farm lobby appeared strongly opposed to any liberalization – with production control programmes in mikan oranges underway, and the vested interests of licensed orange and beef importers and privileged beef processors making their political muscle felt. But Keidanren, the economic ministries and the media favoured a gradual liberalization in beef and orange imports. With the US threatening with an anti-Japanese import control bill to be passed by Congress, and after considerable inter-LDP/ministerial in-fights, in January 1978 a first agreement between US STR Robert Strauss and Nobuhiko Ushiba (Foreign Economic Affairs Minister) provided for an additional 10 000 tonnes as hotel beef quota and 45 000 tonnes of oranges. The result was soon ridiculed as amounting to a hamburger and 3.2 oranges per Japanese per year,[14] and awakened US producer interest in the Japanese market. This compelled Strauss to ask for a further enlargement in the quotas. Previous Japanese farm protests and inter-ministry/LDP disputes were rehearsed, high level Zenchu and LDP missions once again dispatched to the US (and were, as usual, forced to soften their hardline views). By December 1978, in Geneva's MTN, Japan then announced it would unilaterally enlarge her annual *erga omnes* orange quotas to 82 000 tonnes and her beef quotas to 30 800 tonnes by 1983. In spite of the US's use of strong-arm tactics, an escalation of the conflict was avoided. As a partial result in 1982, 44% of all US citrus fruit exports (orange, grapefruit, lemon and lime) – or 330 000 tonnes – and 62% of US beef exports (53 000 tonnes) went to Japan.[15]

This success encouraged the US to pursue relentlessly their policy objective of 'fair access' to Japan's food market in early 1982. Initiating Phase III, the US demanded a complete liberalization of beef and orange imports into Japan.[16] In response Zenchu and its Nokyo activists collected 10 million signatures to reject the demand, and 150 Dietmen, led by the chairmen of the respective Diet Leagues for the Livestock and Pomiculture Industries, Yamanaka and Higaki, voiced their 'absolute opposition' to the US demand in February 1982.[17] There was considerable confrontation between Zenchu and Keidanren (fearing for the future of Japan's industrial export to the

Table 9.4　The Brock/Yamamura agreement of April 1984[19] (term of agreement: four years; in tonnes)

	Import framework for FY 1983	Average annual growth volume	Import framework for FY 1987
Beef	30,800	6,900	58,400
Oranges	82,000	11,000	126,000
Orange juice	6,500	500	8,500
Grape fruit juice	6,000	–	Imports to be liberalized as from fiscal 1986

US), in which heavy-weights like Kakuei Tanaka, then the undisputed leader of the LDP's largest faction (and representing nothing-but-rice producing Niigata) took Keidanren's side (endorsing a concept providing for gradual liberalization with deficiency payment compensations to affected producers).[18] Finally in April 1984 William Brock (Special Trade Representative) and Shinjiro Yamamura (MAFF Minister) were able to conclude once again a compromise deal in the form of a phased quota enlarging agreement (see Table 9.4).

While these quotas in principle are *erga omnes*, in the case of oranges seasonal quotas allow target imports of fresh products according to certain origins (California vs. Florida vs. Brazil); in beef, the LIPC's import monopoly specifies *ad hoc* types and grades of beef to be imported: e.g. Australian beef (67% of Japan's imports in 1983) is largely a grass-fed low-to-medium quality product for use in manufacturing (such as hamburger beef, etc.). US exports are grain-fed higher quality dairy beef, used mainly as 'hotel beef' in restaurants.

The 'liberalizations' in 1987, amounting to 4% of Japan's orange and 37% of her beef production, certainly did not 'wipe out' domestic producers as Zenchu in 1982 had alleged. But given Japan's persistent industrial trade surplus, the writing is on the wall for further quota concessions ('Phase IV').

In order to forestall likely US pressure for beef and rice liberalization, MAFF in January 1987 let it be known it was ready to lift import controls on oranges from FY 1988. Seasonal and quality differentials would continue to protect Japanese mikan 'mandarin oranges'.[20] With all probability current orange juice blending requirements – the share of imported juice is not allowed to exceed 60% – will be maintained.[21]

On all other agricultural issues in which the US have export interests, liberalization demands are on the table, though with less political priority. These concern tobacco, to which the Japanese after protracted negotiations agreed to respond by 'privatizing' their government monopoly, the JTS, in April 1985 and by abolishing the cigarette import tariff in 1987. They also concern meat preparations, fruit pulp and juices, confectionery, beans, peanuts, tomato juice and ketchup, and food additive legislation.[22] The US Chocolate Manufacturers Association in 1985 threatened to file a 'section 301 trade case' with the STR, which if successful, would authorize the President to restrain the imports from a country which 'unreasonably restricts' its markets. Japan's respective tariffs in excess of 20% would constitute a convincing case, the association felt.[23] On rice, a similar suit by the US Rice Millers Association was rejected by the STR on political grounds,[24] probably fearing that an attack on rice, the sacred cow of Japan's protectionists, was premature and poorly justified (given the US's own heavy subsidization of the product). The Association alleged that $1.6 bn (2.45 m tonnes) in potential export sales were lost due to Japan's import prohibition.[25]

The Nihon Keizai Shimbun then criticized the resulting outcry by the Japanese lobby: nationalistic and emotional sentiments superseded economic logic when it came to rice. MAFF and Zenchu had lost all consideration for international economic relations because they had become too used to excessive agricultural protection over the years.[26]

On leather and shoe imports, after losing a protracted GATT case in 1984, Japan offered industrial tariff compensation to the US for an agreed annual estimated loss in US leather sales of $260 m. This offer was accepted by Clayton Yeutter, US Special Trade Representative, in December 1985.[27]

On forestry products, the US continue to insist on the total elimination of all Japanese tariffs – of strong interest to the US Pacific Northwest – in particular on wood panel boards (plywood, veneer and particle boards),[28] and threatened to withhold the raw materials – logs and lumber – for Japan's housing and furniture industry if no agreement were reached.

US rhetoric on these issues is fervently free trading and only too ready to overlook its own protectionist non-grain agricultural policies. This certain measure of bigotry is immaterial, however, because, for Japan, agricultural import policies should be ruled by economic and not by moral considerations.

EUROPEAN COMMUNITY

The EC's food exports, although only 4% of Japan's import total, as processed up-market food and drinks are highly visible. Unlike feeds, which were an essential raw material needed for the build-up of Japan's livestock industry, European food and drink, against all initial official discouragement of luxury imports, had to penetrate successfully Japan's arcane distribution system to reach the consumer. Even before the Commission's exclusive negotiating competence in external trade matters, member states like France in 1963 on cognac and wine quotas, and the UK 1969/70 on whisky, confectionery and footwear quotas and tariffs, negotiated with little success for market opening in Japan.[29] In 1976 the Commission with the cumulative punch of the then 9 European nations, organized the first negotiations with the Japanese which covered dairy, canned luncheon pork, wine, whisky, cognac, tinned tomatoes, confectionery, chocolates, tobacco and leather, demanding enlarged quotas and/or reduced tariffs/taxes on these products.[30] These items represented a 'shopping list' of member states' export interests that had run into trouble, but no clear priorities were given. The Japanese responded with limited selective concessions: in November 1976, they announced their intention to import some 56 000 tonnes of SMP for feed use, and to simplify tobacco imports. In 1977 Mr Haferkamp, then EC Commissioner for External Relations, was assured that Danish canned pork sales to Okinawa (where it is popular as luncheon meat) would continue on a concessional basis.[31]

In December 1981 whisky tariffs were cut by 10.4%, and in December 1982 Japan announced tariff cuts on chocolates, biscuits, tobacco, jams, tractors and agricultural engines. A further round of tariff reductions was made public in July 1985.

These very partial concessions – most tariffs on sensitive foods and drinks remained well above 20–30% – failed to have perceptible effects on EC exports, as MOF continued to stall on 'its' competent issues: tariffs, tobacco marketing and excise duties, while MAFF resisted all quota enlargements, particularly so on dairy and meats.

The Community's ageing demand for reduced tariffs and a non-discriminatory excise tax system for imported liquor and wines – emphasized by Giscard (for cognac) during the 1979 Tokyo summit, and by Mrs Thatcher (on Scotch) during the May 1986 summit (held also in Tokyo) – finally in 1986 was defined by the Community as a priority sector and declared as a symbolic 'test case for Japan's willingness to reduce import barriers'.[32]

Table 9.5   Whisky producer prices, retail prices, taxes and tariffs (1984, in yen)[34]

	Producer price/bottle	Retail price/bottle	Taxes	Tariffs
Special grade	350	4,150/10,000	2,098 *	332/litre **
1st grade	260	1,620	1,011	
2nd grade	200	900	296	

 * Levied on top of cif cum duty value ('tax on tax').
** Until April 1987; thereafter: 246.4/litre.

The EC Commission, as the Community's negotiator, demands for liquor and wines that a single tax rate on volume of alcohol should replace the current excise taxes based on quality grades. Tariffs should be reduced to EC levels.

Also legal labelling rules should be established specifying the raw materials used and the method of preparation. Clear rules of origin should prevent Japanese consumers from mistaking domestic 'Chateau', 'Reserve', 'Cuvée' and 'Grand Vin' blended plonk from French imports. Further, more flexible licensing should allow more alcoholic drink sales in supermarkets.[33]

Japan's liquor grading system essentially provides for three grades taxed according to quality:

Imported liquor is automatically graded special grade and hence taxed out of the mass take-home market. EC liquor sales to Japan, currently at around ECU 170 m per year, are estimated to double should discriminatory taxation be removed.[35]

In Japan, ministerial and LDP tax commissions late in December 1986 after considerable disagreements were able to present a liquor 'tax reform', which was immediately rejected as window dressing by the EC's liquor exporters' association,[36] a view shared by the EC Commission. Given the popularity of low-taxed second-grade sake and shochu among their voters, LDP politicians found the withdrawal of fiscal privilege from their traditional local brands too hard to stomach. In spite of top level (Mr Nakasone's) advice to consent to more conciliatory ministerial proposals, the LDP Tax Commission[37] led by Sadonori Yamanaka, already renowned as a battle-hardened beef protector, was only able to agree on a merging of special and 1st grade taxes from 1988 on. Excise taxes on the new top grade would still remain 5 times higher than for 2nd grade. Proposed tariff concessions (cuts by 30%) against which local whisky producers were particularly opposed,[38] left the duties for imported liquor and wines still far above comparable EC and US levels.

With no satisfactory solution in sight, the EC asked for a GATT arbitration panel (Art 23(2)), to investigate Japan's wine and spirits tariffs, taxes and labelling practices.[39] A finding of unfair trade practices could then allow retaliatory Community action.

On wines, subjected to a uniform tax system from FY 1987, and for which in December 1986 the industry agreed to new labelling rules, an amicable solution is probably closer, although higher tariffs for imported bottled wines will continue to favour imported bulk for domestic bottling. Depending on the blend, such wines, from 1987 will either be labelled 'domestic wine, using imported wine' or 'imported wine, using domestic wine'. Also names of specific grape varieties are not to be used, unless at least 50% of the wine actually was derived from these grapes. A vintage will only be admissible if at least 75% of the grapes were harvested in that year.[40]

After liquor and wine, there is no shortage of processed agriculture issues as candidates for future sectorial focusing: enlarged quotas in processed cheese, butter, starch and pork; reduced tariffs on a series of dairy, confectionery, sausages, tomato products, jams, juices, instant coffee, chewing gum, leather and furs – further, to increase the EC's shoe import quota allocation beyond the annual 2.4 m pairs,[41] to abolish import controls on silk worms and fabrics from the EC, to ease quarantine controls on flower bulbs[42] and other phytosanitary barriers, the removal of similar non-tariff barriers in Japan's food additives legislation, veterinary controls on meat imports, and retests of agrochemicals.

These requests have in common that they focus rather on market opening of processed food than on raw material agricultural products. Farmers' shares in these items are often very limited. Consequently resistance to liberalization is often stronger on the part of the processing industry than by the farm organizations proper.

OTHER PARTNERS

US and EC liberalization requests are certainly not isolated. Most of the tariff quota and NTB complaints are restated leitmotiv-like by the other developed and developing agricultural exporter nations. *Australian* officials negotiate for reduced tariffs on sugar, beef, and wheat gluten, for enlarged beef quotas, and complain about the length of time to resolve quarantine disputes impeding horticultural trade.[43] On Australian citrus exports it had taken 20 years to clear the quarantine problems. *New Zealand*, for which Japan has become the largest single export customer, faces essentially the same access problems on its SMP, butter, beef, timber and fruit exports.[44] *ASEAN* nations on their poultry and rice (Thailand), palm oil (Malaysia) bananas and sugar (Philippines), and similar exports competing directly or indirectly with temperate Japanese agricultural products, are vocal in their dissatisfaction in being prevented from utilizing their competitive advantage,[45] which Japan since decades is able to exercise in industrial products on their respective markets.

MULTILATERAL ISSUES

Japan is a member and significant contributor to all major international organizations dealing with agricultural questions: *GATT*, the major negotiating forum, which seeks firmer agricultural trade rules and freer agricultural trade; the *OECD*, which through in-depth agricultural policy and market analysis attempts to induce more economic rationality into farm policy-making in developed countries; and the various talk shops of the UN: *FAO*, *World Food Council*, *UNCTAD*, and their better reputed development agency *IFAD*. Japan also participates in various commodity agreements: the arrangements on temperate commodities (dairy, beef, sugar, wheat) which usually do not contain economic provisions, require little more than the supply of statistical information and of membership fees. Tropical commodity agreements (on coffee, tea, cocoa, natural rubber), concluded under UNCTAD auspices, still – to the extent that they remain operational – contain 'stabilized' export prices through export quotas and buffer stock provisions to be respected and financed by importing industrial nations, such as Japan, which in these forums maintains a position of healthy common sense against intemperate LDC demands insisting on over-high producer prices (which invite overproduction and 'illegal' exporting, thus blowing the agreement).

The International Tropical Timber Agreement (ITTA), whose organization since 1986 has had its headquarters in Yokohama – Japan being the world's largest tropical timber importing nation – has more realist objectives: striving to preserve tropical rain forests and to encourage processing in LDCs, it promotes R&D, collects market information, and supports re-afforestation and forest management.[46]

As economic common sense does not necessarily apply to her own agricultural policies, in GATT and the OECD, Japan's representatives, though basically committed to the free trade principles which made Japan's post-war growth possible, stick to a fairly low profile and when challenged, like some other excess protectionist nations, stress the virtues of food security and the 'specificity' of agriculture legitimizing exemption from liberal economics. Protectionist sinning on part of most fellow OECD nations (notably virtuous exemptions being Australia and New Zealand with more cattle and sheep than inhabitants) facilitate the justification.

The Tokyo Summit of May 1986, however, in its final Communiqué also commits Japan to seek adjustment policies. The heads of state or government concluded that 'a situation of global structural surplus now exists for some important agricultural products . . . likely to aggravate the risk of wider protectionist pressures'. They further agreed that 'when there are surpluses, action is needed to redirect policies and adjust the structure of production in the light of world demand'.

The OECD Ministerial meeting of April 1986 had agreed to a similar resolution, calling for reduced assistance to agriculture, a theme which in Punta del Este in September 1986 was taken up as a GATT ministerial commitment to start the new Uruguay Round which in the field of agricultural trade aims to achieve greater liberalization and stricter and more efficient GATT rules in:

(a) improving market access;
(b) increasing discipline on the use of all direct and indirect subsidies, and
(c) minimizing the adverse trade effects of sanitary and phytosanitary barriers

In a subsequent policy document produced by the Agricultural Policy Council – hence likely to be adopted by the Cabinet – Japan asserts to be strongly in favour of strengthened GATT rules for agricultural trade.[44]

Though the success of the Uruguay Round is by no means assured, the new rules are also likely to pertain to facilitated import access – though currently the more urgent international problem area concerns competitive agricultural export subsidization, which so far is not practised by Japan.

Since their tender beginnings in the early 1960s, Japan's development aid having reached $3.8 bn in 1983 on a net expenditure basis of
which 25.6% was spent on agricultural development, Japan's OAD
has increased rapidly since 1978 and is now the world's second largest
(after the US) spent for independent developing countries.

Two-thirds of this aid continues to be directed to Asian nations
(China, Thailand, Indonesia, the Philippines, etc.) with which Japan
shares relatively strong economic, cultural and historical bonds. Only
for the latter half of the 1980s Japan's development aid is planned to
be retargeted towards sub-Saharan Africa.[48] Japan's agricultural aid
is largely bilateral project aid: training manpower, dispatching ex-
perts, supplying facilities (including Japanese-made fertilizers, agricultural chemicals and machinery) for well-defined limited crop,
forestry, livestock and fishery projects mostly in South-East Asia, to
whose monsoon climates and paddy cultures Japan's technologies are
easily transferable. Public OAD cash (Y4.1 bn in soft loans) is also
given for the ambitious Cerrado joint Brazilian/Japanese commercial
venture, attempting to turn 150 000 ha of semi-arid wilderness
around Brasilia into soybean, maize and other export crop
production.[49] This project could be seen as part of an agricultural
alliance with Brazil, which would help Japan to diversify her feed
supply sources from their dependence on the US. Ultimately the
cooperation agreement between the two countries envisages some
5 m ha to be producing about 100 m tonnes of grains and oilseeds
(which would imply a tripling of current Brazilian output!). Two
major shortcomings usually haunt agro-business megaprojects in
Brazil: transportation problems and the shortage of climatically
adapted seed varieties for planting.[50]

After having supplied some surplus rice in the late 1970s to Pakistan and Indonesia as *ad hoc* food aid, Japan is now committed to
more orderly regular annual food and donations of 300 000 tonnes of
wheat (or equivalent) under the Food Aid Convention of the International Wheat Agreement. This grain is bought in third countries, such
as the US, but preferably through local procurement in Asian and
African LDCs to cut transport costs and to enhance regional food
self-sufficiency by giving incentives to efficient producers,[51] in the
knowledge that food aid supplies alone do probably more harm than
favour to the recipient regions in the long run.

The question of *whaling* concerns a multilateral issue which for
Japan found its probable final solution not subsequent to multilateral
persuasion, but due to bilateral arm-twisting. Japan, then the world's
major whaling-ship operator, in 1982 in the good company of the

USSR and Norway, had rejected the International Whaling Council's three-quarter majority's recommendation to end commercial whaling after the 1985 season,[52] claiming that the whales hunted by Japan (minkes, sperms and Brydes) were plentiful and by no means threatened by extinction. Also whale meat was used for human consumption, and not as pet food (as with the Norwegians) or thrown away (as done in the 19th century by US and European whalers interested only in oil, baleen and in the bit of ivory found in sperm whales). Japan in 1981 also claimed in the IWC that whaling still constituted an 'irreplacable means of livelihood for many Japanese fishermen'.[53] For the same year Japan's *Statistical Yearbook* indicated exactly 437 workers employed in factory ship whaling. With IWC's moral persuasion falling on deaf ears in Japan, the US Congress with its Packwood–Magnusson Amendment stipulating that any country not complying with the IWC's moratorium would see its fishing quota in US waters automatically cut by 50%, got a more receptive audience. Instantly applied to the USSR, the Japanese, after negotiations with the US Commerce Department, seemed to get exemption for the vague promise to cease commercial minke whaling in 1988. It was Greenpeace and other anti-whaling groups which successfully sued the US administration for an equitable application of the law. MAFF quickly making its sums with a Y130 bn annual fisheries catch in the US 200-mile zone in jeopardy – ten times the value of her whaling catch (Y13.7 bn in 1984), then decided that Japan would terminate her whaling operations with the end of the 1986 hunting season,[54] ending 400 years of a largely coastal whaling history. However, some whaling in the guise of 'research' continued.

SUMMARY

Japan reacted to the continued international challenge to her protectionist agro-food system in the last 20 years with protracted and uninspiring rearguard actions. In the end Japan always gave in: be it on beef, orange or leather quotas, confectionery and wine tariffs, or the tobacco monopoly. But it was always too little and too late. Year-long domestic compromise seeking was perceived as delaying tactics, and resulting liberalization offers were too often half-hearted or phoney, hence disappointing and further straining the already streched patience of her overseas partners. Whenever more meaningful liberalizations were finally arrived at, the political gain to be expected was already used up in the exhaustion of decade-long prior negotiations.

A corporatist decision-making structure, such as Japan's, is always introvert and slow-moving at best. Vested producer and processor interests are allowed to exercise a near-veto position. Ministries – even bureaux within – engage in the promotion of 'their' clientele industries' sectoral interests, and, largely unchecked by any firm political leadership at cabinet level, succeed in defining these parochial interests, such as the ones of peppermint growers in Hokkaido, or of whalers in Wakayama, as the national interest.

LDP Dietmen – due to the particularities of Japan's election system and the party's resulting factional structure – are even more committed to pork barrel politics and to the vigorous pursuit of local interests in Tokyo (the pursuit of which is perceived as the major indicator of laudable political success by voters back home). Japan's former Prime Minister, Mr Nakasone, a committed and energetic reformer, still takes pride in having exempted *konnyaku*, Devil's Tongue Root, a raddish produced in his native Gumma prefecture, but also in some other East Asian countries, from his liberalization programme.[55]

Traditionally, Japan appears to have done pretty well – though at considerable political cost – to have liberalized only when she was sure of having developed the industry in question to a level and scale able to withstand international competition. In the agro-food sector, the systematic neglect of structural adjustment has induced a severely retarded sector which, with its excess-protection levels, appears to be safe from liberalization. Decades of sheltering have produced a myopia of parasistic rent-recipients creating a web of mutually shared benefits in which all participants of the system: the agricultural bureaucracy, the farm politicians, the co-operatives, the traders, processors and the suppliers, are tangled. The difficulty in unravelling this network of structural corruption in a corporatist consensus-oriented national decision structure is evident. Japan's negotiators were usually instructed to adopt a defensive and low profile role, and to use persuasive approaches ('explain fully'), but rarely were able to obtain a genuine negotiating mandate with fall-back positions. They had little choice but to stick to the usual and unconvincing tear-jerker theme of a small, typhoon- and earthquake-ridden mountainous island nation, where hardworking decent (pro-US) conservative farmers eke a miserable living out of flower-pot sized paddy fields, and rich consumers are only too happy to purchase their unique semivegetarian diet at excess prices for the sake of food security and for sponsoring their beloved needy country folk.

Countries with an agro-food exporting interest to Japan hence face two tactical negotiation options:

1. *The tough and consequently politicized approach*: to threaten with retaliation if certain well-defined import barriers are not dismantled within a given period, and to have one's top political leaders hammer home the message and the threat both to the Japanese and to the domestic public.
2. *The soft and bureaucratic approach*: to attempt to sell sectoral liberalization measures to the Japanese by pleading with common sense and technical detail. Instead of threats only vague warnings are sounded, rhetoric is kept in check, and the political leadership is only routinely involved.

The first approach – obviously with some, though equally limited, success pursued by the US – is a high-risk strategy, which entails the possibility of a political backlash, as such politicized demands antagonize some of the LDP's most faithful voters. For obvious reasons, the LDP's continued rule is dear to the US administration, which would abhor to see the quarrelsome and unpredictable opposition parties, decrying the US import demands as 'economic invasion of Japan',[56] taking over the country. Equally, too harsh public criticism of Japan could fuel US domestic protectionist pressure (disguised as dubious 'reciprocity' legislation) beyond control.

The second approach with less obvious success, but with certainly reduced political risks and costs, is pursued by the EC, Australia, New Zealand, Canada, ASEAN and other agricultural exporters. This choice may be conscious in order to contain the temperature of world trade disputes – dominated by the saga of US–EC farm trade warfare – or in the knowledge of one's own protectionist sinning, or due to disagreements over a negotiating strategy, or simply for the lack of stick as potential bargaining leverage.

To Keidanren, and the other economic organizations dominated by Japan's export industries, to the more 'international' ministries – MFA, MITI, the EPA and to the major dailies, the risks and costs of continued stalling on agro-food access requests have become more aware since 1980. It is probably due to the US bargaining stands that 'zaikai' now has come out in active support of a gradual liberalization programme and uses its considerable political muscle for its implementation. On one such item Keidanren proudly reported:[57]

Camomile tea is a herbal preparation made from the camomile plant. Through it is popular in Europe, it could not be sold in Japan without special permission because it was classified as a drug under the Pharmaceutical Affairs Law. In response to submissions from Keidanren, the Ministry of Health and Welfare carried out safety studies and subsequently agreed to treat the product as a food item beginning from April 1, 1983. The ministry stipulated only that the tea should not be sold in a way that might create the impression that it is a drug and that it should not be advertised as a medicine effective, for example, in curing colds or as a diaphoretic.

Behind the curtains, however, liberalization pressure on politically more sensitive issues can be expected. Fear of a resurge in protectionism as a threat to Japan's industrial exports, has led the more enlightened sections in the Japanese political establishment (which includes the economic ministries) to strongly support the new GATT Round, which is to include agricultural trade. The version of an 'internationalized' economy finally also moved the PM's Agricultural Policy Council in 1986 to recommend policy adjustments which by the mid-1990s should create a revitalized agro-food structure in Japan able to withstand international competition. In preparation, Japan's import quotas and variable levies should gradually be replaced by straight tariff protection,[58] which would permit to signal international market developments to domestic producers.

Though, to no one's surprise, current trade disputes have not improved perceptively, as the *ad hoc* and compartmentalized ways of bureaucratic politics continue to govern most such issues, a gradual reorientation in Japan's farm trade policies could now be hoped for.

With persistent global excess production, continued commodity price depressions, and resulting growing trade tensions, Japan – just at about the right time – could also signal to share her part of the burden of the needed international agricultural policy and production adjustment through reduced producer subsidization and more significant market access.

Notes

1. In variations these arguments are found in the following publications: Yukata Yoshioka (Chairman, Japan Intl. Agric. Council), 'Business before Politics', *Speaking of Japan*, no. 7, May 1986, pp. 22–6; Yoshio Okawara (Japanese Ambassador to the US), 'Japan's Farm Policy', *Speaking of Japan*', no. 5, Feb. 1984, pp. 7–10; Hidero Maki (Deputy

Dir. Gen. for Int. Aff., MAFF), 'On Japan–US Agricultural Relations' in JIAC (ed), *Views from Japan on Farm Trade Issues* (Tokyo 1985), pp. 1–5; Keiki Owada (President, Agric. Pol. Research Committee), 'Japan's Agriculture and US–Japan Agricultural Trade Issues', op. cit., pp. 5–9, Hiroya Sano (Dir. Gen., Econ. Aff. Bureau, MAFF) 'Towards a Mutual Solution of Japan US Farm Issues', op. cit., pp. 10–12; Yukata Yoshioka, Foreign Trade – Tool or Weapon?, op. cit., pp. 15–19; Iwao Taki (Insp. Gen., Japan Consumer Information Centre), 'What Agriculture Means to the Japanese', op. cit., pp. 19–22; Yasuji Ota (President, Japan Meat Info. Center) 'Perspectives on the Japanese Beef Market', op. cit., pp. 22–6; Ichiro Nakagawa (then Min. of Agric.) and Susumu Yamaji, 'Foreign Expectations of Japan's Agriculture Are too High', *Look Japan*, 10 Mar. 1978, pp. 1–4: Nobuo Imamura (Dir. Gen. Econ. Aff. Bureau, MAFF), 'Japan's Food, Agriculture and Trade', op. cit., pp. 3–4; Eichi Nakao (Chairman, Diet Agric. Forestry and Fishery Committee), 'Japan–US Trade and Japan's Agriculture', op. cit., p. 5; Saburo Fuyita (President, Zenchu) and Osamu Morimoto (President, Norinchunkin Bank) 'Better Understanding of Japan's Agriculture Needed for Trade Negotiations', op. cit., pp. 6–11; Gebhard Hielscher and Yutaka Yoshioka, 'Ministry Defends Present Trade Policy', op. cit., pp. 8–9.
2. Iwao Yamajuchi (Zenchu Senior Executive Director), 'Establishing New Rules on Agricultural Trade' in Zenchu (ed.), *Position of the Japanese Farmers on Farm Trade Issues* (Tokyo, 1984) p. 25.
3. H. Maki, op. cit., p. 4; Y. Okawara, op. cit., p. 7.
4. A first indication of this policy shift was given by Y. Yoshioka, op. cit., (1983) p. 18. For details see Agric. Policy Council, *Basic Directions of Agricultural Policies towards the 21st Century* (Tokyo, Nov. 1986).
5. Adapted from MAFF, *Japan's Market for Agricultural Products* (Feb. 1986) p. 4.
6. Adapted from JETRO, *Japan's Agricultural and Imports of Agricultural Products* AG-9 (Tokyo, 1982) pp. 7/8; and: *Focus Japan*, Jan 1984, JS-A.
7. UNSO Contrade.
8. Jetro, 1982, op. cit., p. 11
9. MAFF, 'Japan's Market', op. cit., 1986, p. 6
10. *Japon Economie*, no. 174, July 1984, p. 8
11. John R. Block, 'An Agricultural Alliance', *Speaking of Japan*, no. 5, Aug. 1984, p. 1
12. Earl L. Butz, 'Trouble Down on "Japan's Farm"', *Speaking of Japan*, no. 6, Jan. 1986, p. 21.
13. Hideo Sato and Timothy J. Curran, 'Agricultural Trade: the Case of Beef and Citrus' in I. M. Dester and H. Sato (eds), *Coping with US–Japanese Economic Conflicts* (Lexington, Mass.: Lexington Books, 1982) 121–83.
14. Murray Sayle, 'Resisting the Japanese Invasion', *New Statesman*, no. 96, 1978, pp. 207–9.
15. MAFF, 'Agriculture in Japan', *Japan's Agricultural Review*, no. 10, Mar. 1984. p. 21.

16. *Frankfurter Allgemeine Zeitung*, 13 Nov., 82
17. *Sentaku*, Mar. 1982.
18. Tsugio Ibayashi, 'Domestic Adjustment for Japanese Agriculture', *KKC Brief* no. 19, May 1984.
19. *The Oriental Economist*, June 1984.
20. *Asahi Evening News*, 5 Jan. 1987.
21. David R. Tallent, 'Japan's Trade Barriers Pose Problems for U.S. Citrus Exporters', *Foreign Agriculture*, Oct. 1983, p. 21.
22. Yukata Yoshioka, 'Domestic Scope for Agricultural Issues', *Look Japan*, 10 July 84.
23. *Financial Times*, 20 Sept. 85.
24. *Japan Agrinfo Newsletter*, no. 4, Nov. 1986, p. 4.
25. *Financial Times*, 12 Sept. 86 and 23 Oct. 86
26. *Nihon Keizai Shimbun*, 15 Sept. 86
27. *Financial Times*, 5 Dec. 85 and 23 Dec. 85
28. Block, op. cit., p. 2.
29. Albrecht Rothacher, *Economic Diplomacy between the European Community and Japan 1959–1981* (Aldershot, Hants: Gower, 1983) pp. 103 and 147.
30. Ibid., pp. 219, 228, 232.
31. Ibid., p. 235.
32. Willy de Clercq (EC Commission Extl. Aff. Commissioner), quoted in the *Financial Times*, 27 Nov. 86.
33. *Agence Europe*, 19 July 86.
34. PA Consulting Service, *EC Wines and Liquor Study*, vol. I, Tokyo, 1985, pp. 23 and 50; European Business Council, *The Japanese Whisky Market*, Tokyo 1985, Section 4.5.
35. *The Economist*, 25 Oct. 86.
36. *Financial Times*, 30 Dec. 86.
37. *Financial Times*, 4 Dec. 86 and 8 Dec. 86.
38. For a revealing insight into this opposition, see the interview with Keizo Saji (President of Suntory) in *Economisto* (Tokyo), 22 Feb. 1977.
39. Community Statement, *Panel EC–Japan* (Wine and Spirits) 26 Nov. 86; *Kyodo News Service*, 4 Feb. 1987.
40. *Japan Times*, 25 Dec. 1986.
41. *Financial Times*, 28 Jan. 86.
42. *Kyodo News Service*, 17 May 85.
43. *Agra Europe*, 21 June 85, *The Age*, 16 May 86.
44. *Financial Times*, 26 Oct. 84.
45. *Financial Times*, 24 June 84.
46. *Japan Agrinfo Newsletter*, no. 4, Aug. 1986, p. 6; *Financial Times*, 10 July 1986 and 30 July 1986.
47. Agric. Policy Council, *Basic Direction Of Agricultural Policies Towards the 21st Century* (Tokyo, Nov. 1986) p. 19.
48. MAFF, 'Japan's Overseas Agricultural Cooperation', *Japan's Agricultural Review*, no. 12, 1985, p. 11.
49. Ibid., pp. 25–36
50. *Agra Europe*, 15 Nov. 85.
51. *News and Views from Japan*, Brussels, 23 Dec. 85

52. *Economist*, 13 Apr. 85
53. For the Japanese position see Japan Whaling Association,*Whaling: Questions and Answers* (Tokyo, 1983); C. W. Nicol, 'The Whaling Controversy', *Look Japan*, 10 Oct. 1982; Kunio Yonezawa (counsellor to the Japan Fisheries Association), 'Japan: a Whaling Nation', *Speaking of Japan*, Dec. 1981, pp. 10–11.
54. Shuji Kori, Fisheries, *Japan Economic Almanach (1986) p. 69; Süddeutsche Zeitung*, 29 Oct. 86.
55. *Financial Times*, 31 July 85.
56. Hemmi, Kenzo. in Castle/Hemmi (eds), op. cit., p. 244.
57. 'Keidanren Proposals for Widening Market Access Implemented', *KKC Brief*, no. 35, Sept. 1986.
58. Agricultural Policy Council, op. cit., 1986, p. 16.

10 The Future of Japan's Agro-Food Sector

This concluding chapter will summarize the major challenges facing the farm sector and its associated upstream and downstream industries: structural shifts, the problems of demography, the challenges arising from biotechnology, environmental concerns, internationalization, and changes in the political economy equation.

Excess protection for Japan's agriculture has affected profoundly the working of the economic and political variables of the sector. It appears that the very 'success' of these policies may finally prove to trigger their own demise. In early 1987 it was apparent that the movement for agricultural policy reform was finally gaining momentum worldwide. In LDCs awareness grows to stop the discrimination of the sector. In the countries under Communist party rule bureaucratic stifling is reduced and market elements reintroduced; and in the OECD world, the beginning new Uruguay GATT Round promises to reduce direct and indirect subsidization of agriculture in long negotiations. The result of these reforms could be a world agriculture more in line with economic logic: with welfare gains to all concerned. Japan's experience of excessive protection helpfully teaches a lesson to those who, particularly on the old Continent, are reluctant to join the needed internationally coordinated adjustment effort: the inevitable consequences and monstrous costs of isolating a key economic sector, of 'freezing' structures and of lavishing open-ended (consumer paid) subsidy rents on it. If Europe has a lesson to learn from Japan with reference to a low-budget government, efficient industrial R&D, dynamic international marketing, positive labour relations, and a future oriented outlook of society at large, Japan's agricultural policy offers equally strong lessons of pitfalls to be avoided.

STRUCTURAL CHANGES

The consequences of the development of 'prospering farmers' with 'ruined farms' are bound to become more acute. Too many operators enjoying strong price and tax incentives to stay in the sector, continue to squeeze out entrepreneurial professional talent willing but unable

185

to make a full-time living off the land. As old-timers stay and retired people move in, by 1990 50% of all male farmers will be 60 and above. By 2000 this percentage will have increased to 60% nation-wide, in some regions exceeding 70%.[1] Entire villages will be without 'youngsters' below 60.

According to an extrapolation made by the National Land Agency, Japan's farm population will shrink from 6.9 m (1980) to 3.4 m (2000), and further to 840 000 by 2025.[2]

It is evident that socially this tendency implies the end of rural society, in which specific rural norms rule based on the needs for the survival of farm households. Rural social life gradually vanishes: with its customs forgotten, youth and women's associations defunct, fire brigades starved of members, women disliking hard and dirty farm work, most farms lacking a successor, relationships to the land turning utilitarian (as it is no longer essential to family survival), the hamlets having lost all administrative, economic and finally most social functions. Metropolitan Japanese norms have conquered the land with their primordial importance placed on proper schooling and salaried white-collar work. Villages will face either abandonment or suburbanization.

To the economic, ideological, social and demographic erosion of the farming community, eventually and inevitably their political demise will follow.

This development was perfectly foreseeable. Already Dore in 1963 observed[3]

> There is no doubt what the ministry of agriculture wants. An increasing proportion of part-time farmers is a messy solution, implying – and the point is made by charts in its reports showing the 'feminization and gerontization of the farm labor force' – that agriculture is left with the least active and least enterprising work-ers. Weekend and womenfolk farmers do not have their heart in farming and are loath to invest money in it. Only the full-time operators of large holdings can begin to reap economies of scale and to afford the experiments and the risk-taking which alone can make agriculture a viable industry.'

In the long run, the adverse demographic structure may be a boon. 840 000 farmers operating on Japan's 5.4 m ha farmland, with a 6.4 ha average operation would perhaps provide (under the proviso of redressed excess protection) a healthy competitive structure of about 150 000 full-time crop farmers running 30 ha farms with the rest pursuing part-time or speciality livestock or greenhouse operations. Per hamlet this would amount to 2 or 3 full-time farmers at most. Obviously expansion of scale operations would only imply a gradual transfer of land titles, as already now a wide variety of tenant and contract labour schemes apply and are likely to spread.

Hayami found that economies of scale effects have been increasing.[4] Average costs in rice production had widened from 30% (1970) to 50% (1980) between small (below 0.3 ha) and large (above 3.0 ha) farms, with progressively reduced costs for labour and machinery. According to our own calculation (Tables 5.1 and 5.2) not surprisingly the rice biased particularities of Japan's price policies make crop production more profitable a pursuit than livestock production. Gross profits (i.e. returns net of cash outlays) for crops varied between 85% and 45%, those for livestock between 54% and 7%. Net profits (gross profits minus opportunity costs for capital and land) on farm product sales confirm this observation which motivates part-timers to stick to their additional activities in the paddies as long as possible. Even Zenchu, champion of part-timers, had to acknowledge that demography and low land mobility began to erode Japan's food supply capacity.[5] Sakaki admits 'It is hopelessly difficult to solve problems now facing Japan's agriculture by simply following the conventional policy line'[6] and proposes new variety introductions, systematic cost cutting and collective utilization of farmland for scale operations. This would indicate a direct farming role for Nokyo, which could thus expand further its current frequently monopsonic contract farming role in many products. Should the Nokyo system be able to overcome its management problems and possible cuts in the subsidy flow and statutory privilegization, a transformation into an agro-business and services Keiretsu appears possible, focusing on both food production/processing/marketing and on a full range of services for the rural prefectures (integrating and expanding current roles in banking, insurance, fuel trading, real estate development, education and travel) largely for the non-farm population.

The Agricultural Policy Council in its recommendations for policy reform (November 1986) emphasizes the strengthening of individual farms with, aiming at a competitive structure of 12/24 ha medium-sized and 30/45 ha large-sized farms.[7]

Even taking into account the continued existence of farmers and farming by retired people for which public subsidization is likely to be cut, those figures imply a drastic reduction in farm numbers and labour used in agriculture.

Those recommendations, however, are not so innovative as they may seem. The Council in 1982 already, in line with MAFF's traditional orientation, had asked for structural policies aiming at improved productivity through reduced producer prices in the long run, and a more viable rural society.[8] Since then little policy change has been perceptible.

Related to the structural transformation of Japan's agriculture and countryside are two 'new' challenges: biotechnology and environmental protection.

ENVIRONMENT

Agriculture is both a culprit and a victim of pollution. Japan's agriculture still suffers from irrigation water for paddies polluted in earlier mining, industrial or household use (the latter particularly in suburban areas).[9] Damage to crops is also done through heavy metal residues stemming from air and water pollution. The sorry condition of Japan's rivers and coastal production sites contributed a serious environmental deterioration of coastal fishing grounds.[10]

An OECD Report already in 1974 identified 3 sources of agricultural pollution in Japan:[11]

1. Pesticide residues – such as DDT and BHC (their use was prohibited in 1971) – which had polluted the soil and through milk, vegetables and fruit entered the food chain.
2. Fertilizer application in the paddies, however, is not considered by MAFF as contributing to soil pollution, perhaps because drainage flushes the chemicals out into the sea.
3. Intensive livestock holdings, like elsewhere, produce excess manure whose disposal risks water and soil pollution. Particularly in urban areas, smell can be a considerable nuisance.

The Forestry Agency's timber factory approach destroying natural forests and landscapes and transforming them into terraced forest monocultures has more recently come under public criticism.[12]

It is evident that Japan's agriculture particularly with its paddy orientation performs an important function for national water and soil management and in maintaining a varied landscape. As in Japan a health-food boom is equally in fashion, there should be economic incentives for farmers to move to a more ecological and extensive mode of production. Excess protection has so far largely prevented these market signals offering premiums for ecological quality to reach producers, for which current support policies continue to encourage high-cost intensive production.

BIOTECHNOLOGY

Biotechnology refers to a variety of new (and not so new) processes which have in common that they are based on biological and biochemical reactions and deal with living organisms. Their importance to the agro-food sector which deals with the same kind of raw materials and processing technology is evident. In Japan, often seen as the second innovative revolution after electronics, total biotechnology sales by the year 2000 are forecasted to multiply by 23 times their current levels, to reach totals between Y3–4 trillion and Y5.7 trillion in Japan alone,[13] 35% to 50% of it in the pharmaceuticals' sector (for insulin, interferon, growth hormones, etc.). In the food industry, fermentation in bioreactors will create new products – often with more healthy propensities – substituting for traditional dairy and meat products (beyond the traditional margarine and soy milk). Processing will be innovated, and shelf-life prolonged while making chemical additives largely redundant.

In agriculture, both for crop and livestock farming tremendous productivity gains are imminent. In livestock, embryo transfers will help to increase the quality of a national herd much faster than through artificial insemination alone. New feeds, such as single cell proteins through cell mass cultivation will be created.

Genetic engineering now already creates new hybrids which are more productive and/or more resistant to pests, diseases or climatic hardships. Seeds as genetic pools have already acquired a strategic value. MAFF whose control of rice, grain and soy seed development has stifled the development of new seeds, is now worried about the US MNCs edge in grain seeds, such as corn. With bureaucratic hindrances (eager not to increase rice productivity), and a plant genetic pool of only 34 000 species, Japan's private sector so far was only able to achieve a competitive edge in cabbage and broccoli seeds.[14]

Currently about 150 companies in sectors such as chemicals, food and drinks, which otherwise face fairly stable growth prospects, engage in biotechnology research, expecting that successful R&D may create shifts in the competitive edge in their respective oligopolist subsectors.

Public support and subsidies are abundant. They are dispensed from MITI's Bioindustry Office, the Science and Technology Agency, the Ministry of Education, Keidanren's Life Science Committee, and the National Land Agency for its Regional Technopolis plan.[15]

A wide subsidy and R&D race is on between Europe, the US and Japan. The scope for innovation is truly impressive. Currently 90% of human food is derived from 30 cultures alone. But some 10 m kinds of plants and animals are known to live on this earth. Their genetic resources offer fascinating (and perhaps on occasion frightful) possibilities for new breeds and hybrids and for agricultural productivity growth. However, only an entrepreneurial, viable agricultural sector will be able to absorb and utilize adequately the potential offered by biotechnology.

INDUSTRY CHANGES

High margins supported by excess protection, complex distribution routes and government intervention all along the food chain, create strong incentives for short-cuts through vertical integration. This takes the form of both forward integration (by feed suppliers) and backward integration (by meat processors and supermarket chains) into the livestock sector. The agro-food business which so far was not a typical component of the Keiretsu's core business (apart from some, however, more peripheral import food processing, such as grain milling, beer brewing, sugar refining and feed compounding), as concentration proceeds, now appears to become more integrated into the Keiretsu conglomerates, on which they rely for more efficient overseas sourcing, and increasingly also for export marketing and biotechnology R&D financing needs. However, full vertical sectoral integration under Keiretsu auspices is still fairly distant. Costs and legal barriers prohibit any significant agro-business penetration into crop production (one frequent alternative being contract farming, particularly in fruit and vegetables, but also the intensive livestock subsector).

The Keiretsu presence is strong in sectors in which their sogo shosha handle bulk imports and affiliate and/or subsidiary companies manage the subsequent processing, subcontracting and marketing. Pork and chicken feed compounding and grain milling are typical examples for possible full vertical integration. Zenno with its own direct dairy processing and marketing facilities and its affiliated Snow Brand Milk Products attempts a similar integration in dairy and meat production, as well as direct processing/marketing in the fruit and vegetable sectors.

Pressure for expanded scale and better capitalized operations in the food processing sector (i.e. also for horizontal growth), derives from related challenges:

1. the gradual rationalization of the distribution sector (with increased bargaining power on the part of the larger, fast growing operators);
2. the costly effects of non-price competition (advertising expenditure, financing and pampering of distribution channels, new product development and promotion);
3. the double challenge of 'internationalization': the advent of often superior (largely Anglo-American) world food MNCs, and the growing awareness to turn to overseas marketing and processing faced with only moderate growth prospects at best and high raw material costs in the home market; and
4. finally the biotechnology challenge with its variety of new products and processes in the offing, requiring high, frequently uncertain and long-term R&D outlays.

Small businesses, the second tier of Japan's agro-food sector, will survive only due to this (historically proven) adaptability to service special needs and demands faster and more flexibly: to produce traditional and quality products (e.g. in confectionery and sake brewing) and special services (in restaurants and retailing) for which affluent consumers are willing to pay premiums. The quality criterion also applies to small-scale primary producers – i.e., farmers – who want to guard their independence: ecological production, special qualities and products (not standardized run-of-the-mill production covered by stabilization price bands and government intervention) will allow for better prices and a stronger sales position.

Though Japan's food and drinks industries – to the extent that they are not yet already locked into cartellized oligopolies (as in grain milling and sugar refining) – gradually move towards concentration, they remain small by world standards with still only an embryonic international marketing presence on aggregate. This also applies to

Suntory, though today the world's largest whisky blender. Kikkoman and Ajinomoto, which succeeded in making soy sauce and monosodium glutamate respectively international seasonings, are rare exceptions. The current worldwide health food boom occurs unexploited by Japanese food processors.

Burdened with excessive raw material costs, sheltered consequently from import competition, the processors of the primary processing stage to a large extent still appear content with earning government-facilitated low-effort oligopoly rents. Their excess costs and margins are often transmitted to either captive small secondary processors (for which a fragmentized distribution sector permits to pass on costs and margins) or to large oligopolies – enjoying near-monopolies in some regional or product segments – whose market power facilitates the same effect. The laws of fierce non-price competition also make for high mark-ups. In dairy products administered prices rule, as do intervention purchases propping up meat prices. Tobacco farming, processing, and distribution finally is entirely regulated.

Evidently the food industry's structural set-up, for the most based on permanent government intervention to stifle competition – from primary production/importation to retail distribution – makes for a costly, inefficient and uncompetitive processing sector.

The agricultural import supplying industries appears as similarly harmed by official support policies.

Farm machinery producers still suffer from the overcapacities created during the policy-induced machinery boom of 1972–76. Zenno, due to the Nokyo's semi-statutory privileges, can compete under unequal conditions – allowing for non-competitive pricing and for captive markets (part-timers) – thus forcing independent feed compounders and agro-chemicals producers either to affiliate with the sogo shosha or with Zenno proper. Again competition appears less price based, but to be maximizing efforts to captivate the clientele. As a result, more and more farmers end up as high cost contract operators, whose output is exclusively purchased by the input producers.

THE CONSUMER ECONOMY

The multi-layered wholesale system with its parcellized retail outlets – similar to the secondary tier of the food industry and the eating out sector – put in Marxist terms, represents a high industrial reserve army. The levels of overstaffing of under-utilized, low-skilled manpower can safely be considered as a large private funded, publicly sheltered employment programme. Yet, as mentioned, in spite of all regulatory discouragement, high margins once again offer incentives for entrepreneurial short cuts and rationalization. Producers move into wholesaling operations (thus putting pressure on retailers) while large retailers expand their operations (thus being able to squeeze processors and producers). Franchising systems and electronic shopping are fast to innovate time-dishonoured trade habits. International chains and their concepts may finally move in.

The same applies to the eating out sector, where US chains' success in low-market fast food has triggered Japanese responses in the middle-market family restaurant sector. Traditional family-managed restaurants will survive, but turn more and more to speciality and up-market services. There would also be an attractive and growing international market to Japanese restaurant chains and operations offering Japanese cuisine abroad.

Japanese consumers can be counted on to remain demanding and health conscious clients. Though the consumption of over-priced rice will decline, with livestock products growing in demand, a proper carbohydrate/fat/protein balance in a varied, fresh food based diet will maintain fairly stable caloric average intakes. Yet, an ever more affluent consumer economy with more women working, having less time available with higher disposable incomes, will increase the demand for more processed convenience foods and eating out facilities. But as weekend leisure time expands, there will also be a growing market for gourmet cooking and its sophisticated requests.

INTERNATIONAL RELATIONS

Japan with her 120 m prosperous consumers and elavated food price levels constitutes an impressive lure to agricultural exporters suffering from depressed world prices and the contraction of commercial demand elsewhere. Obviously a formidable array of protectionist devices prevents most of them taking advantage of this. Depending on bargaining power, the choice between negotiating strategies is made among Japan's external partners: the US, for domestic purposes largely, has adopted a fairly heavy handed, highly visible approach demanding the liberalization of key agricultural markets:

beef and oranges having gained most notoriety (with 'Phase VI' just in the offing). Whaling had been a similarly emotive issue. So far the US's high risk and politicized approach – threatening with straight retaliation especially on Japan's industrial exports – has shown more visible success than the more subtle soft spoken and bureaucratic approach pursued by the European Community, Australia, Canada and the ASEAN nations. Japan, with agricultural imports in volume increasing at the rate of 5% p.a., in strategic terms fights a continuous rearguard action to maintain its import protection as long as possible. Delaying tactics then appear as a successful means, but in the long run continuous 'too little, too late' concessions erode her partners' patience and waste Japan's political and bargaining capital acquired when eventually giving in.

These delayed responses are a result of the veto position vested interests enjoy in Japan's corporatist decision-making. The LDP's factious structure – supported by the electoral system the set-up of clientele ministries and a national tradition of consensus decisions, easily permits local parochial interests to be defined – for some time at least – as the national interest.

Decades of systematic sheltering have bred a considerable infrastructure of parasitic protection rent recipients in significant segments of the agro-food sector. They range from vested bureaucratic interests in some MAFF bureaux, its agencies, to farm politicians, Nokyo officials, meat processors, privileged traders, and finally 5 m part-time farmers and farm-land owners owing capitalized subsidies and lucrative side incomes to the system. Liberalization is not facilitated by the fact that most subsectors of Japan's agriculture, as the result of protection, is starved of entrepreneurial talent and even the more modern concentrated productions (poultry, pork, dairy, vegetables) appear still too cost intensive to forego all protection (though tariff protection may suffice). Since the 1960s Japan has only liberalized, once her ministries were convinced that the industry in question was sufficiently competitive to withstand the foreign onslaught.

With political and economic costs of border protection increasing, demands for reform on the part of the export industries, the business federations (Zaikai), the economic ministries, the media, and gradually also from politicians representing urban constituencies have intensified. The beginning new Uruguay GATT Round as indicated in its Punta del Este opening declaration of September 1986 will focus amongst others on the reduction of 'direct and indirect subsidization' of agriculture. Japan will be asked to shoulder her part of the burden in the needed international adjustment efforts to solve the OECD world's agricultural surplus crisis. Reduced producer prices and enhanced import access will be inevitable.

FOOD SECURITY

Food Security is a red herring in Japan's protectionist rhetoric. Three scenarios are usually quoted: global crop failures, a world war, civic disorders or transportation strikes blocking maritime food shipments to Japan, or the beginning of a Malthusian food crisis.[16] In the public debate food security is often equated with current self sufficiency levels. High domestic production may be helpful in the case of global crop shortfalls – leaving aside Japan's feed import dependency – but they are fairly useless in the more serious case of short-term military aggression threatening food supplies both domestic and imported.

UNCTAD more sensibly has differentiated three types of stock-holdings:[17]

1. strategic reserves: 'intended for use in national emergencies resulting from war or blocked trade routes';
2. economic reserves: 'intended to cushion the impact of less serious supply disturbances – i.e. limited to one or a few commodities', or for the event when prices rise abnormally high; and
3. surplus inventories: products in excess of demand, stored by governments to maintain minimum prices.

Strategic reserves would probably need to be integrated into a concept of civil defence, with decentralized emergency stocks, possibly held in households' storage or in air raid shelters. These would contain essential provisions for a limited period of hostilities. Essentially modern civil defence – for which Japan is completely unprepared – has nothing to do with agricultural policies: to wait for harvesting time or to plough up golf courses for potato crops would certainly be too late.

Keeping economic reserves are an alternative to paying scarcity prices which occur worldwide for some commodities (such as sugar) every 7 or so years. The reserves certainly are, however, the more expensive option. As aggregate crop levels in most temperate countries, such as Japan, vary surprisingly little from a good year to a bad year – with about 10% fluctuation margins for the standard commodi-

Table 10.1 Japanese Grain LTAs (1986)[19]

Commodity	Quantity (m tonne)	Supplier country
Wheat	1.2	Canada
Wheat	0.9	Australia
Coarse grains	2.4	China

ties, the issue is not one of starvation in industrial countries, but one of prices. Still, the Food Agency, in addition to normal commercial stock levels, keeps wheat and feed grain for about 2–3 months of national consumption in store.

Japan has also concluded a series of long-term grain supply agreements (Table 10.1).

In order to redress the political fall-out of their soy embargo of 1973, the US in 1975 concluded the Abe-Butz agreement, guaranteeing a minimum supply of various grains and soy beans. Japan, however, faced with the prospect of ample supplies decided not to renew the agreement in 1978.

To prevent Malthus's predictions becoming reality effective agricultural development and birth control programmes are needed in LDCs. Particularly South Asian and Latin American nations have shown significant progress in both respects, thus increasing the likelihood of proving Malthus wrong.

In short, food security is not an argument for agricultural protection but for an efficient and competitive farm sector, the existence of which, as this study attempts to prove, is put into jeopardy by protection reaching excess levels.

THE POLITICAL ECONOMY SHIFT

The writing is on the wall for Japan's agricultural protection. Prime Minister Nakasone in January 1987 made agricultural policy reform one of his priorities.[20] This could be an indication for a gradual realignment in Japanese politics. Instead of courting the diminishing rural vote, Japan's parties might begin to fight over the huge and growing urban middle classes. The Socialists following their 1986 Diet election defeat already indicated their policy reorientation. In May 1986, the Diet decided to add eight seats to urban constituencies, and to remove seven seats from rural districts. It is likely that further corrections of the rural/urban bias in Diet seat allocations will accelerate the trend.

In November 1986 the authoritative Agricultural Policy Council had finalized its recommendations demanding more restrictive price policies, structural policies and a revised paddy conversion programme to create a competitive structure of large (30–45 ha) and medium-sized (12–24 ha) farms by 1995.[21]

The Nokyo system, the standard bearer of agricultural protection, for the first time ever has come under official scrutiny. The Prime Minister's Administrative Management Office began an inquiry into its management practices, reflecting increased public criticism of this privileged rural agent.[22]

Since the 1950s Nokyo and its activists had become closely integrated into the LDPs' factional and personalized power structure. Since then a mutually beneficial, almost symbiotic coalition relationship has developed. Rural votes and organization were reliably traded for clientele-oriented price policies and increased statutory and semi-statutory cooperative functions.

Zenno became the Food Agency's exclusive rice collector; as 'producer organization' it receives storage subsidies for beef, pork, silk and other 'stabilized' products. Its local Nokyos control all deliveries made to the dairies. Public deficiency payments and production control subsidies are made to Nokyo chapters for processing milk, soy, rape and oranges, which after deducting their commissions, transmit the remainder to their members. The LIPC benefits Zenno through lucrative import beef allocations at bargain prices, award storage subsidies and project grants for cooperative livestock schemes. Zenno also runs exclusively the government's extension services and since 1986 has been charged to administer the paddy conversion programme locally.

Japan's growing budget deficit first put pressures on Nokyo's appetite for subsidies. Since 1983 the MAFF budget was gradually reduced – even in real terms, though some of the apparent reductions were recovered in subaccounts through increased import levies. In rice price setting the transfer burden was equally shifted from the taxpayer to the consumer, and made less visible in the process.

While farmers grew richer – they are significant net creditors in Japan's financial system – the structural consequences of subsidy-based wealth became all too evident. Also stimulated by international pressure, the urban majority awoke – led by Keidanren, followed by the economic ministries (MITI, MOF, the EPA), the MFA, the media, the industrial unions (Domei) and reform minded LDP politicians of the Sogo Noseiha group – linked to MAFF which has also favoured structural policies for sometime. The cosy LDP/Nokyo fraternity is now in the process of gradual erosion. Though policy reform can safely be expected to be incrementalist and move only slowly towards the smallest common denominator, both the LDP and Nokyo will need to design their post-protectionist political and economic future. For the LDP the imperatives of the urban vote will require agricultural liberalization and food industry deregulation; for Nokyo the future points to a painful awakening to the competitive realities of agro-business and the service industries. As such, modernized mutual interests do not need to become antagonist.

THE EFFECTS OF EXCESS PROTECTION

Japan drew up her support policies in an *ad hoc* and incrementalist manner, with a set of different instruments applying to each commodity, with alterations and complications ever since the original mechanisms were designed 30–40 years ago. Table 10.2 gives an overview of the basic policy instruments employed. The mix of price support cum production controls (voluntary and/or compulsory) cum state trading in their combination already indicates a strong protectionist orientation. High price support for abundant crops also then stimulates production-oriented deficiency payments (as opposed to deficiency supplementary income payments) for alternative crops (wheat, soy beans, etc.) to be augmented either directly or through diversion premiums. The deficiency payment instrument is then little else than price support paid from the budget. Several factors coincided in Japan's post-war development to create what was to become an excess protectionist system in the late 1970s to early 1980s.

Most importantly, the land reform of 1946 had created a mass of small owner farmers who had abandoned their left-wing tenant movement and turned into more or less solid LDP Jiban members, their Nokyo run by LDP-affiliated (Koenkai) local chieftains. But their farms – lightly assisted and left behind in Japan's rapid industrial growth after 1955 – were too small-scale and undercapitalized to offer any prospect of prosperity in remaining on farm without supplementary income from seasonal or part-time off-farm labour.

Japan's political establishment in this high growth period faced the

Table 10.2 Support policies pursued

Policy type	Products covered	Structural effect	Income effect	Budget costs	Consumer costs	Demand effect	Output effect
Price Support	Rice, beef, pork, sugar, starch, silk, tobacco, dairy products	stabilizing (capitalization in land value)	largest benefits to large farms	low	high	reduction	increase
Deficiency payments (production-oriented)	Processing milk, soy, rape, veal, eggs, veg., fruits for processing	could allow for adjustment	permits targeting	high	low	increase	reduction
Production limitation	Rice, mikan oranges, eggs, pork, poultry, milk, tobacco	slowed adjustment	stabilizing (+ capitalization of quota value)	neutral	high	–	freeze
State trading	Rice, wheat, barley, beef, tobacco	stability	–	revenue raised	high	reduction	–

alternative of either forcing Japan's agriculture to adjust (thus adding to the political unrest and social turmoil of the early 1960s and alienating the LDP's staunchest supporters) or to attempt to preserve rural structures by doling out cash in the politically least painful way (i.e. introducing automatically indexed price guarantees to be paid by consumers). In 1961, when the Agricultural Basic Law was drawn up the policy-makers' choice was clear.

The protectionist choice was facilitated by structural factors: rapid economic growth and concomitant rising disposable incomes reduced the Engel's coefficient, consumers' relative food expenditure. It had also reduced the relative and absolute size of the agricultural sector to be supported while its political muscle was maintained. Ideological factors played their role: remnants of Nohonshugi, the widespread notion that farming – especially rice growing – was a particularly support-worthy occupation, related to traditional values, the beauty of Japan's landscape, one's ancestors' origins and their way of life. The notion of food security, however vaguely defined, helped the public impression that more national food production was better than less. The ill-effects of agricultural protection were less visible at the time as these policies still appeared to fit Japan's yet protectionist industrial policies. Agricultural protection – freezing obsolete production structures – in reality was a far cry from the ruthless domestic competition and systematic subsequent liberalization practised in industry.

The set up of agricultural protection – as Figure 10.1 illustrates – spreading from rice price support systematically eliminated and distorted market signals which led to decade-long resource misallocations, until the entire sector found itself thoroughly mis-structured and drained of most entrepreneurial talent. It is only very recently that Japan's urban majority noticed that their food bill is the costly substitute for a rural pension scheme. Excess costs which have been created have maintained and further stimulated competition stifling government intervention all along the downstream chain. The loss of dynamism and price competitiveness created networks of rent-pocketing profiteers and unproductive bureaucracies. The Nokyo system alone counts 6000 full-time directors and 290 000 employees. MAFF has a staff of 73 000. Distortion was so systematic as to create a mutually reinforcing subsidy spiral (Figure 10.1), spreading protection horizontally – across commodities – and vertically in the processing sequence. Excess-Parkinson requires systematic control: further intervention in order to award margins in order to reduce

Figure 10.1   Causes and effects of excess protection

Policy measures	Effects
Land Reform of 1946 ⟶	Parcellized, uneconomic units
Indexation of rice support (1961) ⟶	Overproduction, reduced demand
Diversion programmes (1970), increase in other crop support ⟶	over production spreads (mikan, vegetables, tobacco, livestock products)
Extended production limitation programmes and subsidization ⟶	increased input costs to livestock sector
Compensatory subsidies and price support ⟶	increased costs to primary transformation sector
maintenance of production quotas (sugar, cereals), monopoly operations (rice, tobacco), import protection ⟶	increased costs for secondary transformation sector
Toleration of cartellized oligopolies, import protection ⟶	transmission of excess costs and margins to distribution sector
Local and national policies to limit retail and wholesale restructuring ⟶	consumers foot the bill

political costs and organized resistance to protectionist policies.

Milling and refining processing quotas, import licences, import beef allocations (even to consumer organizations) all create vested interests in the system. Corporatist decision-making has always been at the expense of the general public. But the welfare losses of agricultural protection are usually better hidden and argued than those for other subsidized and failed white elephants.

While Japanese consumers still spent 20% of their disposable income on food with little public complaint, it is the structural and the international costs that stimulate the current debate on policy revision. The structural effects – rural depopulation, less and less 'serious' part-timers, and more obvious Nokyo mismanagement – have equally reduced the political clout of the farm lobby. Yet the inevitable policy adjustment will be a hard, long and winding road, painful to both policy-makers and the farming community. There is an iron law of political economy which says: the higher the political rent, the tougher the lobby and the vested interests and their resistance to rent withdrawal.

Structural adjustment will take time for resource reallocation and partial withdrawal from the sector. Policy reform – in a continued consensual corporatist manner – will also be gradual at best: reducing price support from part-time crops, targeting direct income aids to genuine full-time farm professionals, introducing decent rural pensions, increasing farm land taxation, allowing full competition (including anti-cartel provisions) in all segments of downstream processing and distribution sectors, and replacing import quotas and licensing arrangements by import tariffs.

Excess protection might take decades to reverse. In Japan this could well last into the 21st century.

Notes

1. Sakaki, Haruo, (Zenchu Exec. Director) in *Zenchu News*, no. 12, Dec. 1982, p. 6. A report on the long-term prospects of Japan's Agriculture adopted by the Nokyo convention in Tokyo on 7 Jan. 1982.
2. *Japan Agrinfo Newsletter*, no.2, Aug. 1984.
3. R. P. Dore, 'Beyond the Land Reform: Japan's Agricultural Prospect' in J. Livingstone *et al.* (eds). *op. cit.*, vol. 2, p. 563.
4. Hayami, Yujiro, 'The Roots of Agricultural Protectionism' in Anderson and Hayami (eds), op. cit., p. 36.
5. Sakaki, op. cit., p. 00.
6. Sakaki, H. in *Zenchu News* no.14, 1983, p. 6.
7. Agricultural Policy Council, op. cit., 1986.
8. Agricultural Policy Council, op. cit., 1983.
9. *Zenchu News*, no. 22, Mar. 1986, p. 2.
10. Japan Fisheries Association, *Fisheries in Japan* (Tokyo, 1984) p. 16.
11. OECD, *Agricultural Policies in Japan* (Paris: OECD, 1974) p. 39.
12. *Time*, 24 Mar. 1986. For a description of the official approach, see: Forestry Agency, *Forestry in Japan* (Tokyo, undated), pp. 41–55.
13. The first estimate: *Focus Japan*, Feb. 1985, p. 6; the second estimate: *Japan Economic Journal*, 14 Oct. 86.

14. *Japan Economic Journal*, 8 Feb. 1986.
15. Neil W. Davis, 'Biotechnology', *The Oriental Economist*, Apr. 1985, p. 19.
16. Yujiro Hagami in *Toyo Keisai*, 8 Mar. 1980.
17. UNCTAD, *Report for the Committee on Commodities Relating to Disposals of Surpluses, Strategic Reserves or other Government-held Noncommercial Inventories of Primary Products* (July 1986).
18. Uchimura in *Toyo Keisai*, 8 Mar. 1980.
19. OECD, AGR/WPI (86) 14, pp. 16–17.
20. *Financial Times*, 26 Jan. 1987.
21. Agricultural Policy Council, *Basic Direction of Agricultural Policies towards the 21st Century* (Nov. 1986).
22. *Nihon Keizai Shimbun*, 28 Sept. 1986; *Japan Agrinfo Newsletter*, no. 4, Nov. 1986, p. 2.

Bibliography

Agricultural Policy Council, 'Basic Direction of Agricultural Policy in the 1980s', *Japan's Agricultural Review*, no. 3, 1980, pp. 12–16.

Agricultural Policy Council, 'On the Implementation of the "Basic Direction of Agricultural Policy in the 1980s"', *Japan Agricultural Review*, nos. 7 and 8, 1983, pp. 1–38.

Agricultural Policy Council, 'Basic Direction of Agricultural Policies towards the 21st Century, unpublished, Tokyo, Nov. 1986.

Agricultural Policy Research Committee, *Beef Situation in Japan* (Tokyo, 1984).

Anderson, Kym and Yujiro Hayami (eds), *The Political Economy of Agricultural Protection: East Asia in International Perspective* (Sidney: Allen & Unwin, 1986).

Aqua, Ronald, *Local Institutions and Rural Development in Japan* (Ithaca, NY: Cornell University Press, 1974).

Asi Market Research Inc. Market Studies, *Jams and Spreads*, *Dairy Products*, *Processed Meat* (Tokyo, 1979).

Bale, Malcolm and Bruce Greenshields, 'Japan's Agricultural Distortions and their Welfare Value', *American Journal of Agricultural Economics*, no. 60, 1978, pp. 59–64.

Beardsley, Richard K., John W. Hall and Robert E. Ward, *Village Japan* (University of Chicago Press, 1972).

Bernstein, Gail Lee, *Haruko's World: a Japanese Farm Woman and her Community* (Stanford University Press, 1983).

Block, John R., 'An Agricultural Alliance', *Speaking of Japan*, no. 5, 1984, pp. 1–3.

Bureau of Agricultural Economics, *Developments in the Japanese Beef Market*, Beef Research Report No. 17 (Canberra, undated).

Burton, Jack, 'Philip Morris – Puffing Away in Japan', *Journal of Japanese Industry and Trade*, no. 5, 1985, pp. 45–7.

Butz, Earl L., 'Trouble Down on "Japan's Farm"', *Speaking of Japan*, no. 6, 1986, pp. 21–5.

Campbell, John C., *Contemporary Japanese Budget Politics* (University of California Press, 1977).

Castle, Emory M. and Kenzo Hemmi (eds), *United States–Japanese Agricultural Relations* (Baltimore, Md.: Resources for the Future, 1982).

Central Union of Agricultural Cooperatives (Zenchu), *The Status Quo of Japanese Agriculture and Our Position on the Current Trade Issue* (Tokyo, 1983).

Central Union of Agricultural Cooperatives (Zenchu), *Agricultural Cooperative Movement in Japan* (Tokyo, 1984).

Central Union of Agricultural Cooperatives (Zenchu), *Position of Japanese Farmers on Farm Trade Issues* (Tokyo, 1984).

Coyle, William T., *Japan's Feed–Livestock Industry*, Foreign Agricultural

Economic Report, no. 177 (Washington, DC: USDA, 1983).

Curtis, Gerald L., *Election Campaigning, Japanese Style* (New York: Columbia University Press, 1971).

Davis, Neil W., 'Biotechnology: Future Growth Industry', *The Oriental Economist*, Apr. 1985, pp. 18–20.

Davis, William L., 'Japanese Market for U.S. Wine is Improving with Age', *Foreign Agriculture*, May 1985.

Dodwell Marketing Consultants, *Market Studies: Chocolate, Biscuits, Confectionery* (Tokyo, 1979).

Donnelly, Michael W., *Political Management of Japan's Rice Economy*, Ph. D. thesis, Columbia University, 1978.

Dore, Ronald P., *Land Reform in Japan* (Oxford University Press, 1959).

European Business Council, *The Japanese Whisky Market* (Tokyo, 1985).

European Business Council, *Free and Fair Trade in Wines and Spirits* (Tokyo, 1986).

Forestry Agency, *Forestry in Japan* (Tokyo, undated).

Francks, Penelope, *Technology and Agriculture in Pre-War Japan* (New Haven, Conn.:Yale University Press, 1984).

Fruin, W. Mark., *Kikkoman: Company, Clan, Community* (Boston, Mass.: Harvard University Press, 1984).

Fujita, Den, 'Golden Arches on the Ginza', *Speaking of Japan*, no. 7, 1986, pp. 24–7.

Fukawa, Mitsuo, 'Edible Oil Demand Reflects Living Standard Level', *Business Japan*, Feb. 1984, pp. 72–4.

Fukui, Haruhiro, 'The Japanese Farmer and Politics' in Isaiah Frank (ed.), *The Japanese Economy in International Perspective* (Baltimore Md.: Johns Hopkins University Press, 1975), pp. 134–67.

Fukutake, Tadashi, *Rural Society in Japan* (Tokyo University Press, 1980).

Hall, P.K., 'Japan's Farm Sector, 1920–1940: a Need for Reassessment', *Journal of Agricultural History*, 1985, pp. 598–616.

Harbison, Mark A., 'Sake and the Japanese', *Look Japan*, 10 Feb. 1985.

Hasumi, Otohiko, 'Rural Society in Postwar Japan', Parts I and II, *Japan Foundation Newsletter*, vol. 12, nos 5 and 6, 1985.

Hayami, Yujiro, 'Rice Policy in Japan's Agricultural Development', *American Journal of Agricultural Economics*, vol. 54, 1972, pp. 19–31.

Hayami, Yujiro, *A Century of Agricultural Growth in Japan* (Tokyo University Press, 1975).

Hayami, Yujiro, 'Trade Benefits to All: a Design of the Beef Import Liberalization in Japan', *American Journal of Agricultural Economics*, vol. 61, no. 1. 1979, pp. 342–7.

Hemmi, Kenzo, *Agriculture in the 21st Century: A Japanese View* (New York, NY: Philip Morris Inc., 1983).

Horikoshi, Hisamoto, 'The Changing Rural Landscape', *Japan Foundation Newsletter*, vol. 13, no. 1, 1985, pp. 1–11.

IRM Inc., *Market Studies: Soups, Alcoholic Beverages* (Tokyo- 1979).

Ishida, Akira, *Food Processing Industry in Japan* (Tokyo: Japan FAO Association, 1978).

Japan Company Handbook (Tokyo: Toyo Keizai Shinposha, 1985).

Japan Economic Yearbook, 1981/82 (Tokyo, 1982).

Japan Fisheries Association, *Fisheries of Japan* (Tokyo, 1984).

Japan International Agricultural Council, *Views from Japan on Farm Trade Issues* (Tokyo, 1985).

Japan Machinery Exporters Association, *Japan Agricultural Machinery and Land Internal Combustion Engines* (Tokyo, undated).

Japan Whaling Association, *Whaling: Questions and Answers* (Tokyo, 1983).

Japon, Le *Bulletin d'information de la mutualité agricole*, no. 378, May 1986, pp. 23–30.

JETRO, Access to Japan's Import Market Series, *Agricultural Machinery*, no. 3, 1979; *Biscuits*, no. 30, 1984; *Canned Fishery Products*, no. 26, 1980; *Chicken Broilers*, no. 7, 1981; *Cocoa*, no. 1, 1979; *Coffee*, no. 2, 1981; *Feed and Roughage*, no. 19, 1979; *Food Processing Machinery*, no. 17, 1981; *Natural Cheese*, no. 29, 1984; *Nuts*, no. 18, 1983; *Processed Foods*, no. 11, 1980; *Tapioca*, 1978; *Vegetables*, no. 27, 1980; *Wine*, no. 15, 1983.

JETRO, Your Market in Japan. Mini-Reports: *Beer*, no. 7; *Biotechnology Equipment*, no. 3, 1984; *Health Food*, no. 19, 1986.

JETRO, *How to Approach the Japanese Food Market*, AG-13, 1984.

JETRO, *Food Processing Industry in Japan* (rev.), AG-12, 1984.

JETRO, *Japanese Forestry and Forestry Product Trade*, AG-10, 1983.

JETRO, *Japan's Agriculture and Imports of Agricultural Products*, AG-9., 1982.

JETRO, *Dine-Out Industry in Japan*, AG-7, 1982.

JETRO, *An Outline of Food Distribution in Japan, Centering on Distribution through Wholesale Markets*, AG-6, 1981.

JETRO, *Keys to Success: Japan's 'Food Lifestyle'*, Tokyo, 1983.

JETRO, *Planning for Distribution in Japan*, Marketing Series 4, Tokyo, 1982.

JETRO, *Changing Dietary Lifestyles in Japan*, Marketing Series, 17, 1978.

Johnson, Chalmers, *MITI and the Japanese Miracle* (University of California Press, 1983).

Kalland, Arne, *Shingu: a Japanese Fishing Community* (London and Malmö: Curzon Press, 1980).

Kaminogo, Toshiaki, 'Beef Prices', *Bungei Shunju*, Mar. 1977.

Keizai Koho Center, 'Domestic Adjustment Measures for Japanese Agriculture', *KKC Brief*, no. 19, 1984.

Keizai Koho Center, 'Cost Reduction by Productivity Increase Is Imperative', *KKC Brief*, no. 11, 1983.

Kishimoto, Koichi, *Politics in Modern Japan*, 2nd edn (Tokyo: Japan Echo Inc., 1982).

Kojima, Kiyoshi and Terutomo Ozawa, *Japan's General Trading Companies* (Paris: OECD, 1984).

Linhart, Sepp, *Sozialer Wandel in Ländlichen Siedlungen der japanischen Nordinsel Hokkaido* (Wien: Institut für Japanologie an der Universitat Wien, 1970).

Livestock Industry Promotion Corporation, *LIPC* (Tokyo, 1975).

Livingston, Jon, Joe Moore and Felicia Oldfather (eds), *The Japan Reader* vols I and II (Harmondsworth, Middx: Penguin, 1973).

Lemm, Wolfgang, *Japans landwirtschaftliche Genossenschaften* (Hamburg:

Institut für Asienkunde, 1977).

Longworth, John W., *Beef in Japan* (University of Queensland Press, 1983).

MAFF, *White Paper on Agriculture*, Tokyo Annual issues.

MAFF, 'Agriculture in Japan', *Japan's Agricultural Review*', vols. 13 & 14, 1986, pp. 1–23.

MAFF, *Outline of the Results of an Inquiry Concerning the Actual State of the Distribution of Imported Food Products*, unpublished, Nov. 1985.

MAFF, 'Japan's Overseas Agricultural Cooperation', *Japan's Agricultural Review*, vol. 12, 1985, pp. 1–31.

MAFF, 'Japanese Experimentation and Research in the Fields of Agriculture, Forestry and Fisheries', *Japan's Agricultural Review*, vol. 11, 1985, pp. 1–20.

MAFF, *Annual Report on Fishery Developments*, 1983 (Foreign Press Center, Tokyo, 1984).

MAFF, *Food Balance Sheets for Fiscal 1983* (Foreign Press Center, Tokyo, 1984).

MAFF, 'Fishery and Fishery Products in Japan', *Japan's Agricultural Review*, vol. 9, 1984, pp. 1–16.

MAFF, 'Forestry and Forestry Products in Japan', *Japan's Agricultural Review*, vol. 6, 1982, pp. 1–12.

MAFF, 'Japanese Dietary Habits', *Japan's Agricultural Review*, vol. 5, 1981, pp. 1–16.

MAFF, 'Long-term Prospects for the Demand and Production of Agricultural Products', *Japan's Agricultural Review*, vol. 3, 1980, pp. 1–11.

MAFF, *The Ministry of Agriculture, Forestry and Fisheries* (Tokyo, undated).

Marubeni Corporation, *The Unique World of the Sogo Shosha* (Tokyo, 1978).

Matsuura, Akira, 'Japan's Agricultural Policy', *Japan's Agricultural Review*, vol. 1, 1980, pp. 1–20.

Matsuura, Tatsuo, *The Livestock Farmers of Japan* (Tokyo: Japan International Agricultural Council, 1984).

Matsuura, Tatsuo and Morio Morisaki, *The Japanese Feed Market* (Tokyo: Japan International Agricultural Council, 1985).

MFA, *Agriculture in Japan: Facts about Japan* (Tokyo, 1981).

Miller, Geoff, *The Political Economy of International Agricultural Reform* (Canberra: Department of Primary Industry, 1986).

MIPRO, *Survey Report on the General Market in Japan for Special Foodstuff Products* (Tokyo, 1981).

Motiki, Ryo, 'Pomiculture Promotion Deliberation Council', *Kankai*, May 1982.

Naito, Satoshi, 'The Tobacco Monopoly Goes Private', *Economic Eye*, June 1985, pp. 30–2.

Nakajima, Tomio, 'Alcoholic Consumption Well-Established in Japan', *Business Japan*, Aug. 1984, pp. 37–40.

Nakamura, Takefusa, *Economic Development of Modern Japan* (Tokyo: Ministry of Foreign Affairs, 1985).

Nakao, Mitsuaki, 'Inside the Beef Industry', *Japan Echo*, vol. 11, 1984, pp. 64–72.

Nicol, C. W., 'The Whaling Controversy', *Look Japan*, 10 Oct. 82.

OECD, *Ministerial Council Mandate on Agricultural Trade. Country Report – Japan*, AGR(86) 10 Aug. 1986.

OECD, *Agriculture in China* (Paris: OECD, 1985).

OECD, *Les industries alimentaires de L'OCDE dans les années 80* (Paris: OECD, 1983).

OECD, *Structure, Performance and Prospects of the Beef Chain* (Paris: OECD, 1978).

OECD, *Agricultural Policy in Japan* (Paris: OECD, 1974).

Ogura, Takekazu, *Can Japanese Agriculture Survive? A Historical Approach* (Tokyo: Agricultural Policy Research Center, 1979).

Ogura, Takekazu, *Agricultural Development in Modern Japan* (Tokyo: Fuji Publishing Co., 1963).

Okawara Yoshio, 'Japan's Farm Policy', *Speaking of Japan*, vol. 5, 1984, pp. 7–10.

Okita, Saburo, 'The Proper Approach to Food Policy', *Japan Echo*, vol. 5, no. 2, 1978, pp. 49–57.

Oshiro, Kenji Kenneth, *Dairy Policies and the Development of Dairying in Tohoku, Japan*, Ph. D. thesis, University of Washington, 1972.

Otsuka, Keijiro and Yujiro Hayami, 'Goals and Consequences of Rice Policy in Japan, 1965–1980, *American Journal of Agricultural Economics*, vol. 67, 1985, pp. 530–8.

PA International Consulting Services Ltd, *Study on EC Wines and Liquor Exports to Japan* (2 vols), Report for the Commission of the European Communities (Tokyo, 1985).

Rothacher, Albrecht, 'The Political Economy of Japan's Agriculture' in Erich Pauer (ed.), *Silkworms, Oil and Chips*, Proceedings of the Economics Section of the 4th International Conference on Japanese Studies. Bonner Zeitschrift für Japanologie, 8, Bonn 1986, pp. 133–46.

Rothacher, Albrecht, 'Das japanische Unternehmen', in Sepp Linhart (ed.), *40 Jahre Modernes Japan* (Wien, 1986) pp. 93–103.

Rothacher, Albrecht, 'Wirtschaftsbeziehungen Japan–Europa', *Shiosai*, July 1986, pp. 9–12.

Rothacher, Albrecht, *The European Community and Japan: Crises and Crisis Management*, Berlin, Occasional Papers no. 42, Ostasiatisches Seminar, F.U. Berlin, 1984, reprinted in *East Asia*, vol. 3, 1984.

Rothacher, Albrecht, *Economic Diplomacy between the European Community and Japan, 1959–1981* (Aldershot: Gower, 1983).

Sabouret, Jean-Francois, *L'autre Japan. Les Burakumin* (Paris: La Découverte–Maspero, 1983).

Sakai, Yoshiaki, 'Four Myths about Rice', *Japan Echo*, vol. 5, no. 2, 1978, pp. 58–66.

Sanderson, Fred H., *Japan's Food Prospects and Policies* (Washington, DC: Brookings Institution, 1978).

Sato, Hideo and Timothy J. Curran, 'Agricultural Trade: the Case of Beef and Citrus in I. M. Destler and H. Sato (eds), *Coping with US–Japanese Economic Conflicts* (Lexington Books, 1982) pp. 121–84.

Sato, Yoshio and Koichi Ito, 'A Theory of Oligopolistic Core and Competitive Fringe: Japan's Wheat Flour Milling Industry', *Keio Business Review*, no. 13, 1974, pp. 17–41.

Sato, Yoshio, 'The Silk-Reeling Industry and the Catch-up Case', *Keio Business Review*, no. 11, 1972, pp. 63–78.

Sekiya, Shunsaku, 'Agricultural Land System in Japan', *Japanese Agricultural Review*, vol. 4. 1981, pp. 1–32.

Shimpo, Mitsuru, *Three Decades in Shiwa* (Vancouver: University of British Columbia Press, 1976).

Smith, Robert J., *Kurusu, The Price of Progress in a Japanese Village* (Stanford University Press, 1978).

Social Science Research Institute, ICU, *Transformation Process of a Suburban City in Japan* (Mitaka, Tokyo: International Christian University, 1966).

Tachibana, Takashi, *Nokyo* (Tokyo: Asahi Shimbun-Sha, 1980).

Tachibana, Y., 'Are Farmers Really Victims?', *The Oriental Economist*, June 1984, pp. 6–9.

Takeshi, Domon, 'The Sorry State of Rice Breeding', *Japan Echo*, vol. 12, no. 1, 1985, pp. 30–7.

Tallent, David R., 'Japan's Trade Barriers Pose Problems for U.Ş. Citrus Exporters', *Foreign Agriculture*, Oct. 1983.

Tsubota, Kunio, 'Agricultural Policy in Japan', *Journal of Agricultural Economics*, vol. 36, 1985, pp. 365–75.

Ushiomi, Toshitaka, *Forestry and Mountain Village Communities in Japan* (Tokyo: Kokusai Bunka Shinkokai, 1968).

Ushiomi, Toshitaka, *La Communauté Rurale au Japon* (Paris: Presses Universitaires de France, 1962).

World Bank, *World Development Report 1986* (Washington, DC, 1986).

Yamaguchi, Iwao, 'Irreparable Trouble if Policies Don't Change', *Japan Times*, 19 Ap. 1985.

Yoshikazu, Kano 'The Growth Potential of Japanese Agriculture', *Japan Echo*, vol. 9, no. 2, 1982, pp. 65–73.

Yoshioka, Yutaka, 'Business before Politics', *Speaking of Japan*, vol. 7, 1986, pp. 22–6.

Yoshioka, Yutaka, 'Domestic Scope for Agricultural Issues', *Look Japan*, 10 July 1984.

Yoshioka, Yukata, *Food and Agriculture in Japan* (Tokyo: Foreign Press Center, 1979).

Yuize, Yasuhiko, 'Liberalizing Beef and Oranges' in Keizai Koho Center (ed.), *Economic Views from Japan* (Tokyo, 1986) pp. 3–7.

Yuize, Yasuhiko, 'Six Simulations for Rice Decontrol', *Japan Echo*, vol. 12, no. 1. 1985, pp. 22–29.

Yuize, Yasuhiko, 'U.S.–Japan Rice War', *Gendai*, June 1984.

Index